PUSHING BUTTONS

Future Works by Rozerik Ross and The MADPENS Project

Reimagining Terror Management, The Podcast
Conversations Defining Ever-Present Trauma in the Everyday

The Periodic Table of Parenting:
Dramatic Elements of Family Life

Living With The Hulk Syndrome:
Intense Perspectives on Monumental Meltdowns

Enough With The Eggshells:
Escaping the Prison of Parental PTSD

madpens   mimemo

SHOULD THE ELEVATOR DOORS
FAIL TO OPEN,
DO NOT BECOME ALARMED.

THERE IS LITTLE DANGER
OF RUNNING OUT OF AIR
OR OF THIS ELEVATOR
DROPPING UNCONTROLLABLY.

PLEASE USE THE BUTTON
MARKED "ALARM"
OR TELEPHONE (IF FURNISHED)
TO SUMMON AID.

ELEVATOR COMPANIES
ARE ON CALL
24 HOURS A DAY
FOR EMERGENCY SERVICE.

PUSHING BUTTONS

UNSETTLING STORIES OF LIFE'S UPS AND DOWNS

STORYRUNNER
ROZERIK ROSS

mimemo

Pushing Buttons
© Copyright 2025 by Rozerik Ross

All rights reserved. No part of this publication may be reproduced, distributed, or transmitted in any form or by any means, including photocopying, recording, or other electronic or mechanical methods, without the prior written permission of the publisher, except in the case of brief quotations embodied in critical reviews and certain other noncommercial uses permitted by copyright law.

Adherence to all applicable laws and regulations, including international, federal, state, and local governing professional licensing, business practices, advertising, and all other aspects of doing business in the US, Canada, or any other jurisdiction is the sole responsibility of the reader and consumer.

Although the author and publisher have made every effort to ensure that the information in this book was correct at press time, the author and publisher do not assume, and hereby, disclaim any liability to any party for any loss, damage, or disruption caused by errors or omissions, whether such errors or omissions result from negligence, accident, or any other cause.

Neither the author nor the publisher assumes any responsibility or liability whatsoever on behalf of the consumer or reader of this material. The resources in this book are provided for informational purposes only. Please always consult a trained professional before making any decision regarding treatment of yourself or others. The content in this book should not be used to replace the specialized training and professional judgment of a health care or mental health care professional.

For permission requests, write to the publisher at:
Mimemo LLC
13351-D Riverside Drive #635
Sherman Oaks, CA 91423
www.rozerikross.com

First edition: 2025
ISBN Hardcover 979-8-9910622-0-6
ISBN Paperback 979-8-9910622-1-3
ISBN Digital 979-8-9910622-2-0
Library of Congress Control Number: 2024914240

Published by Mimemo, Printed in USA
Los Angeles, California

SHOULD THE ELEVATOR DOORS FAIL TO OPEN, DO NOT BECOME ALARMED.

THERE IS LITTLE DANGER OF RUNNING OUT OF AIR OR OF THIS ELEVATOR DROPPING UNCONTROLLABLY.

PLEASE USE THE BUTTON MARKED "ALARM" OR TELEPHONE (IF FURNISHED) TO SUMMON AID.

ELEVATOR COMPANIES ARE ON CALL 24 HOURS A DAY FOR EMERGENCY SERVICE.

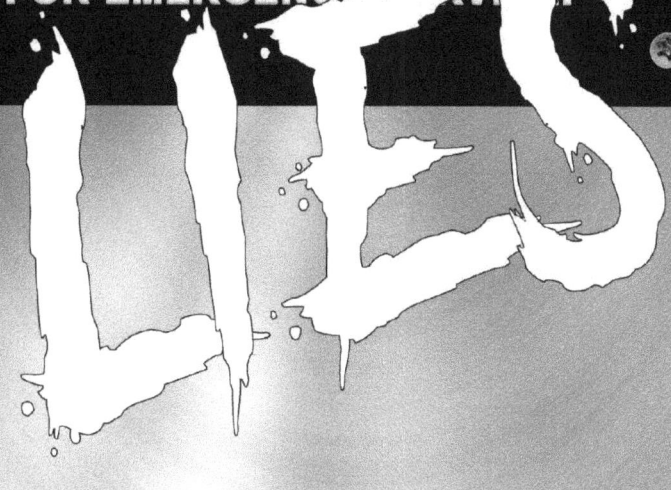

LIES

Dedication

To My Wife, Jodi and My Daughter, Layla,
to whom I dedicate this first book of many.
Our life has had many ups and downs
(mostly ups) and has absolutely pushed my buttons!

To My Dad,
We were so close to you seeing this book.
There's at least one story about Heaven,
and I expect you can read it there.
I love you and miss you.

How To Use This Book

Disclaimer

The content presented in this book has dubious informational and educational value. The author is not a licensed healthcare provider (not yet, anyway), and the information provided should not be used to diagnose or treat any health condition or disease.

End of Chapter Codes

At the end of each chapter, you'll find codes showing which elevator etiquette rules were followed or ignored. The explanation of the codes can be found in the Etiquette chapter towards the end of the book. In real life, follow the rules or don't — it's your call. Either way, you'll find out what happens...

Reality Check

Life is messy and so is this book. This work discusses various sensitive topics that may be unsettling for some readers.

A list of stories, organized by genre, is provided in the next chapter. While genres like comedy, fantasy, romance, and science fiction are *generally* more light-hearted, the other categories explore more intense and potentially distressing themes.

Reader discretion is advised.

Stories Categorized by Genre

[xx] Chapter numbers

COMEDY
- [25] Chaos Without Movement
- [10] Cheapest Rent Available [i,m]
- [17] Dishonorable Discharge
- [01] Elevator Pitch
- [32] Lost In an Elevator
- [11] Minyan Man and The Krimson Angel
- [42] Muzak [i]
- [43] New Elevator Boy
- [03] No Spritzes to Give [i]

DRAMA
- [45] American Paternoster *
- [47] Cover Girl [i]
- [46] Foreign Exchange *
- [28] Hellavator
- [14] Minimum Wage Face [m]
- [29] Pearly Gates
- [16] Sirens, Lights, and A Skunk, Oh My [m]
- [24] The Chute [i]
- [04] Thompson Twins
- [15] What the Skunk? [m]

FANTASY

[38] Anime Girl

[50] Floor B Leprechauns *

[08] Love Like You're Dying

[06] Mark of a Man

[48] Reverie

[44] Sleepy Time

[07] Supernatural Scorn, Metaphysical Mayhem

[13] The Unbearable Presence of Fairies

ROMANCE

[02] Disco Man [i]

[53] Disco Man Takes A Lover

[09] Love Rising *,[m]

POLITICS

[34] Full Transparency [m]

[26] I Take The Stairs

[49] Let's Go Brandon

[19] The Elevator State [i,m]

[33] The Four Snowflakes Hotel

[18] Toiletpapermageddon

BY GENRE   xv

RACISM

[35] American Shame [i,m]

[52] Spider on the Wall [m]

HORROR

[21] Cirque de la Mimique [i]

[40] I Hear You [i]

[23] Mama Bear [i]

[22] No Help is Coming [i]

[39] Professional Help [i]

[30] St. Monica's Children's Hospital [i]

[31] Santa Muerte's Children's Hospital [i]

[41] The Sign Lies [i]

SCIENCE FICTION

[20] 23rd Century Fishbowl

[51] Digital Vision

[54] Jump Before Crashing

[05] Portal *

[12] Secret Sequence Scheme [i]

[36] Space Elevator

[37] Space Heist!

[27] Timeline

(i) Intensely influenced by psychological or medical factors
(*) LGBTQIA2S+ positive content
(m) marginalized communities

Contents

Acknowledgements	XX
Foreword	XXIII
Preface	XXVII
Introduction	XXIX
1. Elevator Pitch	1
2. Disco Man	5
3. No Spritzes To Give	9
4. Thompson Twins	16
5. Portal	25
6. Mark of A Man	33
7. Supernatural Scorn, Metaphysical Mayhem	41
8. Love Like You're Dying	48
9. Love Rising	56
10. Cheapest Rent Available	65
11. Minyan Man and The Krimson Angel	70
12. Secret Sequence Scheme	78
13. The Unbearable Presence of Fairies	85
14. Minimum Wage Face	92

15.	What the Skunk?	96
16.	Sirens, Lights, and a Skunk, Oh My	101
17.	Dishonorable Discharge	107
18.	Toiletpapermageddon	113
19.	The Elevator State	119
20.	23rd Century Fishbowl	128
21.	Cirque de la Mimique	133
22.	No Help Is Coming	139
23.	Mama Bear	144
24.	The Chute	151
25.	Chaos Without Movement	158
26.	I Take The Stairs	162
27.	Timeline	165
28.	Hellavator	175
29.	Pearly Gates	183
30.	St. Monica's Children's Hospital, Guidelines for Behavior	189
31.	Santa Muerte's Children's Hospital, Guidelines for Behavior	198
32.	Lost In An Elevator	209
33.	The Four Snowflakes Hotel	212
34.	Full Transparency	215
35.	American Shame	231
36.	Space Elevator	237
37.	Space Heist!	244

38. Anime Girl	254
39. Professional Help	261
40. I Hear You	265
41. The Sign Lies	273
42. Muzak	277
43. New Elevator Boy	282
44. Sleepy Time	285
45. American Paternoster	290
46. Foreign Exchange	298
47. Cover Girl	303
48. Reverie	311
49. Let's Go Brandon	316
50. Floor B Leprechauns	318
51. Digital Vision	322
52. Spider On The Wall	328
53. Disco Man Takes A Lover	332
54. Jump Before Crashing	336
Afterword	345
Contributors	347
Elevator Etiquette Rules and Codes	349
About the Storyrunner	357
Join The MADPENS	359

Acknowledgments

The Above and Beyond list

The below kind souls were *instrumental* in creating this book. Many also participated in building the infrastructure to create new works by crowdsourcing. Your efforts are appreciated, and I am filled with gratitude.

(in Alphabetical Order)
Amery Bruce
Andrea Colocho
Andrew Burk
Brian Green
Charles Milstein
Dan Watanabe
Donna Fields
Ellie Shoja
Gina Freyre
Hannah Lorenzo
Heather Butterfield
Jamie Martinez
Jennifer Grace
Jodi Milstein
Lahn Elise Matelski
Lisa Chow

ACKNOWLEDGEMENTS

Loren Weisman
Luisa Bravo
Molly Minogue
Myrna Milstein
Randall Libero
Sloane Milstein
Summer McStravick
Tomi Alo
Warren MacEvoy
Zach Hunchar

Furthermore, the *Contributors* section, which follows the *Afterword*, recognizes those pivotal in writing the stories, creating The MADPENS Project, and founding Mimemo, the publisher of this book. I am indebted to you all.

Foreward

I love elevators. Love them.

With no entrance list, we are randomized and anonymized people thrust together. For a magically brief time, social survival depends on rigid observance of personal space and restraint. Riders must maintain a fierce determination to look forward. Yet, most people ultimately miss an elevator's true value. Beyond the usefulness of getting to your destination, the elevator provides you with the most precious resource of all: time.

Many misuse this time to contemplate the mundane: work, bills, where you parked your car, and whether they validate here.

Instead, go deeper. Ask yourself why you're on the elevator. Or where you came from? What brought you there? What series of choices put you in that moment? Your decisions may seem inconsequential, but rarely do they impact only yourself. Sometimes, small actions can change the course of the world. And occasionally, an elevator can remind you of that.

Years ago, I went on a trip to Washington, DC with my wife, who was doing business with our representative in the House — a portion of our trip involved meeting with her mother's cousin, Representative Henry Waxman. Generously offering a tour, he took us into the Capitol and the main chambers. We used the non-public underground trolley system, which many representatives used to get around. It's both clever for expedience and sobering that they have legitimate security concerns. At the end of the tunnel, an elevator stood with a crowd of people waiting.

One person turned to introduce himself, but he didn't need to: civil rights hero John Robert Lewis. To say I was in awe would be an understatement. The history in that place was suffocating on its own, but this encounter took my breath away. He was thoughtful and gracious and filled most of the space where my words would have gone if I could speak. I wondered how much time he spent reflecting upon his choices that brought him to such a place in public service and changing the tenor of our nation. And I only got that experience because the elevator was slow.

Elevators don't have to be solemn and profound experiences. There is the opportunity for chaos and laughter, born from the unity we experience on those single-axis rides, especially when we push the wrong buttons. Everything is a choice in an elevator, and sometimes we make the wrong one.

At the San Diego Comic-Con in 2011, I was leaving a party with a friend and wasn't looking around when I entered the elevator. Glancing to my left, I noticed actress Jennifer Carpenter from the television show *Dexter*. I turned and nodded, and in the 'coolest' voice I could conjure, said, "Hey. How you doing?" I didn't see that she blocked my view of Michael C. Hall, her husband at the time, and the Dexter in *Dexter*. He leaned forward and, with little sympathy, said, "She's doing fine." Sometimes, you wish you could pry the doors open, so you could jump down the shaft. Needless to say, when we reached the ground floor, I waited for them to leave first. Afterward, my friend laughed without mercy, and I couldn't argue.

All of that was because I made a choice. Perhaps silly, but one I won't forget. Like much in life, choices have all sorts of meanings and impacts that ripple beyond what we can ever know. Often multiple at the same time. These choices are thrust upon us, and we usually try to make the best of them — but not always. And we rarely get to choose when this happens.

The collection you're choosing to read is all about choices, consequences, and the general absurdity that is life. And by letting each of the authors share a little something with you, you'll be forever altered. Possibly even in a good way.

So, get out there! Push some (elevator) buttons. See what floor you land on. You might love where you end up, and even if you don't, the journey was worth the ride.

Zachary Hunchar
Los Angeles
June 2024

Preface

On November 20, 2017, Post Malone had a number #1 single, and for a writing class assignment, I posted a god-awful Haiku on Facebook.

> Who was this Otis?
> Elevator sometimes works.
> Name in dirty steel.

Now, years later, after this writing class post, we have *Pushing Buttons: Unsettling Stories of Life's Ups and Downs*. It's high concept elevator fiction that no one asked for but everyone needs — for enjoyment, for use as a doorstop, or to help grandma see over the steering wheel. For this class, I surrendered to the first topic that came into my head, Elevator Etiquette. Fortunately, the scope grew well beyond that 17-syllable haiku inspiration.

The inside of my mind is like a pinball machine. Ideas rattle around in there, get stuck, and break free at seemingly random times, usually connecting to something else in a way only warped people like myself can fathom.

Are you warped enough to fathom? I suppose you'll see.

Introduction

"There are only three times in our lives that we enter a small, windowless, enclosed space that has no ready exit: the womb, the tomb, and the elevator. The elevator is the only one we share with strangers." -Lane A. Longfellow, PhD

Sadly, I occasionally suffer from claustrophobia, whether inside a hot car, while relying on a scuba tank, or like that one time I jumped out of a perfectly good airplane. Under normal circumstances, the anxiety might surface from enormous stress. Curiously, it has never surfaced in an elevator, and I hope it never does!

Phobias are never convenient, and our nervous systems grab our attention with an overwhelming panic. As Jon Kabat-Zinn says, "Wherever you go, there you are." And in an enclosed space you can't control, you must account for both the people and your emotional reactions. Our thoughts, like some entities in my elevators, can't be fully contained. Our minds can be frightening. I know it's not just me.

Every character in this book has to *deal with* unsettling company in a confined space of about 30 square feet. Not all passengers are dark; some are quite pleasant. I hope you are fortunate enough to ride with those.

Dear reader, a stranger is holding the elevator door open for you. You're just a few feet away. Will you take a bold step into the unknown, or send them on their way? I hope you are one of the brave ones.

Rozerik Ross, Elevator Operator

Elevator Pitch

60 Seconds To Change Your Life, Go!

pitching you is easy
Watch and Follow for the cues
to mold yourself, Bide your time
-Amery Bruce

Consider this. If you had to convince someone to hire you in less than a minute, what would you say? This scenario is better known as the "elevator pitch," and people phrase it in various ways. It all boils down to the same thing: getting your point and goals across in the time it takes an elevator to reach its destination. For most people, it's merely hypothetical, but for me, I made it happen.

The irony was that I had only been by Jacobson and Silver for some light reconnaissance, just to get a sense of the building and the people in it. I hadn't planned on doing the interview today, only to drop off my application in person. The plan was to take the elevator from the ground lobby to the sixth floor and hand my resume directly to Bob Flenderson in HR. (I had tried reaching out to him on LinkedIn, but I knew he was busy handling all the applications.)

Easy peasy. That was before the elevator stopped on the third floor and opened up to…THE head of the firm!

At first, I was understandably star-struck. The head of my dream firm was standing next to me in the elevator. There was an aura of assertiveness all around him. He pressed the button for the upper lobby, and it hit me — my elevator pitch. I had a completely unique opportunity here; it couldn't possibly hurt to try. I could introduce myself and land the job right now, without a formal interview. So I took a deep breath and stuck out my hand.

"Hi, I'm Ann."

He smiled and shook it. "Nice to meet you, Ann. I'm Grey."

I took another deep breath and started my speech about why I wanted to join his firm. I talked about my experience at my previous firm, working for the county, my GPA, and my qualities. I spoke right up until the elevator door opened. We stepped out of the elevator to the upper lobby on the fifth floor, and Grey shook my hand again, looking interested, before heading off quickly. I really admired his commitment to getting to work right away.

I decided against going to the sixth floor and handing in my resume to HR. I believed that building a close relationship with Grey would better solidify my position at the firm. I wouldn't be like all the other candidates with overly edited resumes. I would make my presence known in more creative ways. So, when I returned to the ground floor and left, I began to do more research. It was surprisingly easy to not only get his email and phone number online but also learn about Grey's background and personal life. This would definitely show how dedicated I was and how I could pay attention to detail.

I went to work emailing him to remind him who I was and to develop a friendly relationship with him. I asked about his hobbies, interests, and professional goals. His online profile included pictures of him and his children, so I learned their names and where they went to school. I thought it would be a great idea to volunteer at their school fairs and sporting events so I could help Grey with his busy schedule. I could always be right there if they needed rides or tutoring, just like a family friend.

I began emailing him more frequently, three to four times a week, in fact. I wanted him to know that I thought constant communication was the key to success. I also tried calling at least once a week, though he never answered, which was okay since I was sure he was busy being the head of the firm and all. So I left detailed voicemails on his work and home landline. Grey was also very active on his personal X account (I made sure not to call it Twitter — attention to detail, amirite?). Anyway, I made sure to follow him and like and comment on every single post he made, even dating back to years ago about his college life and family. I friended him on Facebook, but I haven't received a response yet. I don't think he uses it very much. I felt like I knew him as a person, not just as a potential boss.

A couple of weeks passed since I applied at the firm with my elevator pitch to Grey. I wasn't sure why they hadn't contacted me for an interview, but maybe they were finalizing the candidate choices. I thought of giving Grey another call that night just to ask what the progress was with my application, but thought better of it. I wanted to be respectful of the time he spent watching *Monday Night Football* after work; I knew he liked to relax with two Corona Lites during the game, one before halftime and one after....I found this out when I peeked through his living room window for research and all.

Anyway, the next morning, I decided to drive by Grey's daughter's school to see if I could catch him there for a conversation. As I locked the front door of my apartment, a man in a gray suit approached me.

"Excuse me, are you Ann Sanders?"

"Yes, I am."

"Well hello, I represent Jacobson and Silver. I have an important document to hand deliver to you."

I grabbed it, heart hammering, excited to see what was so urgent. Did Grey really go all out for me? Maybe I got my dream job after all my hard work. My hands shook with anticipation as I prepared to shout with joy. I carefully opened it...

...and instead found a restraining order, requested by none other than Grey himself.

See the end of the book for elevator etiquette rules followed or broken. Elevator Etiquette Codes: 1C, 2A, 2C, 2D, 2F, 3D, 4A, 6B, 6C, 6H

Disco Man

A Disco-verse Story

"Surrender is like a fish finding the current and going with it." -Mark Nepo

Consider this. Judy was running late. Her alarm didn't go off and traffic was a bitch with a capital B. Still, she played the not-late-yet game with herself. It wasn't officially late until nine o'clock; and today, she had blasted her way into the lobby with her hair on fire by 8:54. She had six minutes to spare, and the only thing between her and another late arrival was the elevator ride to the 7th floor. She could still make it. She was not late yet. Judy pressed the button to go up and waited. The elevator was known to be slow, but today, it was moving at a snail's pace.

"Come on!" She pressed the call button again as if it would help summon the elevator faster. It made her feel better, at least.

The elevator dinged, and she eagerly waited for the door to slide open. Three possible banks were going up, each converted into state-of-the-art DJ booths. And unfortunately, every day was elevator roulette. Because Lady Luck frowned upon Judy this morning, the door opened and she was faced with her worst enemy.

Occupying elevator car #2 was Disco Man. This was not her first encounter with the notorious character, a legend in his own mind. He engaged his deck and immediately started playing the track "Here We Go Again" by Aretha Franklin, and Judy was not amused. She felt the bass as she stood outside the elevator, evaluating her options. With repeated exposure, Disco Man's afro, shades, and low-cut shirt had been burned into Judy's retinas. His tune selection and elements of surprise set Disco Man apart in the art of transportation delay.

Disco Man had made her late on several occasions before, and her boss warned her about being overdue for work again. She couldn't wait for another elevator, and her chronic fatigue, which started around the same time Disco Man came on to the scene, made the stairs impossible. Judy hated waking up exhausted and getting more tired as the day went on. Yet here Judy was, staring at a man that made her consider, welcome even, those seven flights of steps.

Ultimately, reason set in and she decided that as bad as Disco Man was, she had fewer than six minutes to go. She said no words to him as she entered the elevator. What was there to even say at this point? He had no words for her, either. Disco Man communicated through bass, scratches, and beats per minute. She knew his game, and he knew hers. He cross-faded directly into the chorus of "Bad Luck" by Harold Melvin and the Blue Notes, and Judy gave him the finger.

She was running late (not late yet), and it was Disco Man's job to punish her *in advance* for her potential tardiness. Her boss didn't care about the Disco Man's antics. He was the one who hired the DJ, but why has always remained a mystery. She thought of Disco Man as sanctioned cruelty, an inhuman tool of corporate oppression. Why couldn't she just get up a few minutes earlier? Fatigue, anxiety and depression, that's why.

It was 8:55 now and Judy stared down at her foe. Her posture ensured she could cover his proprietary "tardy panel" and keep Disco Man from pressing his button, which would ensure her lateness. Disco Man's button was not hard to miss. It was shaped and textured like a disco ball and jutted out prominently from the elevator panel. It was really just an Emergency Stop button, but whatever. She knew by now not to watch his eyes, those damn hypnotic eyes. It was his feet she would have to worry about. But now, Disco Man's shades made it impossible for Judy to see where he was looking, anyway. In a blink, he matched the beat to the Bee Gees' "Tragedy," and as the music changed, Judy knew time was running out.

It was at 8:56 when Disco Man turned his head. Judy was ready. He was about to make his play. She readied her stance, like a linebacker about to go for a tackle. She kept her gaze on his feet. When 8:57 came, he cued up the next track but didn't make his move. Except for the metal clanging of the elevator, it was silent. This made Judy nervous. Disco Man had a crisis of conscience, but it was short-lived. She glanced at him and that's when he made his move. Disco Man pulled his shades down, revealing something new and far more sinister. It wouldn't have startled her as much if it weren't for the fact that his eyes were now disco balls. It made total sense; and yet, it took Judy completely by surprise.

This was enough to throw Judy off-balance, and with her critically low energy level, there was no chance she could overcome Disco Man's slick moves. He grabbed her by the hand like he had done many times before and twirled her away from the panel and into a "Disco Inferno". But this time was different; he'd had a true change of heart. Disco Man pressed his blinged-out disco button and gave Judy a sincere, reflective look. In a blur, he changed the vibe with the next track. A glittering disco ball descended from overhead, and the cramped space began to rock and roll. The loud and rhythmic falsetto disco of Bee Gee's "You Should Be Dancing" played on. Disco Man bobbed his head up and down as he noticed Judy was feeling better. Her fatigue was starting to lift, if only for a minute. For once, Disco Man's lips trembled with unfamiliar movements. He cracked a smile.

The elevator stopped as Disco Man pressed the next button in his sequence so he could break it down. In a flash, the final song changed again to "Found A Cure" by Ashford and Simpson, and although Disco Man wouldn't (couldn't) talk, his message was loud and clear. The doors opened and Judy exited as a woman with hope. With her head held high and a groovy pep in her step, she clocked in just in time. Maybe the boss knew something no one else did about Disco Man, or maybe not. But for Judy, she was "Born to Be Alive", and that was the best she had felt in years.

See the end of the book for elevator etiquette rules followed or broken. Elevator Etiquette Codes: 2B, 2D, 3A, 3B, 4A, 5E, 5F, 6B, 6C, 6H, 9B

No Spritzes To Give

Using Alcohol, Not Abusing Alcohol

"Spread Kindness, Not Germs." -Carson Dellosa

Consider this. French housekeeper Yvette Delacour was working in the penthouse of the Maestro Hotel and Casino. She had just finished wiping clean the mirrors on the walls near the elevator when she reached into her cart to disinfect. Yvette found her spray bottle, but her worst nightmare came to life: it was empty! How was she to sanitize the mirrors with an empty disinfectant bottle? This has never happened to her in all her years of working at this hotel. Was it sabotage? She had paper towels, toilet paper, mini soap bars, little shampoo bottles — and an empty disinfectant spray bottle; those did not satiate her compulsive objective to vanquish germs.

When the government initiated COVID-19 protocols, Yvette had raised the bar of ultimate cleanliness and germ mitigation, making sure her supplies were stocked! Running out of supplies always happened to someone else, not Yvette Delacour. Yvette raged inside as she returned to the elevator to ride it down to the basement where the supply closet was located.

She was proud that her boss relied on her when a recent disaster occurred in the hotel, but he interrupted her lunch and rushed her to clean with this joke of a cart. She ruminated on her preparation prior to her boss's catastrophe. Before leaving the supply room in the basement, she tapped her cart seven times, a ritual to bless her with luck so she wouldn't encounter anything unsightly. It didn't always work. Immediately, she guarded herself with an N95 mask as a precaution. She inspected all four corners of the elevator as she entered, keeping a three-foot distance from the control panel and other items in this germ box. She planted herself firmly in the center and stared wide-eyed at the door, looking out for anyone who might come in and invade her three-foot personal space with the coronavirus. Extreme? Nah. She could stop with these compulsions any time she wanted to, but she never wanted to.

A spot on button 3 drew her attention. How she wished she had her Driftwood Waters disinfectant (not an antibacterial) with her. With viral COVID-19 now running rampant, an antibacterial would have been no match. She had an almost overwhelming urge to sanitize this button that so many guests, so many fingers carrying so many germs, had pushed. She smiled as she imagined a germ-free button. Whenever she spritzed, the saltiness of the scent overwhelmed her nostrils, and a lightness took her into a sea of serenity.

A hand confidently and purposely reached past her and pushed the button for the casino on the first floor, snapping her out of her Driftwood Waters daydream. Regrettably, the hand belonged to Antonella Clemente, a rival housekeeper. She must have entered the elevator while Yvette was enraptured in her trance. Antonella had the odd rooms; Yvette had to clean the evens. This arrangement worked because Yvette never wanted a room that ended in 13 and Antonella acquiesced. She greeted Yvette with a warm smile, which was more than she expected from her nemesis. They have known each other ever since they began training in the cleansing arts at the Housekeeper Certification Academy. They always acted competitively toward each other, seeing who could clean the best over the 17 measurable and subjective metrics created by the HCA.

Though Yvette was highly trained in her duties, especially in stayover cleaning, her mysophobia often got the best of her. She spent too much time focused on buttons due to her inflated fear of infectious germs. She'd imagined all the possible scenarios in which a room would get dirty and start all over to prevent an unlikely tragedy. Remote control buttons, safe buttons, vending machine buttons, elevator buttons. So many buttons! This conscientiousness led to Antonella being praised by the hotel owners for her efficiency, while Yvette's pay was adjusted for the opposite reason. Antonella never spoke of her successes to Yvette, but that little smirk she gave irked Yvette every day because she knew. She knew.

Yvette wasn't innocent in this game either, especially when she would steal and hide cleaning supplies from Antonella's cart (Yvette had her own blends; she did not covet Antonella's toxic hotel-issued sprays), and turned her back when her frenemy would suffer accusations of theft. They never spoke to each other anymore, but they recognized who to hang their hatred on during this silent sport of escalation. Of course, they knew.

The long-drawn silence felt daunting in the elevator as the two women stared straight ahead, patiently waiting for the elevator to descend to the next floor. Yvette tapped her foot repeatedly to a song only she could hear while Antonella slowly steamed and waited for the ding to alert her that the waiting nightmare with Yvette was over. Finally, the elevator came to a halt, and the doors opened on floor 2, where the seafood buffet was.

Cough! The harsh discordant sound of sickness rippled through the air, echoing like sharp dissonant notes. Yvette popped her head out of the elevator, yet no one was there — until she looked down and saw Leandro The Slug, an ungodly sight that made Yvette sick to her stomach. He was still dripping from the pool, shirtless, morbidly obese, and wearing a very form-fitting, stained yellow Speedo called the Man Jammer. Leandro was clutching a beach towel in one hand and two crab legs in the other. His fingers clenched around the seafood like a toddler clutching his prized marbles. What was even worse was that he was wheezing like an alley cat with asthma. The hacking and coughing left a thick and sticky mucus mist that could be traced to Leandro, this man-thing, a resident psycho with a drooling problem. The Slug was sweaty and didn't feel the need to make an effort or use a previously recommended wheelchair, so he chose to crawl, dirtying his beach towel and his lunchtime leftovers. Antonella squeezed herself to the back of the elevator to watch "The Yvette and Leandro Show." Yvette tried to slow her descent into personal madness by presenting him with a mask — those she had plenty of. With one hand covering her closed eyes, Yvette reached her other hand out as far as she could towards Leandro. She quickly pulled her hand back as soon as the mask left her grasp out of fear of his contamination. He confirmed her suspicions by messily cramming the mask into his mouth after dropping his towel.

Yvette, almost about to throw up from the number of germs she visualized lying ahead of her, had no choice but to get back to work. Using her elbow, she chaotically pressed the button to the gaming floor since Leonardo always goes there. She grabbed the essentially empty bottle and frantically squeezed the trigger repeatedly. Out came tiny drops, which barely dampened her washcloth. Her attention shifted to Leandro as he tore the mask from his gaping maw, and the crunchy mask dropped to the elevator floor. In the busy corners of her mind, she chanted, "Give me strength, heavenly spray, serenity now!" But that affirmation did nothing to ease her anxiety, and the lack of her treasured Driftwood Waters frustrated her return to her own private Idaho. Leandro's droplets contaminated the air with utterly foul detritus, his revoltingly moist nature on the floor she had recently cleaned! Preparing to double down on her war on germs, she tightened her grip on the spray bottle until her fingers were purple, and on the verge of bruising.

The polluted mask landed close to Yvette's feet, and she started to back away from it as if it were a dangerous creature. She looked at Antonella, who smirked and motioned for her to pick the mask up. Yvette ignored that shit. Her face screwed up in discomfort, trapped in her world of germs, filth, and The Slug, now in his third year of living at the hotel.

Yvette noticed a benign disorder in her cart: the bleach bottle was not supposed to be mixed with the scent bottles, nor was it supposed to be hidden under dirty linen. Yvette stiffened as she carefully picked up the bottle so that her hand would not bump into Antonella. However, the bottle slipped out of her hand instead and crashed to the floor. The trigger cracked, releasing a wave of strong, irritating odor. Antonella now started sneezing and without a mask. Jesus! Yvette cringed and handed Antonella a tissue and a mask from her apron. Leandro unexpectedly picked up his contaminated mask and smeared it all over his face. Yvette winced with every coarse rattle of his diseased lungs and started to hyperventilate and feel dizzy. She immediately turned away from both of them, held on to the bar handle attached to the wall, and regained her composure. She intently focused her eyes on the panel that needed one good spritz if it needed a thousand. Yvette wanted everyone and everything to dissolve away so that she could properly and perfectly clean the elevator. It was her duty, her desire, and her fixation to accomplish this benevolence.

Finally, the elevator opened to reveal the casino floor, smoky as it was. Saving the mask for later, Leandro, all teary-eyed from the bleach exposure, shoved the biohazard down the side of his Speedo to both Yvette and Antonella's disgust. (They agreed on something!) Then to add insult to injury, Leandro crawled away without ever saying a word, leaving a monstrous fetid blob of sweat and saliva behind, along with his beach towel and one of the crab legs. Yvette couldn't help but dry heave.

Antonella stepped into the gaming arena, but not before looking deep into Yvette's soul with an unexpected but pleasant warm smile. Antonella handed her a disinfectant spray bottle, one with the scent of Driftwood Waters! Yvette wasn't sure what to make of that, but perhaps they were at a peaceful stalemate for now.

Holding back her own tears, Yvette blinked a couple of times. It could have been joy, or maybe a residual reaction to the bleach. She relieved the sting in her eyes and the grateful lump in her throat. Yvette carefully took the spray and watched as the maskless Antonella walked through the casino to exit out to her car without another glance back.

After the elevator door closed and when Yvette was alone with her thoughts, she was an unstoppable force. The floor and mirrored elevator walls were almost transcendent, shining a beam of light to where all the surfaces reflected off one another, the light bouncing into infinity. She returned to the penthouse, where she transformed the place into the clean, bright scene that was a dead ringer for the photo in the brochure. She imagined there to be a Mt. Rushmore of Cleaning where one day she would join Martha Stewart, Alice Nelson from *The Brady Bunch,* and of course, Mr. Clean.

At last, her shift ended, and it was time to head home, where she could relax in her hypoallergenic bubble of safety and control, where masks were plentiful and her favorite disinfectant spray even more so.

See the end of the book for elevator etiquette rules followed or broken. Elevator Etiquette Codes: 3A, 3F, 3G, 4A, 4B, 4C, 5C, 6B, 6C, 6E, 7B, 8A, 8B, 8C, 8D

Thompson Twins

Fractured By Time, Never By Heart

"Separation and division is not a natural state; it is an unhealed state." -Teal Swan

Consider this. When Tryp Thompson walked into the run-down bar, his reflection stared back at him as if he was looking into a mirror. The only problem was there was no mirror in front of him.

He had come to the Nighttime Awake bar every Thursday afternoon for the last month. The dive bar was a staple in the community, one of the few 24-hour joints in Parsippany that satiated both the night crowd and the third-shift workers who needed a drink when they clocked out at five in the morning. Since the bar had a public officer discount, the police looked the other way as it served liquor past when legally allowed. The first thing someone noticed about the bar was that Nighttime Awake was eclectic. The bar was built into a refurbished hotel lobby. There were couches scattered throughout, worn down and steeped in the smell of cigarettes, bourbon, and G-d knows what else. Each couch faced a single stage centered in the bar. The stage was Nighttime Awake's pride and joy, built into the large elevator that had once functioned in the hotel. They had taken the doors out, hollowing the center and strengthening it with an upgraded support structure. The result was an open box wide enough to fit a full band set. The glass walls that made up the elevator made it so the band playing could be seen from every angle. LED lights and strobe lights lined the glass, the flashing synced with the rhythm of the music. It was a hot spot for any aspiring musician to play and get videos for their socials.

Nighttime Awake hosted live music every night, making it the perfect place for Tryp to search for new talent. He had been a talent agent for three years but had barely signed a handful of bands in that time. His hopes of managing a band were fading. The pressure of making his rent loomed over him, driving him to walk into Nighttime Awake every Thursday. It was his only day off from his part-time job as a grocery store checker, so he went to the bar at 4 PM to watch the band performing that night. Tryp had always believed the true nature of a band could be seen before their set ever began. Every night there was music, but Thursdays were specifically set aside for bands that had never performed at Nighttime Awake before. A flier for tonight's band, Theorycraft, had been pinned on a pole outside the store. The picture of their lead singer, Oscar, was promising enough to Tryp.

The stage was where Tryp saw his face, sitting atop the shoulders of the bassist on stage.

He had never seen the man before, but there was no mistaking how much they looked alike. The musician had the same sandy brown hair, hazel eyes that were more green than brown, and sharp facial features as Tryp. The man on the small circle stage was slightly taller and a bit more muscular than himself, but that was the only obvious physical difference between them. He was so distracted that he paused right in front of the door. A man barreled into him from behind.

"Shit, sorry Cam," he frowned at Tryp. "What are you doing? I thought you wanted to be set up by five-thirty."

"I do," the bassist called back without turning from the speakers he was placing across the stage. "That's why you're supposed to be helping me."

It only took a few seconds for Tryp to see the shock on the guy's face as he registered it wasn't his bandmate standing in front of him. His eyes widened, lips parting into a gaping mouth as he stared at Tryp like he was something supernatural.

"I was going to help you, but I think I just found something a little more important. Camden? You gotta turn around."

The man, Camden, made a low sound in his throat, similar to a growl. Tryp was so in shock that he hadn't said a word since he'd stepped in the door. He just stared at the bassist.

"I swear to G-d, Oscar, if you brought in another kid's toy to play one of our songs with, I'm going to lose — oh." Camden cut himself off, attention landing on Tryp. He looked over the talent agent's form, from his business slacks and button-up to the top of his identical head. "Who are you?"

"I'm Tryp," he said, finally recovering enough to form words. "I'm a talent agent. I came here to watch your band play. You're the bassist?"

"Camden, bassist and founder," he said, hopping off the raised elevator stage to shake Tryp's hand. Everything seemed so surreal as Tryp met his grip. "When's your birthday?"

"August seventeenth. When's yours?" Tryp asked, already knowing the answer.

"August seventeenth," Camden confirmed.

"No way," Oscar laughed, startling them both. Tryp had forgotten the man was there. "Did you just find a long-lost twin? That's so cool."

"Can you finish this up?" Camden asked, nodding toward the stage. "I think we have some things to talk about."

Oscar agreed, and Camden led them around the elevator-turned stage, past the kitchenette, toward the back door of Nighttime Awake. The cooks chopped ingredients on a cutting board, garlic and onions wafting through the air like an air freshener as they prepared Happy Hour appetizers. Mozzarella sticks sizzled in the fryers. Tryp's stomach growled at the aroma of his favorite appetizer, but he ignored it in favor of following his twin into the back alley.

"Those are my mozzarella sticks if you want some," Camden said. "I order them at every bar we play at. It's like my good luck charm."

They settled on a wire table set, complete with two rickety chairs propped against the brick wall of the alley. Camden pulled out a pack of cigarettes, offering one to Tryp. He declined.

"I have so many questions, but I don't think there are many answers. How were you living? In foster care? Adopted?" Camden asked, and surprise ran down Tryp's spine at the realization that Camden didn't even know if they had a mother.

"I grew up with my — *our* — mom," Tryp said.

"Our mom?" Camden parroted, saying the words like they were foreign on his tongue. "I thought she was…"

"Dead?" Tryp finished, sensing why his brother was trailing off. "Why would you think that?"

"That's what Dad told me," Camden said. His face was passive, but Tryp recognized the questions swimming in his eyes. They were ones Tryp had often thought of himself. *Why didn't Dad ever visit me? Did he care about me at all?* There was little point in speculating, but it was impossible not to.

"Why would he tell me that?"

"To act like we never existed, I would assume. They each erased the other half of our family completely," Tryp said. "Mom never spoke about Dad, and when I asked about him, she would just completely shut down."

"That's so fucked up," they both said in unison.

"How is she?"

"Mom's in the hospital," Tryp said slowly, realizing that was the first time he'd told anyone that. He looked pointedly at the cigarette in Camden's hand. "Lung cancer."

Camden sat up straight, putting the cigarette out on the table. He pulled the pack out of his pocket, setting it away from him. "How bad?"

"Stage two. There's a lot she has to go through, but we're optimistic," he said. Tryp had never been keen on discussing his family with strangers, but the words were coming easier now. He supposed it was because she was something like Camden's family, too. This was terrible for them both.

"Are there visiting hours at the hospital?"

"You want to visit her?"

"I--," Camden struggled to speak. "I guess. I don't know."

Tryp couldn't blame him. Finding out a family member had cancer was heartbreaking, but adding the hurt and confusion over a mother who wrote you off as if you never existed muddled those feelings. Despite their blood relation, Camden had practically no ties to the woman he called mom. Tryp had always thought he didn't have a dad.

Turns out he did, just one that hadn't wanted to be his father.

"You don't seem all that surprised to find out you have a brother," Tryp said, changing the subject to give Camden time to think. He didn't need to decide if he wanted to see their mom right now.

He shrugged. "Growing up, I never really felt like an only child even though it was just my dad and I. He never talked about the day I was born, and there were very few family pictures. They might have come with the frame, I don't know. I had my suspicions, but I had no proof."

Tryp wondered if he had ever even looked. "I always thought something seemed to weigh Mom down, like a regret she couldn't shake off. The way she would dismiss me completely when I asked about Dad made me believe it was about him."

"That's how Dad seemed, too. I always wondered what I got passed down from Mom," Camden said, carrying on. "I guess it was a nicotine addiction and depression."

"Not that. Your love of music is from her," Tryp explained, shaking his head. "She was in a band called Fear Grin growing up. There are pictures of her everywhere with teased hair, leather pants, and an electric guitar."

Camden smiled. "Why didn't you end up--?"

"In a band too? I got the love of the music, but none of the rhythm. I can't even read music," he said. "It's like a foreign language to me. I chose the next best thing."

"That's how Dad was," Camden said. "He showed up to every one of my performances, bought me any instrument I wanted, but he was tone deaf something awful."

Tryp's heart squeezed at the similarities between himself and a man he had never met. It intrigued him that they both had qualities of the other parent, even after all the years they had been separated. Maybe nature was stronger than nurture sometimes. "When did he pass?"

"Two years ago," Camden said. "We were about to sign with this big agency, but right before the meeting, he had a heart attack. I rushed to the hospital instead, and we lost the deal."

"I'm sorry," Tryp said, leaning back and crossing his arms over his chest. He didn't know how he could feel any loss over his father, but something inside him darkened anyway like he was shifting into mourning for a man he never knew. Tryp struggled with the fact that he would never meet his biological father. If he were alive, would he have reacted well to Tryp entering Camden's life? Despite the unanswered questions, he couldn't help the sense of awe that lingered between them. Camden had lost a parent, while Tryp hoped his mom wouldn't pass. They were on the verge of sharing a specific feeling no one ever wanted to face. It felt like a sign that Camden had experienced the loss that Tryp hoped every day he wouldn't go through. He had not only found a twin but maybe someone he could seek comfort in.

"I don't regret it," Camden shrugged his shoulders, and Tryp realized they were sitting in the same position, arms folded over their chests. "I would have chosen him a thousand times over, but it sucks that Dad's situation may have messed up us being signed."

He reached for his pack of cigarettes on instinct, but Tryp snatched them from the table. Camden tensed, fingers curling into a fist, but then thought twice. He waited, afraid he had crossed a boundary with someone he really didn't even know, but Camden didn't seem angry. If anything, he looked at Tryp with a little respect. Camden busied his fingers by checking his watch instead, sighing at the time.

"I have to get back inside. We start rehearsal in less than an hour." He stood up, Tryp following suit. "Are you going to stay and watch the show?"

Tryp nodded. "I don't need to in order to know I'm going to sign you, and there's no way I'm not going to watch my brother's band. I'm not some big talent agency, though."

"Are you serious? Being able to tell the guys that we have anyone looking into us at all is amazing," Camden said, rushing his words like he was afraid Tryp would change his mind. They walked back inside Nighttime Awake, Camden crackling with energy. "You can decide for sure after you hear us play."

"I'm not going to change my mind. Consider it a family favor."

After promising he would stay, Camden left Tryp. He slid onto a stool at the bar, the cracked cushion on the swivel chair squishing underneath him. The bartender cut fruit for garnishes, preparing for Happy Hour and the long night that would follow it. Marveling at his luck, he ordered a double shot of Johnny Walker Red on the rocks, treating himself to the top-shelf liquor today. He sipped the blended scotch whisky, surveying the servers as he waited for his brother to take the stage. As it burned in his throat and buzzed in his head, he noticed one server in particular. She looked incredibly familiar.

Tryp wondered if he was going to see his features on every person he saw from now on.

See the end of the book for elevator etiquette rules followed or broken. Elevator Etiquette Codes: 1C, 2B, 2C, 4D

Portal

Mama Said Knock You Out

"Most people are completely oblivious to eternity. They look at the sky at night and they think that's eternity; it is just the senses having contact in the sense world. There are other dimensions." -Frederick Lenz

Consider this. Marge hated taking the elevator to work. She would avoid it whenever she could. Sure, the fact that she had access to other dimensions via elevators sounded marvelous. However, when she was 13 and a bit reckless, she met her doppelgänger from the Westphall dimension. Her name was Clarice and when Marge entered her world, it felt comfortable, so Marge hung around for a bit. Clarice took Marge home and showed her the place. Even though they shared virtually identical DNA, they both lived completely different lives and only Marge was supernatural. Clarice loved the arts and was honored to decorate most of her three-story house with her paintings and sketches.

Everything was great until Clarice's very religious and excitable mother came home one day and saw her little angel standing next to Clarice. She thought Clarice must have spawned a demon. Marge's mom looked the same as hers but had no powers and was a fanatically religious woman. Clarice's mom panicked, lost her shit, and threw all kinds of crap at Marge and Clarice. Her mother shrieked **daemonium** in frantic repetition and freaked everyone out. Clarice didn't even know her mother knew Latin and wondered what else she was hiding. After Mom's fierce insistence on an immediate exorcism, Marge ran out of the house and back to the elevator she came from. Since then, she has been very choosy about opening portals and entering dimensions that opened up for her, especially the mirror dimensions.

Now, almost twenty years later, Marge sighed in exasperation as she stared at the sign on the stairwell door:

STAIRS CLOSED FOR QUARTERLY
DISINFECTION.
KINDLY TAKE THE ELEVATOR.

Marge liked to keep it calm and simple at work. So at the office, Marge was a stairway gal and usually marched right up those stairs. But today the elevator was her only option to make the Q3 meeting, and it was essential she be on time. Marge was teased before for taking the stairs in outrageously sexy 6-inch heels, and Marge had hit her limit by being the butt of jokes at work. As far as she was concerned, the additional steps kept her fit and helped her manage her weight. She could not imagine the things she'd hear if "Marching Marge" revealed her supernatural abilities as well. Screw her mother for passing down these elevator portal powers.

Marge waited patiently in the lobby outside the god-forsaken elevator. She took a deep breath and pressed the shining gold button to go up. When the ding sounded, Marge braced herself for what may come from the other side of the doors. While Marge was proficient at bending reality, there were rules. Outside of the elevator, it was difficult for her to control the location on the other side of the door, one of the many downsides her mother had told her to be careful of. However, since Marge was in a bit of a rush, she hoped the elevator would simply open to her actual reality and take her to the 10th floor. She wished to arrive at her meeting without incident. Marge needed a break.

Unfortunately, that would not be the case for Marge. The elevator door opened, and a gust of cold wind hit and snow flurries beat her face. Three men in Viking helmets holding pink suitcases greeted her, *"Heil ok sæl, Marge!"* If she had time and was dressed for it, she'd usually hang with the Vikings. Today they would yell and cheer, gripping their pink suitcases in excitement. They weren't that bad to ride with, but today she refused to settle for ear-splitting screams and constant elevator shaking that escalated her nerves and anxiety. If Marge was going to be forced to take the elevator, she was going to hitch a calm and temperature-appropriate ride up. Still, she was intrigued about what was in the pink suitcases and where her Viking friends were planning to holiday.

She nodded and gave them a small smile. "I'll take the next one."

The Viking on the far left looked disappointed, but exclaimed, *"Blessuð!"* and then pressed the closed door button.

As the elevator portal opened again, the smell of grilled hot dogs raided her nose from a competition on a cruise ship. Chants of "Glizzy! Glizzy! Glizzy!" echoed off the walls of the lobby. Marge was not hungry enough to miss her meeting, and besides, it was too early for a snack. A man in a mustard yellow shirt with the words Frank Feeders Referee stepped in front of Marge with his arms crossed.

"Are you joining us for the next round, Ms. Sayyora?" the ref asked as he beckoned her to cross the threshold into his space. Just next to him, she couldn't take her eyes off a man the size of a boulder with a bib that said "Weiner Eater". His system fascinated Marge. After rotating his plate, he would dip the buns in red Crystal Light before tapping the bread on the side of the cup for the excess liquid to drip out. The glizzy gobbler would then grab the hot dog with his right hand and the bun with his left before finally eating the dog.

Marge looked at the ref, and then at her watch. "No, just passing by."

The ref groaned in disappointment and walked away. An air horn blasted in the background, followed by "T-I-I-I-I-M-E". Marge pushed the up button and hoped to not witness any "reversals of fortune" before the doors closed. So what madness awaited Marge next, delaying her now urgent trip to the conference room?

The elevator opened again to reveal Bruno Montacarichi, a tall, shirtless male fitness model flexing his sculpted arms and chiseled chest. This floor was alive with the sounds of weights clanging, accompanied by the grunts of those exercising behind him. Marge had taken the elevator with him only once before. He re-introduced himself and said he wanted to find a beautiful gal to be his gym partner today. Once he saw Marge again, it made his day.

"Mi corazon, will you take my hand and join me?" He asked. Despite his beautiful stature and silky voice, declining his hand was easy for Marge.

"Not today, Bruno. I'm in a rush." Marge let the elevator doors close as his bright smile quickly disappeared.

After a short wait and another ding, the elevator opened again. A short woman with vibrant red hair and emerald eyes smiled brightly at Marge. She bounced slightly and charged at Marge for a surprise hug.

"Sarah!" Marge held the woman close, walking backward and placing a hand on the open elevator doors to keep them open.

Leaning back, the green eyes met Marge's dark gray ones. "I know you told me not to try this, but I missed you and..."

"So you used our in-home elevator? That's only for practice when I'm there; you know that." Marge stepped back and considered her next words carefully. She held Sarah's hand tightly and inquired, "How'd you even know my work elevator would open to the house?"

"I just did the math and a lot of wishful thinking," Sarah explained. "You left home an hour ago, and it takes you about 45 minutes to get there and then about ten more minutes to exit the car, walk across the lot, and then get to the elevator bank. You're not mad at me... are you?" Her eyes watered.

There was only a small chance of this working and she knew it, but the fact that Sarah gave it a shot anyway showed how much she cared about Marge. Marge leaned in and kissed Sarah lightly. "Of course not. I miss you too, but I really need to get to this meeting."

"Right, right," Sarah agreed, as she took a step back in the elevator.

Marge crossed to the elevator's edge and held the door open. She took a deep breath and pressed 1-1-1-2 to manually close the portal. Marge stepped out of the elevator after stealing a kiss from Sarah. "I'll see you back at home then, babe. I love you!"

Sarah waved as the portal shrank. "Of course, I love you too." The doors closed.

Marge turned at the sound of footsteps approaching her. Great. Coming up behind her was Marge's nemesis supervisor, Herman. He was condescending to Marge, and she didn't appreciate that. Marge generally did her work with excellence and minded her own business. Recently he requested, but really demanded, that she finish the rest of a report for him while he handled a family emergency. Of course, Marge agreed and emailed Herman back immediately, sending him positive wishes for him and his family members. Herman didn't show Marge any appreciation, not even a "thank you" for her concern, and, more importantly, for bailing him out. What made it worse was when Marge discovered on Insta that he was really hanging out with Alice from PR that day — at the beach!

Marge was a patient woman, but everyone had limits, and lately, Herman had been violating hers. Marge hated him even more after he took advantage of her repeatedly and lied about it. She'd rather ride the elevator with a hungry crocodile than Herman, but with Marge not wanting to be late, she didn't have many options. However, if Herman wasn't tolerable, Marge wouldn't hesitate to take him on a little trip in the elevator after the meeting.

Herman stepped into the elevator and Marge followed behind him, moving to the farthest corner of the elevator while Herman pressed the button for the 10th floor.

Herman's cologne assaulted Marge's nose, causing her to sneeze.

"I have a last-minute thing for you to do over the weekend —" Herman started.

"No." Marge cuts him off before he can finish.

"Marge, I don't know what has gotten into you —"

"No!"

Herman, a bit on edge now, continued. "You know I can write you up for insubordination."

Suddenly, Marge's mind flashed back, remembering all the unruly tasks and unpaid overtime she had to endure. The number of times he took advantage of her and rubbed her nose in it. Enough was enough. She was going to embrace her inner elevator goddess and assert control!

Marge calmly reached for the buttons and methodically pressed the 8th floor five times, triggering a specific portal. She retreated into the farthest corner of the elevator and gripped the handrails as tightly as she could, sucking in a deep breath and holding it.

"What the hell are you doing?" Herman asked, mocking Marge's closed eyes and scrunched-up face. But soon he would wish he had taken the same precautions as she did. The elevator door opened and the air immediately got sucked into a black void mixed with green glowing specs scattered across space. Because they were in space, no one could hear Herman scream. He tried to grab Marge but was snatched from the elevator and tumbled uncontrollably into the void. He panicked as he entered the expansive cold abyss. Marge's version of the 8th floor was a cold-hearted bitch.

She held on with all her strength as the vacuum pulled her toward the void. It managed to move her foot forward, which she countered by stepping down hard and pressing her forefoot into the floor. Finally, the suction lightened up as the elevator door started to close. Marge slowly relaxed her muscles. She reveled in the instant relief given to her muscles and lungs and allowed herself to smirk. She slowed her breathing and fixed her clothes and hair. Marge rubbed her nose once more and executed a quick makeup check before the elevator dinged for the 10th floor. Marge confidently strutted to her Q3 meeting on time, full of confidence, vim, and vigor.

She'd make sure to pick Herman back up later. He'd probably come back a bit traumatized but not be coherent enough to adequately explain his absence from the quarterly meeting to HR. If Marge was going to get written up for abandoning Herman inside an interdimensional void, she felt she was in the clear, as there wasn't an established company policy for that situation. However, if Herman was gonna Herman, New Marge was gonna New Marge. With a smile creeping across her face, she fantasized about an enlightening trip with her supervisor to the 13th floor, where she would unleash the powers she inherited from her father.

See the end of the book for elevator etiquette rules followed or broken. Elevator Etiquette Codes: 1C, 2D, 2F, 6C, 6G, 9B

Mark of A Man

Mark of A Man Trilogy, Part I

"Our lives are not our own. We are bound to others, past and present, and by each crime and every kindness, we birth our future." -Somni-451 in **Cloud Atlas** *by David Mitchell*

Consider this. Caleb got on the elevator and pushed the button to his floor, wanting to collapse in bed after an awful day. His Spring trip was supposed to be fun, a nice break from high school. Instead, it was tension-filled because he and his girlfriend, Elisa, fought the entire time. Despite that, he wished she was still here with him. Deep down, he hoped Elisa didn't call it quits after she stormed out and that he could still patch things up. She wanted him to step up in the relationship and get over himself; he didn't know if he could. The clock was ticking. After a while, he decided to snoop around her social media to see if she was with someone else and saw that her relationship status had changed to "It's complicated." He felt nothing would ever be good without her; maybe he was right.

His fists clenched, and tears threatened to spill from his eyes. He took a deep breath and punched the button for his floor. *I am a man, and men do not cry.* He was so caught up in his feelings while staring at his phone that he didn't notice the mysterious entity in the elevator. ☐

She was slowly tracing the shape of a flower with her bare feet while saying a few words in ancient Greek. A dark mist appeared on the elevator floor surrounding this sixteen-year-old girl. She sighed for a moment, staring at the dusty floor. The girl glanced up in Caleb's direction, and she smiled. She could have recognized his spirit anywhere. She admired the King Leonidas Lives shirt hung tightly around his body. "Nice shirt," she told him. Her eyes stared at him, pleading as if he was a present for her.

Caleb jumped, startled by her, and then he was embarrassed. She was so beautiful he had trouble focusing.

"Thanks, I just love that movie," Caleb responded, badly faking his usual enthusiasm when discussing it.

Then she asked, "What's the matter? What is your name?"

"Caleb, my name is Caleb," he said curtly. "And I'm fine."

The girl continued to smile as she came closer to him. *My darling, is it you, after all this time? Oh, the gods are smiling upon us.* "I'm Rosemarie, and I'm visiting with my family for —" Rosemarie began. She paused for a moment to read Caleb's mind. "Spring Break."

"I hope you've had a better vacation than me," Caleb responded. *Just leave me alone,* he thought.

"Why? What happened?" Her voice filled with faux concern.

Caleb was about to tell her to go away when he finally held her gaze. He sighed. Her soft brown eyes sparkled in the little light in the elevator. She was beautiful and peculiar at the same time. A voice sounded in his head that seemed to come from nowhere: *No, I won't leave you alone, my King; it has been too long.* "Oh, nothing. I just got into a little fight with my girlfriend, Elisa. She stormed off, saying I was too insecure and possessive." Caleb laughed, but it sounded forced.

Rosemarie pressed closer to him and pushed strands out of his face. She felt his torso pull back, but at least he didn't stop her from running her hands over his body, which she was grateful for. She wanted to familiarize herself with his new features. They were strange to her, but she didn't mind. Words could not describe the feeling she felt touching them after so long. She felt Caleb quivered under her touch.

Caleb stared at her smooth pale skin and flowing red hair. Her beauty so entranced him that he didn't notice the shadows beginning to creep up the elevator walls.

With his girlfriend gone, this will be much easier than I thought. "I understand, Caleb. One should never make their beloved doubtful of their devotion." She pressed against him and smiled.

Her hair shared the fragrance of rosemary, and that scent enticed Caleb. The aroma, now imbued within the fibers of his shirt, was so familiar, yet he could not place it. The elevator stopped, and the door opened. Caleb turned to leave but was conflicted.

No, my love. I won't lose you again, Rosemarie thought, ready to use any means necessary to keep him here with her.

"It was nice to meet you," Caleb said. Her lovely figure aroused him, and he was desperate not to let her know it.

"Stay a second, Caleb." She stepped in front of him, blocking his exit. She flipped her hair and licked her lips.

Caleb blushed a tiny bit. The elevator door thudded shut, causing him to glance over her head in response.

"I just met you, but your soul could light anyone's way in the darkness, maybe even mine," she said. Rosemarie waited for a reaction from him, a bit too long for her taste. *Come on. You have to remember my ουσία της ζωής. You have to, my beloved.*

"Ummm," Caleb began as he laughed nervously.

Her hopes dropped just a little. *He only needs more time.* She stared at the features on his face, from his dark brown hair to his almost black eyes. Rosemarie nearly wept when she saw the raised birthmark on his cheek, shaped like the moon. Rosemarie had received the same crescent moon on her wrist during their binding ritual several centuries ago. The mark was hidden beneath her sleeve. It signaled that she had found her beloved's vessel and her silver moon had returned. Her blessed one. There was no way in Tartarus that she would let him leave this elevator alone. *My love, tonight is a gift given to us by the gods who gave us our joys and greatest sorrows. We must take their blessing now, since they may not give us another.* Rosemarie's heart clenched at the thought.

Caleb stood there in a daze. Her pupils narrowed like a cat's. He felt like he was a canary about to be eaten. Then he perceived the shadows swirling around them. "What the —" Caleb began, feeling the urgency to pry the elevator doors open and get the hell out of there. Then he saw her hand covering the button. "Hey, it's pretty late, and I still have to eat. Would you let me get to my floor?"

"I can satisfy your cravings. Come with me," she voiced as more of a command than an offering.

Caleb tried to push her off the button to his floor, but she slapped his hand away before grabbing his chin, and their eyes met.

"Come to my room," she said as seductively as possible. She began tracing the moon's shape on his pectorals with one sharp nail on her right hand. "We could talk more or perhaps..." Her tone was sensual as she massaged her warm chest against his.

Caleb's face was completely red, his body on fire. He had never gotten this close to a girl who wasn't Elisa. He allowed himself to be pressed into the elevator wall. He barely remembered that they were in one. It was as if his mind were somewhere else as the girl continued her assault.

"It's alright, my love," she told him. A shimmering shadow rolled and followed her movements. "I need you to hold me in your arms forever. I could lose myself when I look into your eyes."

Caleb gave an uneasy smile. Butterflies invaded his chest. Here was the most exotic girl he had ever seen, wanting him and only him. Elisa was still on the fringes of his mind, but just.

"I promised you that no matter what form you took, I would find you," Rosemarie whispered. "Surely, you remember me, don't you?"

Caleb's mind was darting back and forth between Elisa and Rosemarie. He wanted to do the right thing but didn't understand what the fuck she was talking about. *She's hot, but Elisa would hate me forever. Shit.* Caleb flipped between confusion and excitement.

She wrapped her arms around him. "You were never meant for simple girls like Elisa," Rosemarie continued, and her tears fell on Caleb's peculiar birthmark. Rosemarie's mouth slowly turned into a smile without Caleb realizing it.

Her tears softly pelted his skin like warm pearls. Caleb cuddled her, wanting to be closer than their clothes would allow. He knew he was being lured in, but it made it hotter.

That's right, my darling. Remember our caresses. I promise you we will live as King and Queen again. "Let's seal it with a kiss." She closed her eyes and aimed for his lips.

Caleb unexpectedly turned away. The image of his girlfriend in his head solidified. Elisa hadn't said they were officially over; maybe she was testing his feelings and devotion, not as an insecure boy but as a strong man of honor. On the other hand, he was so turned on. And being stuck in the elevator, he had nowhere to go. *Who's going to know?* Caleb assured himself. But something inside him firmly said no, he would know.

Rosemarie's eyes widened with disbelief. Her world shattered, and her happiness seeped from her body. She shook her head in frustration and grabbed both of his hands with her own, trying to keep the hope of having him back with her alive.

The shadows paused to evaluate the scene. Caleb shuddered in fear, sensing their stillness.

"It's alright, my beloved. Let me in, and I can make you forget about Elisa and remember all that is important," Rosemarie whispered. *After all, you swore I was your true love, and no other woman would ever hold your heart again.*

The grin on her face was slightly too wide and sent a shiver down his spine. He noticed the undulating shadows circling them again, drawing ever closer to him. Their shimmer flickered much more rapidly, like sun rays bouncing off glass shards on a windy day.

Empowered that her corusics eagerly awaited orders from their mistress, Rosemarie continued. "We could spend all of eternity together. Never to be separated by death again."

Not hearing what Rosemarie said and forgetting for a moment about the supernatural shadow, Caleb's resolve weakened. He licked his lips and pushed closer to her body, enjoying her warmth. Everything about her seemed enticing to his body, which desired hers. However, a part of Caleb's mind remained firm in the reality that she was a threat. He had no idea how to get out of the elevator without escalating the dangerous situation. Here was a striking girl who desired him as Elisa used to, maybe more. And Rosemarie seemed to admire him, unlike anyone else in his life. "I can't...I won't," Caleb said. He pushed her away.

"Why?" Rosemarie protested.

Caleb replied, snapping back to a harsh reality, "I don't even know you. I'm sorry. I need to go." He reached for the elevator button to open the door.

Rosemarie sighed in frustration, vulnerable momentarily, before signaling to the shadows to attack. One of the shadows, actually a corusic, became aggressive.

Caleb's eyes widened. It took hold of Caleb's hand and pulled him back. He shrieked as the corusic turned him around. As Caleb's eyes locked with Rosemarie's, this shadow creature followed her lead. The urge to flee coursed through Caleb's body, but he was trapped. He noticed Rosemarie's pupils taking on an unearthly quality and became piercing amber coals of despair and desire. Caleb realized that a conniving predator was preparing to consume him.

"Centuries ago, you said that you wanted to be resurrected no matter the cost," she declared, as she moved to cast a spell. "I do not break my word. I swore to you in the name of Hecate."

He watched in horror as dark mist materialized from within the elevator walls and the ceiling hatch. Caleb screamed and writhed against the shadow's grip as more shadows formed and aggressively closed in on him.

TO BE CONTINUED

See the end of the book for elevator etiquette rules followed or broken. Elevator Etiquette Codes: 2F, 3B, 3D, 4A, 5A, 5F, 6B, 6D, 6H

Supernatural Scorn, Metaphysical Mayhem

Mark of A Man Trilogy, Part II

"She's mad, but she's magic. There's no lie in her fire."
-Charles Bukowski

Consider this. Caleb met a mysterious girl, Rosemarie, in the elevator, an enchantress his spirit had known for centuries. After briefly being transfixed by her beauty and mystique, he ultimately stayed loyal to his girlfriend. This did not go over well with Rosemarie, as she expected to be in the arms of her warrior king by now, after searching for hundreds of years for his reincarnation. Scorned, Rosemarie summoned her shadow corusics to trap him and punish him for rebuffing her advances. Rosemarie recalled the last night she spent with her true love many millennia ago.

Rosemarie retired to their bed. A man climbed in and held her from behind. He pressed his face against her neck, and she sighed, full of delight. He stroked her hair before kissing her. "I wish we could stay like this forever," Rosemarie said.

"We will," Aniketos' deep booming voice was filled with confidence. "I'll become like you. Immortal. To you, I promise this."

She lay in his arms. "I wish it were easy to do so, especially hiding the transmutation from the gods," Rosemarie's voice was solemn, "Many have tried, but few have completed the ritual successfully." She caressed his arm. "Simply enjoy the time we have now."

"Nothing shall separate us," Aniketos insisted. "If Zeus himself refuses to grant us this victory, it shall not stop me. For I will always find my way back to you." He pulled her into the bed and kissed every part of her body.

The memory echoed in Rosemarie's mind as she faced Caleb, Aniketos incarnate in this lifetime. That crescent birthmark proved it.

The shadows forced Caleb's arms into unnatural positions, causing Caleb to yelp in pain, but he would not submit. Another shadow poured through the closed elevator doors, dragging Caleb to Rosemarie for a reckoning. The shadows tied him to the brass grab bars attached to the elevator walls with their bodies. He turned his head away and closed his eyes as they poked at his forehead and ears, finally whispering something that Caleb couldn't make out, except for two words: My Lord. *What are these things?* Caleb thought to himself. He could tell that they seemed familiar with him. *What the hell?* His eyelids felt heavier, and his movements became more sluggish. The elevator moved up.

"Come on now, my King, I expected more fight out of you." Rosemarie placed her hand on his chest, grinning, as Caleb hissed.

"But it does not matter. You will be mine in the end." She pushed forward to kiss him, desiring to have his lips on hers once more and erase the bitter memory of her rejection.

Rosemarie was out on the battlefield with King Aniketos. Enemy soldiers howled and pleaded for the gods to save them, to no avail. Aniketos's men slashed through their bodies. Horses fled from broken chariots, sometimes dragging screaming soldiers with them.

Aniketos fought alongside them with his sword, slicing the throats of his adversaries. Rosemarie took the form of a dragon and decimated several men with her vibrant flames and enormous tail. They seemed like an invincible team.

However, the emperor of the invaders prepared for this. He first had his archers coat their arrows with a potion that immobilized witches and had them aim at Rosemarie in flight. In her dragon form, Rosemarie was injured but managed to keep the potion's effects from completely overtaking her. She crash-landed and spat fire upon the men who swarmed her.

The emperor then charged into the fray. The emperor advanced on Rosemarie with his poisonous sword. Her attention was so split that she didn't sense the emperor's advance. But Aniketos did. The emperor lunged to stab, only for Aniketos to throw himself between the sword and Rosemarie's body, blood pouring from his chest.

Rosemarie's whole world exploded. At that moment, charged with rage and passion, she was as powerful as the gods. Her dragon fire first scorched the emperor, then everything else except the fallen Aniketos and his men. The memory fueled Rosemarie's fury like it was yesterday.

The charge of the remembrance dissipated when Caleb broke free of the shadows and shoved her away once the elevator stopped. She telepathically commanded the shadows to prevent him from hitting the elevator button back to his floor.

The shadows took hold of his leg as he reached for the panel. He fell to the floor and frantically grabbed at the air. *There's nothing I can do,* he thought frantically. How the hell am I supposed to keep fighting these things? Elisa's figure flashed right before his eyes. She never left his thoughts since he first met her during summer camp and shared their first kiss in the woods. He could still feel the warmth of her lips. *I have to get back to my girl.* He kicked at the shadows around him, his foot passing through their supernatural form. Frustrated, he discovered that the harder he fought, the tighter the shadow creatures held him. They were using Caleb's life force against him.

His phone fell out of his pocket, and the camera flashed when it hit the floor. The shadows shrieked, and they repelled back just for a moment. That instant was enough for Caleb to get up and snatch his phone before the corusics could steal it. *Now we're talking,* Caleb thought, smirking.

Rosemarie didn't appreciate Caleb's realization and winced at the sharp pain she felt through the shadow hive mind. However, she grinned, knowing aspects of her love remained, but it seemed time was running out for the transmutation. It was wishful thinking, but maybe she wouldn't have to continue harming him to get Aniketos back. "My darling, you were born for greatness. Stop denying who you are and let the flame of our passion consume you," she demanded.

Caleb gave her a crooked smile and continued working the flash on his phone as if he were firing arrows, targeting and shooting any that dared come close. The corusics howled each time.

Rosemarie groaned. She still did not fully understand modern technology and despised it. "Please, my love, if you persist, I will kill you, and we will do this again in another lifetime." Her voice exuded patience despite her actions.

Caleb continued his flashes. *I need to buy time until I can escape.*

Rosemarie's heart began to hurt at hearing these thoughts. Not a single memory of their life remained conscious within his soul. She recalled her final moments with Aniketos.

Drenched in his blood, he lay on the ground as Rosemarie returned to her human form. Rosemarie cried and tried in vain to use her healing magic.

He put his hand over hers and pleaded that she stop, knowing her sorcery had limits, and if she exhausted her power, she would perish herself. He asked, "Promise me you'll find me in the next life."

"I will try, but if you are happy there, My King —" Rosemarie began but was silenced.

"No. Do not find another," Aniketos pleaded. "I shall never love as I love you." He grabbed her chin. "Do whatever needs to be done for us to reunite."

"My heart burns for you, but the gods always brutally punish those who interfere with fate," Rosemarie began. "It never ends well for —"

Aniketos looked into her eyes. "I want to hold you in my arms again. I cannot face Hades knowing I will never see you again; you are worth the risk." His breaths became shallower. "Please swear on Hecate that you will find me and bring me back, no matter what form I take or how long I take to return to this realm."

Rosemarie, sobbing, said, "I swear on Hecate I will."

"I love you, always and for eternity," Aniketos said. As his hand dropped, his eyes reflected death. Rosemarie kissed his still lips.

Caleb looked on as a tear fell from Rosemarie's eyes at the memory. The shadows saw their mistress' distress and became more determined to please her, and Rosemarie realized sadly that she would have to be more aggressive to achieve Caleb's surrender.

One shadow snuck behind Caleb and latched itself onto the back of his knee. The shadow drilled through his skin, and Caleb gritted his teeth in pain as blood pooled on the floor. The crimson liquid soaked his socks and shoes. Before Caleb could turn his phone on that monster, two shadows pinned his arms to his sides, keeping him from a fresh attack. The phone remained in his hands as Caleb tried to take photos without seeing the screen.

"This is getting tiresome. You can't win," Rosemarie assured him, her frustration peaking.

"My Moto G says I can, you bitch!" Caleb said. He tried to twist his body out of the shadow's grip. "I wanna see my friends again. I want Elisa back. You won't take away —." The shadow wrapped around his throat and squeezed. Caleb managed to wheeze out the words "— Elisa from me." Black spots soon dotted his vision. His phone fell from his hands.

"Do not utter her name. She does not appreciate you," Rosemarie said, her voice dripping with arrogance. "You were never hers. She was never yours. You are both children." She took a few exasperated steps towards him. "Besides, *you* swore me to these acts."

Caleb shook his head "no" as he fell to his knees. "You are killing me." The strength he had in him was running out. He pushed himself to remain kneeling until a third shadow shoved him to the floor. Though he was near death, he could hear Rosemarie in his mind. *Please endure this, my love. I prayed Hecate would take pity on us and she would bring us together without all this unnecessary pain.* She summoned the shadows into a single large mass, and they consumed Caleb as one.

He hadn't had the energy to push them back any longer. They went in his nose, filled his torso with blackness, and exited his mouth. His stomach burned as the shadows tore at his insides. *This is how it ends,* Caleb realized. His favorite shirt, which Elisa had bought him for Christmas after they saw *300*, was ripped and stained with his blood. At once, he realized he was weeping, ironically realizing that sometimes men do cry. The wounds on his chest stung every time he moved an inch. His legs were limp, and the blood felt like a blanket. Caleb stared at the darkness all around him. He touched the hem of his shirt, wishing he could see Elisa one last time. Nothingness greeted him as the shadows started blocking every speck of light around him. His energy lessened, as he knew there was no chance for him now. In the distance, he swore he heard the notes of Elisa's ringtone on his phone. She hadn't given up on him. Was he going to give up on her? NO! He was going to prove himself to her. It was now or never.

TO BE CONTINUED

See the end of the book for elevator etiquette rules followed or broken. Elevator Etiquette Codes: 1D, 2B, 2C, 2D, 2E, 2F, 5F, 6H

Love Like You're Dying

Mark of A Man Trilogy, Part III

"Evil lurks where disappointment lodges." -George Foreman

Consider this. Rosemarie was determined not to lose her warrior king again. She wanted to restore the ancient essence of the man she loved by unlocking his dormant memories. However scorned, she used her shadow corusics to pursue Caleb and attempt to bend him to her will. Despite his best efforts, Rosemarie ultimately subdued Caleb with her creatures. She positioned herself to finish him and bring her lover's powerful nature back to her.

The shadows slowly retreated to the corners of the elevator. Their initial mission was complete, and the shadow warriors awaited further commands.

"My darling, be at peace. Everything will go right this time," Rosemarie whispered, her hands petting his chest. Caleb's movements slowed, and Rosemarie smiled, seeing his unmoving form. He would finally be hers.

"That's right, relax, and your transformation will be complete when you awaken." She patted his forehead gently and instructed the corusics to cover his face to start the next phase of the restoration ritual.

As he neared the edge of death, his rebirth as the warrior king was approaching. For a moment, it seemed like he was about to give in to eternal life with this beautiful enchantress and leave his troubled teenage life behind. A life that still had value to Caleb. He saw the crescent moon symbol glowing from Rosemarie's shadowy arm as she reached over his face. Caleb's eyes grew heavy, beginning to remember as the ritual continued.

He again was Aniketos, a king in silver armor with the moon nota on his chest, leading an ambush on a larger army. He could feel the pride and glory flowing through him, blessed by the gods. Everything he ever desired would be his if he released this life.

BZZZZZZZ! Elisa sent him a text. On the floor, his phone responds with Elisa's ringtone, "You Were Meant for Me" by Jewel, jolting him back to reality. The image of Elisa overwhelmed his mind, adrenalizing his muscles and allowing him to slow Rosemarie's assault. His hands aggressively fanned the corusics' essence away. Part of himself wanted to grasp the memories Rosemarie had shown him, to relive the excitement. However, Caleb knew they would take over his being and that he would no longer be himself. He would never again be with Elisa. Fortunately for him, the corusics still sensed the essence of Aniketos and would not harm his body without Rosemarie's instructions. He at once felt Antiketos' power. His muscles grew to resemble the wrestlers he admired on TV, and his wounds started to heal. On the other hand, he still had the memories of Caleb instead of his warrior personality. However, as strength surged through him, Caleb realized he could lift entire mountains if he wanted to. He got back on his feet and stepped towards the elevator panel, ready to exit this nightmare. It wasn't easy, but he was rebounding quickly. With the ancient spiritual energy rewriting the DNA of every cell of his body, Caleb knew Aniketos must have been a force of nature, and for a moment, he was tempted to surrender. *I want to be a badass, but I won't erase who I am, even for this power.*

Simultaneously, he heard the elevator and Rosemarie's voice echoing in his head.

"Aniketos, stop this abomination at once!" This unholy combination was not in Rosemarie's plan. She roared like a lioness and transformed. Rosemarie grew taller. Her hair became even longer, taking on the bright fire color from the stars themselves. Her face took on the form of a woman in her twenties rather than a teenager's and was even more alluring and beyond gorgeous. Rosemarie had returned to her true visage. The guise that had made Antiketos infatuated with her.

He grabbed the phone from the floor and snapped a photo of a shadow attempting to latch onto his shirt. *No! I'm my own man and won't sacrifice my life for anything.* Whenever a shadow dared try to drag him back, he took another pic, and with a screech, it backed off. Caleb heard words that didn't sound like Rosemarie's. Due to the corusic drilling into his mind, he could better understand them. *Why, my lord? We only wanted to be at your side again, just like in the old times.* Caleb was stunned for a moment and glared at the shadow. He tried to keep himself standing. But while his body was re-energizing, the blood loss took its toll on him. His body pleaded with him to stop moving just as he became sluggish. His second wind waned as his shirt, pants, and shoes were caked in blood and grime. Regardless, he staggered over to the panel.

Suddenly, a shadow shoved him hard into the elevator doors, denting the metal from the inside. His head hit the metal door, and he fell, dazed, white flecks blurring his vision. His phone slipped from his hand. He couldn't bring himself to move, and his thoughts swirled around. Everything burned within Caleb.

"Perhaps I was wrong," Rosemarie said as she caressed his cheek. "You have Aniketos' fighting spirit, but you are still too wild." Her hand moved his chin and forced his eyes to meet hers. "I will tame you. You must perish under my magic to be reborn as my King."

The corusic creature wrapped its body over his head again, causing his world to fall into darkness. Caleb slumped to the floor as more of his violent past returned to him. He is King Aniketos, the dreaded warrior with his powerful queen, Rosemarie.

Rosemarie clutched his body and sobbed. He wanted to look away but was frightened at how quickly everything that made him Caleb was dissolving. His life with his friends and Elisa began to feel like a dream, and his dreams were fading.

Suddenly, Elisa's figure rebounded in his mind. She placed her hand on his face. "Don't give up, huggy bear. I love you," she told him. Caleb's eyes moistened. Truthfully, he had been waiting for those words. "Channel Aniketos' fighting energy and skill," Elisa continued. "She gave you the key. Make her pay, sweetheart. You can —"

She faded away without another word as Rosemarie cut off the vision. Then she had her shadows cleanse more of Caleb's memories from his consciousness. Caleb fought to keep his eyes open, knowing one moment of weakness could ensure his entire identity was gone. He could feel Rosemarie's magic draining him with his pounding headache. His hands grabbed his head, trying to shake her mental grasp. Her memory ripping was excruciating. *I'm stronger than the pain.* ◻

"No, you're not," she told him. Rosemarie seized his chin, and Caleb's eyes widened as he took in Rosemarie's more mature form. She fondled his cheeks, and he recoiled. She leaned once more for a kiss as she put a happy memory of the two of them in his mind, which he ignored.

With the combined strength of Aniketos, adrenaline, and his passion for Elisa, Caleb pushed himself closer to the elevator panel. And with everything he had left and a bit of luck, his fingers landed on *the* button. He pressed, praying to every deity he could think of, and this was indeed an emergency.

The siren rang out over and over. The strobe lights flashed throughout the elevator. The shadows howled as the flashing lights struck them. They scratched at Caleb's legs, trying to carve shelter in his body. *Please, my Lord, stop this. We only were following your ancient wishes.* With strength beyond restoration, he swatted them away like they were flies. The shadows began to shrivel up like flowers in drought under the relentlessly pulsing lights.

"I'm not your beloved," Caleb said softly.

Rosemarie growled before howling in pain. A single tear fell before she turned to Caleb, her face twisted with bitter resentment. However, her amber eyes dulled. Resignation entered her heart. She tried to push the sad thought away, but there was no denying it now. Her love would not return to her tonight. He wanted a love story, just not with her. She held her hand in a vain attempt to get her shadows to push Caleb down. The corusics squealed louder as they dissolved.

Rosemarie still looked into Caleb's eyes with defiance. A weakened shadow managed to grab his ankle and make him stumble. "You are indeed my King from now and forever," she began. She forced a grin when she found his face close to hers.

He took hold of his phone and hoped there was enough power for one last picture. He snapped a final image, a morbid selfie with a partner from long ago. She shrieked so loudly as she closed her eyes that Caleb thought he would become deaf. Her hair became darker and smoky until it turned into a shadow itself. Her face dissolved into steam. As she fell, her body faded into mist, muscles and bones cracking and snapping, slowly breaking apart piece by piece. Eventually, she disappeared into eternity along with her diffusing corusics.

The elevator was wrecked, with his blood spattered throughout the floor and walls. There was no trace of the shadows. The only sign of her presence was her faint scent of rosemary. He was relieved at her absence, but still, her voice reverberated in his head: *Every time you see a shadow, I will be there. Aniketos, I am coming for you, one way or the other. Just like you commanded, my King.* The young man shuddered. He doubted he would ever feel comfortable in the dark again.

The elevator was stuck between floors, so the only chance of escape was up. A knock echoed throughout the elevator before the ceiling hatch squeaked open. Caleb's heart violently palpitated, fearing Rosemarie had returned.

Caleb pulled himself up to his feet, only to fall back down. His chest was torn, his legs could barely stand, and his head felt like a truck had smashed into it and run him over. As a grotesque consolation prize, his healing body was now super fit, and it looked like that would stay.

"Hey, we got a call that the elevator was stuck and someone was trapped inside. Are you okay down there?" the fireman asked.

"I need help."

"I'm going to throw down a rope to you." A belay rope came down from the elevator hatch. "Young man, please take it," the fireman commanded.

Caleb steadied his hands on the fibers, shaking all the way.

Realizing that Caleb was alone, the fireman frowned when he got a better look at his state. "What the hell happened down there?"

Caleb stared at the wobbling floor. "You wouldn't believe me if I told you."

The fireman was about to press him for details until he realized Caleb's eyes were beginning to close. "The paramedics are coming. Hang on. I'll be right down."

Caleb couldn't stay another minute in the haunting elevator, so he told the fireman, "No, it's alright. I can do it." He forced his bleeding legs up and secured himself to the rope before pulling himself up despite all the pain. The cuts throughout his battle-scarred body burned, but his newly swole form powered on through. He focused on Elisa. He had been missing her pretty black hair and the scent of her lily perfume. Even if she had nothing but angry words for him right now, he still longed to hear her voice.

When he cleared the hatch, another fireman carefully placed his body on the floor of the elevator roof's exterior. Caleb had never felt so grateful. He lay there sore, finally able to rest. He was marveling at his surroundings. He had seen much today, from a frightening shapeshifter to fearsome shadow creatures. No one would believe it unless he showed them the pictures, maybe not even then. "I'm so glad to see you." For a second, he could swear he saw the sliver of a corusic passing underneath the fireman's coat.

"Let's get you to the hospital, son," the fireman said.

Caleb pulled out his blood-soaked phone. "Just a moment, sir. I need to call my girlfriend."

See the end of the book for elevator etiquette rules followed or broken. Elevator Etiquette Codes: 3E, 5A, 5F, 6B, 6H

Love Rising

Love In An Elevator

"Cut the ending. Revise the script. The man of her dreams is a girl." -**Julie Anne Peters**

Consider this. Jacki Epps reapplied her red lipstick. Her long, wavy brown hair was pulled into a ponytail that lay on her back. She glanced at her pocket mirror to be sure she had worn black eyeliner instead of blue. Her father, Al, was funding the production, and he insisted black eyeliner was more professional. Jacki adjusted her earpiece and took one moment to make sure her hands weren't flapping since she had learned long ago that even the slightest bit of fidgeting could be distracting. Once Jacki was confident her look was fantastic, she stepped onto the elevator set. The cameras and the talent were waiting.

"Remember, Jacki, if the pilot doesn't work and we lose our network deal, Dad will disown us," her twin sister, Lynn, warned through her earpiece. The first part was definitely true, the second part Jacki wasn't so sure about. After a pregnant pause, she added, "But you got this. No pressure. Think about the show, not Dad."

Jacki let out a laugh and told her, "Don't worry, everything's fine, little sister."

"No. No. No!" The production assistant was taking abuse. Catherine, the bachelorette-type of the show, screamed, "*I said* I wanted an iced Caramel Macchiato, not whatever this is!" Bachelorette-type, yes, but really no one was looking for marriage here. This show was expected to be much more like Tinder than Bumble. Just as the rear elevator doors opened so the cast could reach the set, Catherine threw the iced coffee in the PA's face.

Oh, yippee skippy, Jacki thought, *and away we go!* Nevertheless, as they began the shoot, Jacki turned it on for the cameras, and the energetic opening theme music enveloped the set. Catherine stood almost two feet away from Jacki once they got settled into the elevator.

"Welcome everyone to *Love Rising*, the only queer dating show set in an elevator, where if your dates don't floor you with greatness, you can give them the shaft. We have tonight's contestant, Catherine Knight, who's looking for, well..." Jacki announced. "Cathy, please tell us why people would want to visit your gayborhood."

Catherine had her red hair done up like a rose. Her amber eyes held a flame that threatened to burn anyone who came too close. Her arms were crossed over her formal red blouse. Her ruby heels clicked as she tapped against the floor.

"Catherine. It's Catherine, with a C," she said sternly. "I'm also an actress who starred in the *Kraken Hooker*, and yours truly was as glamorous... as the Kraken Hooker."

"I'm sure you were. Well, Catherine, what brings you to *Love Rising*?" Jacki asked. "Looking for that special woman?"

"Yes, the perfect one. I've yet to meet a woman who can even come close to meeting my standards."

Jacki turns to the camera. "Here's how our show will go. We have four women: Tyler, Stephanie, Perry, and Jo. They'll each have their chance to win the affection of our lovely Catherine. If she likes them, she'll push the button with the up arrow," Jacki announced. "If the date doesn't go well, she'll push the button with the down arrow, and your date will get the Veruca Salt experience."

Jacki grinned and said, "Catherine, I'm proud to reveal the first contestant here to win your heart."

"JACKI!" her sister uttered curtly. Jacki kept smiling, unsure of why her sister needed to interrupt her exactly at this moment.

"What is it?" Jacki asked through her teeth.

"You're almost out of the shot. You need to stand closer to Catherine," Lynn urged.

Jacki sighed but scooted over a bit. Catherine growled upon feeling a personal space incursion. She whispered in Jacki's ear. "If you come any closer, you will regret it, you U-hauler, I know your type."

WTF! Jacki rolled her eyes. Whatever. If Catherine thought she could intimidate her, she'd have to do better.

The announcer exclaimed, "Waiting in the elevator is the adventurous Tyler!" ◻

The front doors opened to reveal a person clad in scuba gear. Jacki blinked, wondering if the crew had played a prank on them. A form-fitting wet suit covered her from head to toe. A pair of goggles and a snorkel buried the individual's face.

She removed the goggles to reveal a gorgeous woman with waves of blonde hair and bright green eyes. Jacki was relieved when she saw Catherine perk up in fascination.

"Tyler, you look ready to face the Kraken herself," Jacki declared.

"I swim with my mates, the octopuses, whales, and even the occasional box jellyfish. Crikey, I'm a vagitarian from down under—Catherine, I hope you'll visit me there sometime! Jacki, I can definitely tame the Kraken."

Catherine, who entered the elevator to be with Tyler, was entranced by her confidence, golden hair, and the playful lilt of her accent. An intrigued smirk bloomed on Catherine's face.

As the date was moving in the right direction, Catherine initiated the elevator's ascent. The elevator rose as Tyler mesmerized Catherine with tales of her adventures, including a cliff-diving experience where she encountered numerous venomous serpents.

By the end of the speed date, the elevator returned to its original floor, where Jacki was waiting. Catherine pressed the top button, indicating she was considering Tyler. The scuba diver exited through the rear doors, cheering, while Catherine exited through the front to join Jacki.

"Well, that was Tyler for you," Jacki proclaimed. "Quite the sapphic explorer."

The announcer exclaimed, "Waiting in the hardware department is Stephanie!" A put-together woman in a conservative yet sexy dress stumbled out of the elevator from the rear doors.

"Stephanie," Jacki said. "Let's see how you get on with Catherine."

Based on her stylistic approach, Catherine immediately pegged her as a femme, but noticed something was off.

"Thank you, thank you all," the woman said in a saccharine voice as she waved, somewhat confused, to no one in particular. "I am a successful real estate agent, and I want to take my man to my penthouse of passion."

Jacki kept a straight face, despite wanting to burst out in chuckles. She and Lynn had decided to throw in a wild card. They didn't tell Stephanie everything about the new dating show. Lynn wasn't completely sold on misleading Stephanie, but their father pushed the idea, and he was in charge. Jacki also knew Stephanie wouldn't object. In her interviews, she had said she just wanted to be on TV and post on her Insta. For her, those were the *right reasons*.

Anyway, looking in Catherine's general direction, she inquired, "Hey Jacki, who's this?" Catherine responded by staring daggers at her and then gave Jacki the hairy eyeball. Catherine clearly was not taking the wild card well and didn't even bother to enter the elevator.

"No! You're shafted." She flicked her hair at Stephanie and turned her back. Catherine pushed the down button, signaling her immediate rejection.

Jacki pushed her lips into a sly smile.

"Bye-bye, you can go now," Catherine added. The elevator doors closed.

A bewildered Stephanie shook her head and shrugged as the next contestant, Perry, fixated on her phone, bumped into her on her way to the elevator set.

Catherine frowned and shook her head. She had more than enough experiences with straight women to last a lifetime.

"Okay," Jacki laughed. "But what can you do? I wish Stephanie the best of luck on her journey."

The announcer exclaimed, "Coming from the Children's-Ware Department is Perry, an influencer, known for modeling clothes for Kavannah's and is sponsored by Coral's Crystal Cakes."

The front elevator doors opened to show a young woman, Perry, all dolled up in the trendiest clothes Jacki had ever seen. She wore a flowery romper and her sparkly eyeshadow nearly overwhelmed her face. Her black hair was wrapped in a beautiful braid around her crown.

Catherine stared. Some sparkle returned to her eyes. Her hand hovered over the up arrow as she entered the elevator for a promising date.

But Perry's eyes were glued to her phone, her lightning-manicured fingers updating her followers. Jacki urgently had to bring her attention back to the show and, of course, to Catherine, who was *right there!*

Perry glared at Jacki's interruption before realizing the date had begun. She blushed in embarrassment.

The woman got a glimpse of Catherine and sighed in delight, then frustration.

"I'm sorry. Sponsor emergency. Big trouble, gotta go!"

And go Perry did, right through the rear doors. Perry had seemed promising. Catherine stood still for a moment, stunned. Through no fault of her own, she was experiencing strange emotions, feeling rejected and alone. Her eyes turned red as she clenched her fists, spamming the down button.

"What kind of fucking show is this?" she howled as she exited through the front doors. Lynn bleeped Catherine but kind of agreed with her.

Jacki thought about comforting her, though she didn't trust Catherine not to make good on her earlier violent threat. Jo, seeing the encounter on the monitor, approached the rear doors of the elevator with confidence.

The announcer declared, "Waiting in the Women's Lingerie department is Jo."

The elevator doors opened to reveal Jacki's dream celesbian standing before her. Jacki had been obsessed with Jo since she first saw her TV show and listened to her companion podcast, *Field of Love and Teddy Bears*. The host flushed, taking in Jo's dark brown skin, black vegan leather Brando jacket, and short pixie-cut black hair. Jacki's heart stopped, and she gulped. Jo's trans activism practically set Jacki on fire. She wished she could have met her backstage before the show, but there hadn't been time.

Jo stood firm inside the elevator as if she had already won.

"Um, Jo, it is an honor to have you on the show," Jacki stammered. "What can you tell Catherine to seal the deal?"

Jo responded, "I'm a trans woman, my pronouns are she/her, and I'm an Aquarius. I've spent my life advocating for our rights through my media ventures. It's been hard going at it alone — until now." She winked at Catherine.

Catherine ignored the wink. She was frustrated, confused, and unsure of what was happening after the scuba gear, a straight woman, and now ...*this*.

"Cathy, I see you're the lucky girl. Well, if you're up for a ride on my crotch rocket, I'm ready to rev your engine."

Catherine responded curtly, "I don't think so. I don't like dirt or insects or... short hair. And my name is Catherine."

Jacki saw an opportunity. Even though she knew from TikTok that Jo's crotch rocket was a Ducati Panigale V4, Jacki couldn't help but ask.

"You — you have a motorcycle?"

Jo turned to Jacki. "Yes, I do, angel. She's called The Beast."

Jacki's face turned as vermillion as the red devil.

"Jacki," Lynn scolded in a whisper. "No flirting, please. Remember our agreement with the sponsors and with Dad."

Jacki froze, not appreciating the cliterference. She remembered the long scolding Dad had given her. She decided she'd stay as professional as possible and noticed Catherine rejecting Jo.

Catherine stamped her foot and pouted. "Not going to happen." She snorted and pushed the down button.

"Well, that was Jo for you. An intriguing, beautiful woman who will *not* be Catherine's next date," Jacki concluded. "That means Tyler and

Catherine are free to drive off in a Subaru or fly off into the heavens or whatever!"

As Tyler came out of the Green Room to hug Catherine, Catherine was relieved that the nightmare production was over.

Jacki felt a weight had been taken off her when the cameras stopped rolling and the end theme music played. She passed through the rear elevator doors, which led to craft services, and met up with Lynn.

Lynn's face had relaxed. She was waiting to give her older sister a big hug. Whatever hiccups there were with the pilot would be sorted out. As Lynn approached Jacki, she was stopped in her tracks by Jo. Jacki's dream girl walked confidently and with purpose toward Jacki. Jo looked right through Lynn and focused on her mesmerized twin.

Jacki, just as engrossed and turned on as Jo, smiled and said, "Shall we pick up where we left off?" Before Jo could say anything, the two ran out of the building holding hands, focused on being anywhere but the set.

Jacki held tightly onto Jo's leather jacket as her motorcycle took them into their future. A future without cameras, elevators, or black eyeliner, as Jo also preferred Jacki to match the blue of her eyes. If there was a sunset outside, then Jacki and Jo rode off into it, to find their happily ever after together.

See the end of the book for elevator etiquette rules followed or broken. Elevator Etiquette Codes: 2A, 2D, 2F, 4A, 5A, 5D, 6H

Cheapest Rent Available

Ignorance Is Bliss

*Any space in the city can be a home
when all you desire
is a place for what's valuable,
even if there is nowhere to plug them in.
-Amery Bruce*

Consider this. It's not easy to find a place to live in the city. Justice wasn't expecting just how impossible the rentals in the boroughs had gotten. No matter where she looked, it was ludicrously unaffordable for anyone who wasn't a millionaire. Whenever a semi-affordable place was up for rent, it only took days — or hours — before someone took it. Just yesterday, an ad popped up for a new (and more importantly, cheap) apartment complex that was geographically desirable. By the time she'd clicked on it, though, all the rooms had been rented out. Justice wondered if she would have to sell a kidney just for a one-bedroom/one-bath. Maybe the other kidney for a guaranteed parking spot.

The morning after another late night of failed apartment hunting, Justice made her way to the mall for a snack: a soft pretzel smothered in what can only technically be called cheese. She heard the ding of the elevator and entered, mindlessly playing with her nails. At first, she ignored a curious stench that she chalked up to the "cheese" melting through the paper bag. Her foot struck something hard yet had some give, and she stumbled back, flinging her hands in the air to reclaim her balance. "What the hell?" she muttered, tilting her head.

Is someone sleeping in the elevator?

Yes, there was. And that someone was Spike Seeburger. Spike seemed surprisingly cozy in his sleeping bag until he sensed an intruder. He looked up and scowled at Justice. "Watch where you're stepping, sister!"

Justice blinked down at him in confusion. "Are you housing insecure?"

"Hell no, I live here! Cheapest rent in the city, and this space is all mine!"

Justice looked around, raising a brow. "How much are they charging you for this?"

"Five hundred a month. Ain't that a steal for a nice apartment in the city?"

Yeah, she thought, *stealing from you.*

"I got everything I need: a cooler, an Xbox 360, a flat-screen, a toilet, and some toys for when I need a break. My precious is the Sun Star DeLorean with working gull-wing doors. Can't plug the other stuff in, though."

Justice glanced around the elevator, and Spike's exact words echoed in her mind. The elevator was like a giant diorama of what could be a suffocating studio apartment. Inside this tiny space was a flat-screen TV, a bright-yellow Xbox 360 — the 2007 Limited Edition tie-in from *The Simpsons Movie* — and somehow, a pristine DeLorean diecast in the middle of all this (actual) shit.

By the elevator control panel was a nearly full 5-gallon neon-orange Homer bucket with an attachable toilet bowl freshener, scented like Ocean Breeze. She was somewhat grateful for Spike's attempt to diminish the stench of urine and feces, but it wasn't very effective. The toilet bucket was surrounded by four buzzing flies, which Justice suspected were mocking how much Spike was being ripped off. The sight of the makeshift toilet made Justice curl her upper lip and narrow her eyes, shaking her head from side to side, trying not to vomit all over Spike's living quarters. Still, she stayed, frankly bewildered by the scene in front of her, watching as he fidgeted with his toy car, opening and closing and opening and closing the doors repeatedly.

Resting on a self-made stand were books like *Freakonomics* and *The Things I Didn't Say In Therapy* by John Piper.

Justice pointed to a seemingly brand-new copy of *Directing Your Destiny* by Jennifer Grace.

"That's a really good book."

"Yeah?"

"It'll change your life."

"Yeah?"

"Only if you read it and, y'know, apply it."

"Maybe, if I have time."

"What else do you have going on?"

"I'm planning an epic fight for the Grid between Lord Zedd's monsters and Tommy Oliver's Rangers, like a multiverse thing. I got the Mighty Morphin Green Ranger, the White Tiger Ranger, the Red Zeo and Turbo Rangers, and the Black Dino Ranger. I also used to have the Red Wild Force Ranger, but I don't play with that one because, problems." His tone dipped sadly. "Yeah, no, I haven't had the chance to read lately with my ADHD and I lost my meds."

Justice frowned, but her fascination grew as she thought there must be something she could do to help. Maybe her friend Dr. Frey could Brainspot some of the deeper issues with Spike. But for now, her attention returned to the cramped "apartment" in front of her. She inspected every inch of the elevator, which didn't take long. "Hey, I don't see any of those action figures. I hope no one stole them."

Spike slapped his forehead. "Of course! Those and the rest of my gear," he mumbled.

"You have more stuff? Where?"

"At Public Storage. Y'know, my old place."

> *In memoriam to actor Jason David Frank,
> who portrayed fan favorite Tommy Oliver,
> the Green Ranger, the White Tiger Ranger,
> two Red Rangers, and the Black Dino Ranger.
> JDF, you have been an inspiration to millions.
> May you rest in peace.

See the end of the book for elevator etiquette rules followed or broken.
Elevator Etiquette Codes: 2B, 5C, 6C, 6H, 7D

Minyan Man and The Krimson Angel

Some Lines Won't Be Crossed

"A gray area is a world that doesn't like gray areas. But the gray areas are where you find the complexity, it's where you find the humanity, and it's where you find the truth." ▫
-Jon Ronson

Consider this. When Orthodox Jews pray, they prefer to worship as a community, and that means a minimum of ten men: a *minyan*. During the day, I am a humble teacher at the local community college. However, when a synagogue knows they will be short of the ten, they call me, The Minyan Man. I'm not inexpensive or cheap, but I can bring as many Jewish men as needed as long as they get to me before sundown. I can also bring someone who is not Jewish, a Gentile, and you will soon see why that can be critical.

The date was October 31, 2014, noteworthy because not only was it the beginning of Shabbat, but it was also Halloween. On Shabbat, Jews are not permitted to do any work. I mean, any. Brushing hair, flushing toilets, and especially, moving things from place to place are forbidden. In the Jewish faith, even something as simple as pressing a button in an elevator is considered *work*. This commandment, specifically the fourth one, applies even if the button is needed to reach a synagogue located in a penthouse. Alas, such sanction would put me in a predicament of biblical proportions.

I was running late, and the traffic was unbelievable, so what happened next was partially my fault. You see, it was 6:00 on the dot as I ran into the building. I dashed to the elevator at 6:01, out of breath but with a minute to go. Since my client was in the penthouse synagogue, I pressed the UP button. The elevator doors opened at 6:02, and many people darted out excitedly, tired from a long week and longing to be somewhere else. 6:02 — not especially important to them, but of the utmost importance to me — was exactly the time that the sun went down. Shabbat began at 6:02....Then began the problematic cascade. *Ah, khara!*

I, Hiram Goldstein, wearing my Shabbat best, touched the mezuzah on the elevator frame as I entered and kissed my hand. By the time I had crossed the threshold and was actually in the elevator, I was a minute late. Unfortunately, I was now stuck in the elevator, paralyzed by religion and unable to reach my client or the elevator button. Pushing the button after sundown was *asur,* forbidden. I looked up towards G-d— actually, the elevator hatch in the ceiling — and prayed for help. "Hashem, send me an Angel for resolution." I spent 10 minutes alone with my thoughts pacing back and forth, reflecting on all the choices I made today. Then, G-d (sort of) came through....

The hatch slid away, and with the athleticism of a trained gymnast, a college student lowered herself to the floor, attached to a rope anchored somewhere in the expansive darkness of the elevator shaft. White feathered wings swung behind her, and she deftly dropped to the dirty floor. She turned to me and said, "Hello," but nothing else. Oh, and one more thing: she held a case of beer between nails shaped like letter openers. Her red and black Halloween outfit was a cross between Frederick's of Hollywood and Party City's Sexy Angel, complete with a halo, those wings, and a domino mask that disguised her identity. I tried not to stare critically as she ran her horror movie fingers along freshly tweezed brows and messy lip liner.

As an Orthodox Jew, I cannot associate with women who are not my wife or relatives because the interaction could be interpreted as sexual. And it goes both ways. Women couldn't associate with me either, and yet here I was, in an enclosed space with the Krimson Angel (Party City, contact me if you want permission to use that name) who just went back up for more beer. After three more beer runs to the elevator shaft in brutal silence, the Krimson Angel finally freed herself from her harness. She punched the emergency stop button and asked me a very reasonable question.

"Dude, what are you doing here?"

"I could ask the same of you."

I stressed to her my role as the Minyan Man, my prompt entrance into the elevator, and my delay from the hordes of people coming in as their workday was coming to an end. By the time they cleared, it was after sundown, and there were rules and laws I just wouldn't break. Krimson Angel was amused, flashing me a teasing smile. She went over to the wall and seductively moved her hand over the panel. She twirled her finger in languid circles over the penthouse button, then pulled back. A sort of elevator foreplay. "This button, the one marked PH?" she asked coyly.

Yes, that button. And that is why my client should have paid the Gentile insurance. What would have happened if the power went out? What if the lights or the air conditioning were turned off? Nothing. Nothing happens after sundown, except prayer. Never more did I need someone to push an elevator button. Never did I expect to be stuck with a lingerie model with four cases of beer. The desire for *teshuvah,* to repent, is already climbing, hot and urgent, up my throat.

"And your mask? Mine is part of a costume. What's your deal? Are you sick?"

"Has no one heard of the Ebola virus?"

She rolled her eyes and got back to the task at hand. The holy button. "Just ask me, dude."

"I can't."

"You mean, you won't."

"I can't and I won't."

"So, if I ask you if you want me to push the penthouse button, you'll say yes or no?"

"No."

"No, you don't want me to push the button, or no, I shouldn't ask?"

"I can't."

She huffed, rustling some dainty feathers from her cheap wings. "Jesus."

"Jesus has nothing to do with this."

"At least I have a real reason to wear a mask. Halloween and everything."

"I think protecting myself from an airborne illness is a good reason."

She smirked. "I guess at your age it's important to watch out for stuff like that. You must watch a lot of news." Her eyes skirted over my long suit, and she made a flirtatious proposal. "My mask was itchy. I'm thinking about taking it all off, 'Bola Boy." Pointing at her mask, she cooed, "I'll show you mine if you show me yours?"

I inwardly balked at the vulgar request. Yet, mildly intrigued and feeling pretty bored, I responded in kind. "Whatever," I grumbled.

When the masks were removed, my eyes grew wide. The Krimson Angel was none other than Jennifer Quartermain. She was a student of mine, barely 21 years old in the same way that she was barely wearing a proper outfit. Meanwhile, I could tell that she recognized me: her humble teacher and a friend of the family, Mr. Goldstein.

"What are you doing with all that beer, Jennifer?" I was sure she could hear the smirk in my voice.

Jennifer replied, "We're having an underground rager, Mr. G., and I need to chill the suds in the basement. There is kind of a lounge down there."

"I know."

She went to send the elevator to the basement, then paused.

I took a long sigh of disapproval before raising my voice in a complaint. "Jennifer, I need to get to the penthouse. I'm late. Assisting your teacher would be beneficial to us both, wouldn't you agree?"

"I'm not sure that's all you want, Mr. G. Not with your beard and curls and that sexy black hat." As she began to speak, she sauntered closer. She removed another part of her costume, the straps that kept her flimsy angel wings in place.

"Please, stop."

"Let's see, Mr. G. I can do what you asked and push the penthouse button now, sending us right to your clients. What will they see? You, with me and my amazing costume, alone together." Another piece of her costume was removed, a fluffy white choker that exposed an expanse of collarbone.

"Jennifer. Enough...."

"Or, I can push B. I go to my party and you get stuck in the basement and you lose your client and your reputation."

"Please, don't do that. If you do, Ms. Quartermain, I will inform your parents you are drinking, which I believe is in direct violation of your probation."

"All I did was have some fun, like any other college kid."

"You urinated in a bush outside a Sikh Gurdwara because you were so drunk. Not every college kid does something so profane! That's why you had to take a World's Religion class — my class — to broaden your mind on other religions."

"I've been a good girl since then, mostly." She motioned to her angelic costume, a cheeky reference that almost made me snort.

"The public intoxication charge begs to differ."

"They won't believe you."

"Jennifer, you have a tattoo on your shoulder that says 'Let's Get Wasted' in Comic Sans, a choice so questionable that even saying it out loud should be considered offensive. They'll believe me."

She huffed, "I paid attention during the Jewish Studies module, okay? By the time you tell them after the Sabbath, the party will be long over. I know you can't call anyone on Shabbat. Not the police, not my mother. No one, Minyan Man."

I grinned proudly. She was attentive to my class. Now, it was time for my finishing move. "Touche. However, this may come as a surprise to you, but I know your probation officer very well. Yep, Tami Hancock. I play pickleball with her brother." Jennifer's smile evaporated. "So what's it going to be, Ms. Quartermain? I know you are a smart young woman. Can you see a way through this where we both win?"

And she did. She agreed that we would take the trip to the basement, where Jennifer would unload her beer. After it was done, she would send me directly up to the 18th-floor penthouse. Better late than never.

So, The Minyan Man's reputation was saved, as was the Krimson Angel's. The religious services went off without any further hitches. The client was pleased, which was my priority. All things considered, I didn't feel the threats, or the blackmail were entirely kosher, but I had committed to Jennifer's parents to keep an eye on her.

About once a decade, Shabbat crashes into Halloween. When these realms collide, doing the Lord's work can truly be a trial of faith. Luckily, no trial is too tough for the Minyan Man. Thank G-d.

See the end of the book for elevator etiquette rules followed or broken. Elevator Etiquette Codes: 1D, 2A, 2D, 5A, 6A, 6B, 6C, 6D, 6H, 8A

Secret Sequence Scheme

Creativity And Conflict Can Canvas Courage

"Character cannot be developed in ease and quiet. Only through experience of trial and suffering can the soul be strengthened, ambition inspired, and success achieved."
-Helen Keller

Consider this. Stacey pressed two, one, five, one again, and then the ground floor. She put the bottle of bourbon on the elevator floor, steadied her hand, and pressed for the roof. She picked the bottle back up as the elevator ascended.

Stacey looked up, expecting a star-and-smog-spattered sky. Instead, she found a crystal chandelier swaying in the air. Marble statues and walls adorned with Van Goghs and Rothkos watch as she stumbled into the hall, heels reverberating against the cold marble. A "Where the hell am I?" dribbled from Stacey's lips, along with a bit of bourbon, as she took another hit off the bottle.

"My office," a voice creaked.

Stacey strained her tired eyes; a portly man in overworked suspenders sat at a desk.

"Who are you?"

"Mr. Kinsley. Have a seat."

Stacey crossed towards the desk, crashing into the chair opposite the man. "This isn't the roof."

"No, it's not," the man said, eyes never leaving the folder in his hands.

"I wanted the roof."

"Why did you want to go to the roof?"

Stacey drained the rest of the bottle. "To jump."

"Why?"

"Why not?" Her bank account was empty, like the gas tank and her fridge, and now the bottle as she tipped her head back and let the rest of the alcohol trickle down her throat.

"Alright Stacey," the man said, closing the folder.

Sobriety and fear rushed upon Stacey. "How do you know my name?"

"It's my job."

Stacey stood to run away, but sobriety had not reached her body. She made it four steps before she found herself on the floor, vomiting. Mr. Kinsley got up from his chair and waddled towards Stacey.

"Apologies if I startled you. I have no intention of hurting you," he said, extending a plump hand toward Stacey.

Her heart still raced, and the fear had not left her tear-stained eyes, but she took his hand and found herself back in the chair across from the man, letting out a labored sigh as he retook his seat. "Feeling okay?"

Stacey didn't know what to say to that, so she said nothing. Mr. Kinsley sighed, breaking the silence. "Would you believe Picasso sat in that same chair?"

"No."

"He did. 1969. Elevator to the top of the Tour Montparnasse. His code was seven one five, then the roof. Pulled a gun on me, believe it or not."

"I don't."

"Then you wouldn't believe Jackson Pollock sat in that chair, or that Salvador Dali defecated in it. One-seven and two eighty-two respectively, in case you were interested in their codes."

"I wasn't."

"But those are your favorite artists. They inspired you to pick up a paintbrush."

Stacey swallowed nothing but dry air and whiskey-flavored spit. "Yes."

"Are you curious as to why they were here, and you are here now?"

Stacey swallowed again; nothing but more dry air and whiskey-flavored spit. "I want to go home."

"You will, in time." Mr. Kinsley slapped both his knees and struggled to his flat feet. He and Stacey huffed their way up an imperial staircase, leading into corridors of oak floors and green wallpaper peeking out from behind Degas, miniatures of sculptures she did not know the names of, and doorways. Some had books in glass enclosures, some scrawling of poetry or drawings on pieces of paper, some marvelous statues of jade, and one had a series of paintings of doves, with two smoking chairs in front of a mantle awaiting the duo. "Have a seat."

Stacey almost collapsed into the chair. For a long time, they said nothing, both recovering from the walk. Mr. Kinsley was the first to speak.

"Do you recognize the paintings?"

Stacey looked around: tapestries of doves met her eyes everywhere they looked, but recognition did not. "No."

"What about this one?" Mr. Kinsley said, accompanied by a snap of his fingers.

He motioned towards a painting above the mantle. A dove lay amidst dying weeds, only tufts of its down feather remained, bloodied and bruised. The brown eyes closed, open just enough to show fear. The breast had been cut open, revealing a heart, devoid of viscera and gore but full of vibrant color defying the gray of the skies above.

"Do you like it?"

"Not really."

"Shame."

"Did you paint it?"

"No, you did."

"Bullshit."

"It's true, along with every other painting in this room. But this one," he said, a smile coming to life on his face, "this is the one people will know you for, certainly the one that caught my eye."

Stacey said nothing, stuck in the cycle of revelation and shock.

Mr. Kinsley continued. "Stacey, every artist ever worth a damn has been right where you are: looking out into the void, debating a gravity-assisted exit from this world. I'm here to ensure you don't leave before you live up to your full potential."

Stacey said nothing for a good, long time. "Will I be happy?"

"At times, but I'm sure that's not what you meant."

"It's not."

Mr. Kinsley sighed. "You'll find it in puddles of rain, in night skies, and dark alleyways, but never in the morning waiting to greet you, or at dusk bidding you goodbye."

Stacey's eyes had a glaze over them like fresh pottery. "Will I be famous?"

"Your work will be studied for generations to come."

Stacey retreated to silence.

"You cannot jump yet, Stacey; you simply can't."

Stacey remained in silence.

"What do you say, Stacey?"

Stacey woke to another hangover. She tried to rub the sleep out of her eyes but couldn't. She got up from her bed, met by nothing other than an empty bottle on the kitchen counter. She slumped at her kitchen table, staring at the canvas in front of the window, and the sound of cars and birds drifting through. She thought about going to the liquor store for another bottle.

She didn't. Stacey went over to the window. The streets below shuffled cars through their cracked and chipped shoots; windows across from her apartment showed glimpses of people's morning routine; a mother getting her children ready for school; two lovers arguing; a man enjoying a morning cigarette, slightly obscured by a telephone wire; a pigeon came down and landed on the wire, hopping along until it reached the wooden pole between the wires. Stacey watched the bird, and she didn't know if it was from the quirky movements of its head, the brilliant shades of deep green mixed with gray feathers, or the grace as it hopped off the post and took back into the skies, but Stacey found a smile forming on her face as she took up her brush and began to paint.

**If you need help, you can call or text *988*
for the Suicide & Crisis Lifeline. A real person
will be there to support you.**

See the end of the book for elevator etiquette rules followed or broken.
Elevator Etiquette Codes: 2A, 3B, 4A, 6H

The Unbearable Presence of Fairies

Tinker Bell Can Be A Lot

"I am a violent man who has learned not to be violent and regrets his violence." -John Lennon

Consider this. Coming into work is the worst part of most people's mornings, but coming to work for the Human Encounters Corporation? That will drive you mad.

The HEC Building stood enormously tall — taller than even the L.L. Beanstalk Tower. And our company motto, "Making the World of Humans Magical Day by Day," still glittered with fairy magic even though it was considered outdated back when the Grimms were first touring Europe. I combed some hair out of my eyes and was greeted by the front desk Manticore, his lion jowls showing a slight grimace. Evidently, the Sphinx was out sick — just my luck. Either way, neither would let me pass without answering today's riddle. Although the Sphinx would have been infinitely friendlier and offered hints, fucking Manticores just glared at you! And if the Manticore screwed up the puzzle, it was only because he couldn't be bothered to read it all the way through.

Prior security had been put in place centuries ago to guard our workplace against the corporate espionage of a Rakshasa (or any other shapeshifting demons) from rival companies or clans. Finally, that protection had been updated. Now, all employees had to use the company's proprietary "Riddle Password System". Whether human or mythical, everyone had to answer a riddle each morning before gaining access to the building.

Since I was fairly new at the company, I was still getting the hang of the RPS process. At first, it was fun. However, the company's magic mostly erases your memory after the riddle is submitted, making each morning unnecessarily challenging. Exasperating. My brain was starting to fray from dealing with the RPS... Every. Single. Morning.

Ugh! Why doesn't Corporate just switch to regular phone passwords? And why do the passwords have to be longer and more complicated every time? I kept being asked to "Please try again," even though I knew I answered correctly. The password requirements are so stressful because if you don't get it right quickly, you can't even go to work. Even worse, after trying three different answers, the system finally haphazardly accepts one as "the right choice" — how is this supposed to outsmart the Rakshasas? I call bullshit!

If anyone answered today's riddle (which was really the same stupid riddle with randomized new answers) incorrectly too many times, they were in a world of hurt. The Manticore security guards would sting them with their scorpion tails, causing the poor soul to fall paralyzed onto the floor — and obviously miss work. Unfair! Then, the receptionist would have to watch in horror as the lion part of the Manticore tore them limb from limb before eating them alive. Manticores fucking suck!

Finally, the riddle began. "It can't be touched and can't be felt. It can't be seen, or heard, or smelt." The Manticore paused, tilting its head back to recall the rest of the puzzle. "Hmmm, I think it went something like… Ah! It lies behind stars and under hills, and any empty holes it fills. It comes early and follows after, ends life, and kills laughter. What is it?"

I glanced at the paper in my hand. "It's darkness," I hoped. Thankfully, I had made a cheat sheet of likely answers, and it worked *this time*. I stuffed the paper back into my pocket, triumphantly. The Manticore snorted through its feline nose, stood aside, and let me pass as I swiftly entered the elevator to the 14th floor. The Manticore, as infuriating as he could be, I could deal with. As long as I didn't have to share some elevator space with a...

"Hi there!" a squeaky voice assaulted my eardrums.

Ugh. A fairy.

Being stuck in an elevator with a fairy was exhausting. Each flutter of her wings produced a glitter of golden dust that bathed the compacted space, and every garment of clothing I had on for that matter, with a brilliant light. The glitter would magically intensify your feelings, which, in general, is nice — if you're already happy. But today I was just in a mood. Now I had to think only happy thoughts if I didn't want to become a madcap miscreant for the rest of the day.

"Oh, you're not floating from the dust. Does that mean you're not having a happy-filled good morning?" the fairy asked in her squeaky tinkling voice. "Well, I just can't let that abide! After all, mornings are bright and sunny when you have good company." She was giving me an obnoxiously smug smile, fingers to her dimples and all.

"No...please don't. I don't need any, so just..." I tried replying politely, trailing off as I desperately moved to brush off the pixie dust from my person but it was no use. The golden flecks had penetrated. I didn't ask for this, I told her to stop. Dammit Janet.

My temples ached as my thoughts grew louder. Why did we even have to share an elevator with fairies anyway? They had wings, they could just flutter all the way up to the 14th floor if they wanted to. That sounded like pure laziness to me. Not to mention their outfits and pretentious wands were an eyesore. This fairy, for example, wore a business suit clad in acid green and crocodile skin boots. How the Hobs managed to thread them in such a small size baffled me — impressive, though. Anyway, she fluttered back and forth, sparkling with an emerald aura that triggered my gag reflex if I stared at it for too long.

"Wellifyou'refeelingdown, miserylovescompany, astheysay. Andyouknow, justtheotherday..." The fairy's immediate ramp-up of enthusiasm left me mentally stumbling. Her excited arm waving blew even more mood-altering glittery magic into my face.

The fairy went on about her life, failing to notice how little I cared about her endless list of grievances. Like how she thought her boyfriend was such an immature twit, or that he was flirting with the mermaids at the lagoon, just to make her jealous. And I stood there silently as she explained that her boyfriend had broken his condo's HOA rules by getting a large pet — an alligator or a crocodile, I could never tell the difference, and I didn't really care.

Anyway, I lost track of where her speed-of-light rants were going. Something-something about a stupid male gaze dress code (fair). Then it was about some boys who got lost, and a creeper obsessed with leather and velvet. Her boy troubles seemed to never end. Anyways, while she was complaining, her dust had me stewing in some of the most horrid, gloom-inducing scenarios I could think of. My thoughts were just too terrible to share.

The fairy's enthusiasm, endless humblebrag stories, and damn sparkly glitter were making this vertical commute so much worse. It was petty, but I kept thinking about how bad my life was compared to hers. I wished she'd just disappear so my feet would stay rooted to the rising elevator floor. I'd do anything to spite that fussock's cheery attitude.

"Andthat'swhenourdategotinterrupted becausewehadtorushtothevet becausehispetatethealarmclock. Isn'tthatunbelievable?..."

"Yes, unbelievable! To be honest, you're annoying, and I can't stand this anymore. I don't give a flying fuck about any of this!" I'm was really trying to be patient, but the additional emotional hit from the dust was too much, man.

The fairy gasped in horror. It was funny the way their faces get when angry, like bright red cherry tomatoes.

"Oh my!" she exclaimed. "There is no place for that kind of naughty language! You know, at the HEC, that we believe in a family-friendly work environment."

"Family-friendly?! Who made you the language police?" I waved my hand in frustration and she dove to avoid it. "I don't believe any of this. As a matter of fact, I don't believe in fairies either!" As the mean-spirited string of the syllables left my mouth, I realized the consequences of my words.

That annoying little fairy let out a piercing shrill before collapsing straight to the floor. She appeared still and lifeless as the golden glow dimmed. I rolled my eyes before recalling a meeting back at ACRID, the Anthropoid and Creature Resources for Individual Development. The memo had clearly stated that "all employees were instructed not to pronounce their disbelief in fairies out loud, as the act alone would incapacitate them on the spot, or worse." *Or worse.* For a second, I smirked, pleased to have finally shut up that annoying chit-chat of a gnat, but then I considered how murder could definitely get me fired. I gasped in horror as the color around her faded to gray. She was for real dying. "Oh, bugger!"

The elevator was making its way to the 14th floor. What to do? I knelt down by the fairy, knocking on my forehead to remember what to do in a crisis situation. I recalled a CPR seminar hosted by Dr. Barrie on how to revive a fairy should it unexpectedly drop from the air. Reluctantly, I prepared to perform a type of "belief resuscitation." I clapped as hard and loud as I could and chanted "I believe. I believe. I believe. Oh please, breathe." over and over again. It was hard because the damned dust told me she deserved it.

"C'mon, breathe, damn you! I believe!" **I believe!**

Slowly but surely, the golden glitter of her wings expanded, and she began to cough, gasping for air. Regaining color and consciousness, she shot me a stare full of daggers. She flew up to my face before giving me a hard smack of her wand right between my eyes, but a bee sting would've hurt worse. Honestly, the whole ordeal was taxing but finally over. From there on, she turned away from me, pouting as she fluttered out as the elevator doors opened. I sighed with relief after undergoing that seriously unforced error. To my dismay, I was going to remain under the influence of that blasted dust for a few more hours.

Coming to work and dealing with fairies could be a trial by fire every morning. But let me tell you that trying to console a vain Medusa after a makeup disaster in a fully mirrored elevator? Oh well — let's just say that's a whole other story.

See the end of the book for elevator etiquette rules followed or broken. Elevator Etiquette Codes: 2B, 2F, 6B, 6C, 6H

Minimum Wage Face

Minimum Wage Face Trilogy, Part I

"Don't worry about the judgment of others. They are telling you their story, not yours." -Unknown

☐

Consider this. It was a busy summer day. I held my head up high like the Queen I was as the elevator went down to take me to the lobby of my luxury apartment complex. I could tell that I caught the attention of the wannabes in the elevator with my blonde pixie haircut, a stark white pantsuit against my creamy white skin, and six-inch nude heels. Everyone knows my name, Karmen, mostly because my husband, Donny, was one of the top donors of this place. He's gotten into a good position with the complex owner Baldwin Boggs. He's such a darling.

Though, I knew they were also paying the closest attention to what I held with a jewel-encrusted leash: my precious therapy dog, Empress.

This was a very expensive and rare dog breed that I bought for $4k from an established breeder in Sweden. The black, luxurious fur on her petite body was always lavished over at the dog spa I took her to every week. And the white stripe on her fur resulted from the rarest confluence of genetic conditions that made her even more unique.

My therapy dog, wearing an orange ESA vest, was smacking her lips, indicating she was in a happy mood. The others in the elevator pressed themselves to the opposite side of the elevator as they pinched their noses and turned their heads away from me. *Ugh, rude*. Once the elevator door opened on the lobby floor, I immediately walked out first. I am the lady, after all.

All of a sudden, I heard the whiny voice of one of the lobby employees trying to walk up to me.

"Excuse me, Mrs. Karmen? Mrs. Karmen, wait!" I ignored this pissant's request. I didn't have the time to entertain whatever it was she wanted. I rushed to the elevator. "Ma'am, my apologies, but as we have explained numerous times before, this type of animal is not allowed inside the complex." *How dare she!* I wanted to pinch my nose after smelling her rancid breath.

The employee looked down at Empress with a grimace as Empress began scooting her bottom on the smooth, marble floor to clean herself, but I wasn't going to apologize for that. The residents looking for a show had expressions of fear mixed with disgust on their pathetic faces.

I turned and glared with eyes like Medusa at the employee, who cowered in response.

"'Excuse me?' I think you mean, 'excuse you,' little girl," I towered over the employee as I spoke. "I will only say this once: I live here. Not you with your minimum-wage-looking face, so I have a right to bring my emotional support dog, which helps me deal with stress, by the way. I am a busy woman with a very successful mindfulness practice and a nanny that I meticulously supervise to take care of my two beautiful children, so do not dare pick an argument with me right now."

Ugh! If I had to keep speaking to her, her acne-filled, clogging presence would probably infect me. I turned and saw the other residents backing away from the two of us. I wouldn't allow her to continue embarrassing me, so I turned on my heel before saying the last word.

"This is my emotional support dog, and I have all the documentation to prove it. That of which I don't need to show someone like *you*."

With that, I walked away, becoming increasingly tired of dealing with such incompetence. All I wanted was to take my magnificent therapy dog for a walk, but I felt too exhausted and decided to go back up to my luxury apartment.

I walked back to the elevator and pressed the up button. I stood directly in front of the door as I kept pushing the button. Empress cooed excitedly as she always did when she wanted to play. The amount of money my husband paid to keep this complex running, and the fact that the elevator couldn't go faster, is preposterous. Not to mention the employees were imbeciles.

The elevator finally opened up to reveal many more insufferable residents. I walked straight into the elevator. Everyone scattered like roaches the moment their eyes drifted downward toward my dog, sprinting and jumping to get out of my way while Empress purred and galloped alongside me. It was like no one had respect or simple etiquette for others anymore. Feeling inconvenienced, I picked her up to keep anyone from trying to touch her with their disgusting digits.

As the elevator door was about to close, I realized that I wasn't going to be alone. Someone was about to encroach on my personal space in this elevator, and it was a man in a wheelchair. *Oh, hell no.*

I stared blatantly at this man as he tried to make his way inside quickly, and he was past the elevator door before I could press the button to close the door. He wore a plain white t-shirt and black sweatpants with his chestnut brown hair cut short above his ears; he couldn't possibly live here.

When he rolled in on his squeaking wheelchair, Empress began to chirp angrily. The man got so close to me that I felt one of the wheelchair armrests brush up against my leg. *This was madness!* Then, he turned toward my dog, looked at the annoyed expression on my face, and said, "What the skunk is that?"

TO BE CONTINUED

See the end of the book for elevator etiquette rules followed or broken. Elevator Etiquette Codes: 1C, 2A, 2D, 2G, 3F, 3G, 4A, 4B, 6B, 6H

What the Skunk?

Minimum Wage Face Trilogy, Part II

"The wheelchair should not be a symbol of disability. A wheelchair is a vehicle to liberation and freedom, a chariot for independence." -Rick Hansen

Consider this. Karmen was one of the most privileged tenants of her luxury apartment complex and always needed everything to go her way. Things were never up to her level of satisfaction, and this time was no different. She dealt with rude tenants and employees ogling in fear of her skunk, Empress, whom she believed was her emotional support dog. Feeling exhausted and wanting a rose-scented bath after her daily dose of lobby drama, she got back on the elevator. However, Elijah, visiting the complex, rolled in with his wheelchair, and all of Karmen's tolerance and composure went out of the elevator.

Karmen blatantly stared at Elijah with her beady eyes and crow's feet, though Elijah didn't really notice. He was too busy side-eyeing Empress, who began to hiss quietly in Karmen's arms. Its neon orange vest read ESA (Emotional Support Animal), but Elijah was highly skeptical. She dismissed Elijah's exclamation as she moved toward the elevator panel.

After 15 seconds passed, which seemed like an eternity, of still being on the lobby floor, he asked her to press the button for the fifteenth floor. He tried to be as polite as he could while glancing anxiously at the skunk.

In response, Karmen scoffed loudly. "As if you would be on the top floor."

"Pardon?"

"You must be visiting a relative, someone you rely on?" Karmen looked up and down at him with an air of conceit while placing the skunk back down on the floor. "You should know this complex is a bit different. We don't want any solicitors staying too long. Really, we don't want you at all."

Elijah pressed his lips together, not only in suppressed anger but in slight fear as Empress started trotting restlessly, but Karmen pulled her back. The skunk's erratic movement mixed with the overwhelming scent of baby powder and ripe flowers from Karmen's perfume made him dizzy.

"This is not one of those 'donate today' commercials on TV, so I do not have any obligation to help you." Karmen stomped her foot in agitation and stepped on the skunk's tail by accident. She didn't notice her skunk stomp its feet and puff up her fur in response.

"For goodness' sake, I have had to deal with insolent employees all day, and now I have to deal with you? What have you done in your life besides lazily sitting in a wheelchair all day, and you're asking me for this special treatment? How dare you! I have never felt so demeaned in all my life!"

"Ma'am!" Elijah finally had enough, his hands twitching with fury on the worn armrests of his wheelchair. "I am *so* sorry if I inconvenienced you." His eyes couldn't have rolled further back into his head. "But if you do not want to press the button for me, I can certainly do it myself if you would just move back."

The skunk began stomping her feet on the elevator floor; her agitated chirps sounding like a warbler on cocaine. Elijah wished he had a mood-altering substance, too, right about now. He was sweating through his shirt, the air growing heavier, more stifling with each word as their argument escalated, the tension between them thickening like walls closing in around him.

Karmen snapped, breaking the spell. "I will *not* push the button for you." She drew out the single syllable with an odd, exaggerated emphasis. "I have every right to stand where I want, and don't you dare invade my space, or I'll call security!"

"And I'm done with this conversation. Now, *if you don't mind,* I'm getting to my floor whether you like it or not, ma'am."

The man rolled over to the elevator panel and attempted to reach over when she blocked his hand with hers. "If you touch me, I'm suing you for whatever little you may own. And do not dare insult my sweet Empress again with that foul mouth of yours."

But suddenly, Empress hopped up on his lap and looked Elijah directly in the eye, the fur of her tail feeling surprisingly soft as it brushed his arm. He stared back, unsure of what to do.

"Get your filthy hands away from my emotional support dog, or I will let her loose on you!"

Instead, Empress stopped hissing and purred in a way that made it seem like Elijah was her owner. Empress licked and lightly nibbled on his fingertips, which also made him giggle. She then hopped back next to Karmen and slid her bottom back and forth on the floor, as if nothing happened.

"You know what? I'm finished with this, too. I'm choosing my floor and you go from there once *my* travel is completed." Then Karmen lifted her arm to a metallic bracelet on her wrist, pressed a button on it, and said "14," with her brow raised smugly at Elijah.

"There, I informed security immediately as this situation is unsustainable, and no one of my stature should ever have to experience you people," she gloated with her head held high. She finally pushed the button for the fourteenth floor.

Elijah patiently wheeled back to the opposite side of the elevator, almost breathing in the wall. The elevator finally dinged, indicating they were on the fourteenth floor, and the elevator opened. Before Elijah could be at peace without Karmen, whining sirens went off in the hallway. Bright lights flashed by his face as he covered his ears. A group of men with identical blue patrol suits jogged in unison toward them. Karmen seemed unfazed by this, turning toward Elijah to grin mockingly at him, but as she attempted to exit, Empress refused to move. Elijah froze in shock as the skunk sat in front of him, with a mischievous gleam in its tiny eyes.

TO BE CONTINUED

See the end of the book for elevator etiquette rules followed or broken.
Elevator Etiquette Codes: 2D, 2F, 3A, 5F, 6A, 6B, 6C, 6H

Sirens, Lights, and a Skunk, Oh My

Minimum Wage Face Trilogy, Part III

"People didn't always see a person with a disability who had to use a ramp or elevator as people who have been given unnecessary privileges. But I run into that often now. People are saying, 'Why do we have to go to great expense for these people?'" -Major Owens

Consider this. I thought this would just be an average day as I made my way to my father's penthouse located in this overly extravagant apartment complex. Instead, I found myself accosted by an overbearing lady, blaring sirens, flashing lights, and a whole-ass security patrol heading my way.

Before this mess, I was already dreading this visit to my father to discuss his imminent retirement. He would hound me for not taking part in the Boggs family real estate business. My focus was on helping Abili-Max, my nonprofit organization, raise money for disability advocacy and awareness. However, my dad believed that, because of our 'elite' status, I was somehow superior to others who shared my position in this wheelchair. But I knew all this money and prestige couldn't hide my situation, nor should it. This time, though, he was willing to entertain a compromise, and I was willing to listen.

At this point, I barely had the patience to deal with this delusional lady, a woman named Karmen who made the elevator ride a living hell for me. First, she insisted that someone *like me* wouldn't live here and proceeded to act like a victim of someone with a wheelchair privilege. Don't get me started on her emotional support dog or skunk or whatever. If she needs an ESA, she should have one. I truly support that, but her attitude, no one needs.

The moment this woman made a security call from her panic bracelet, I leaned back in my chair and felt the urge to crack up laughing. She was unaware this could be one of her last days at this complex if she keeps up this bullshit.

If she only knew that my father was the owner of the building. She was degrading the son who would likely soon be enforcing the rules. I brushed up on the HOA guidelines for our complex, and *as a public service*, I will investigate her ESA animal. I'm no Dr. Drew, but I'm pretty sure entitlement is not a specific mental disorder.

Anyway, the elevator finally dinged, indicating we were on the fourteenth floor. I was so close to reaching the penthouse right above and being free of her. But as the doors opened, the consequences of her delusions became apparent. The alarm greeted us with sensory overload. I covered my ears and squinted my eyes. There were five men with identical blue patrol suits jogging in unison toward us. The lady seemed unfazed by this, turning toward me with a shit-eating grin while I groaned at my latest obstacle.

As she attempted to exit, her skunk did not follow. I could've sworn I saw the skunk smirk back at me. Skunk smirks are so cute. I exited the elevator and Empress moved forward, stopping directly in front of me when I rolled up to the officers.

The woman attempted to pull her skunk away while yelling at the confused patrol officers. "Officers, please do something about this intruder! He's been a disturbance to me and my precious dog, Empress. Wheel him out without delay!"

"Mrs. Umbridge, please calm down. Kindly explain what exactly is hap—"

"Are you even listening? This man doesn't belong here. He's disturbing me and everyone in this complex with his..."

"'With his, with his?' What ma'am?" I looked her dead in the eyes, but she turned from me toward the security officer and impatiently huffed.

I couldn't help shaking my head vigorously as the officers looked less concerned while they listened to Karmen Umbridge's rant. Her skunk was still in front of me, but it began to puff its chest and hiss like a predatory snake.

As for me, I had enough of this. "Listen, this is a misunderstanding. Now, I completely respect the need for an ESA animal, and you should have one if you so require, but the HOA guidelines clearly state which animals qualify, and by default, skunks are prohibited. *But that's not why I'm here.*"

I was just about to direct the officers to remove her when, suddenly, the ruckus ceased — leaving only the faint sound of a soft stomp, stomp, stomp. I looked down, incredulously, watching the skunk charge aggressively toward Karmen. The officers stepped aside, unintentionally allowing Empress to release her foul-smelling weapon on Karmen.

The woman was hysterical; for me, the situation *was* hysterical. Karmen was screaming bloody murder and she stank. Her next entitled rant didn't improve her situation in the slightest. No one dared come close to help her. Two of the security cavalry escaped down the hall as if they were running from the plague, while the other three vigorously rubbed their eyes. My nostrils burned from the skunk's prank, and I could barely open my eyes. I tried to breathe through my mouth while covering my face with my sweaty shirt. This was terrible. I needed to leave, now.

"Security, thank you for your service. Please escort this woman and her...ESA back to her unit, as I have business to tend to." Gagging and coughing, the woman tried to evade their hands; and from the glimpses of her, I saw her face turn red and blotchy as she became more nauseous. I almost threw up.

I made it back to the elevator once more and pressed the button for floor 15. I was so close. "Get your hands off me!" I heard her helplessly call for Donny on her phone, who I guessed was her husband, G-d bless him. "Donny, get out here this instant. This is all your fault!" Dry heaving, she retched after every word, causing the officers to quickly jump out of the way.

Seriously, everyone needed to leave ASAP, but Karmen and her attitude continued. "All the money we put in this place and for what?" As the skunk's spray lingered, I could hear other residents on the floor opening their doors only to slam them and open their windows. The skunk hissed once more before biting through her gaudy leash and galloping toward the stairs at the other end of the hallway.

"Empress, Empress, I demand you come back here at once!" Karmen screeched as she attempted to run after the skunk, but she was long gone by now. Karmen changed direction towards the elevator, but the officers were able to pull her away, just before her hand reached me. "Citizen's arrest, citizen's arrest, you crip—" The security officer cut her off by grabbing her arm before she could complete the slur. Creating a biohazard lockdown in the building was one thing, but now Karmen had truly gone too far. I'm sure there is something in the HOA that I can review later.

"Citizen's arrest? I don't think so," I replied calmly. "By the way, I'll be chatting with Mr. Boggs, *my father*, about certain over-privileged residents." I relished the realization in her eyes. All she had to do was keep quiet and *walk* away.

A minute later, the elevator doors opened to reveal floor 15 where I *finally* spotted my father waiting for me outside his office at the end of the hall.

"Heard the commotion," he said with a grimace, probably because he could smell me all the way over here. "Another obstacle to you joining the family business, I presume?"

The huge, glass walls of the top floor reflected the sunshine gleaming down on the complex, and as I turned my head to admire the view down below, I saw a little black tail with a white stripe scurry happily into a patch in the front gardens. I was happy for the first time today and turned back toward my father.

I considered my father's query. "Not at all. You know, this floor could be a great headquarters for Abili-Max. I have some ideas on how I can make this work, and I really want to hear what you have to say about your retirement." He genuinely smiled back at me. "But first, Dad, please. For both of our sakes, let me use your executive shower first."

See the end of the book for elevator etiquette rules followed or broken. Elevator Etiquette Codes: 1D, 2B, 3B, 4A, 5E, 5F, 6A, 6B, 9G

Dishonorable Discharge

HOLY CRAP!

*"I learned my lesson long ago:
everyday objects are also weapons of mass destruction,
and women of action win more than women of words."*
-Amery Bruce

Consider this. Pearl, a 72-year-old woman, is taking her poodle Beau Beau to the roof of The Palm and Glades Country Club to relax. They had enjoyed a nice walk on this most perfect day. Pearl, her hair shaved tight, is wearing a sunflower print sundress. She has a large yellow Michael Kors satchel, or it could be Coach. The average person would not recognize it, that's for sure. Beau Beau wears a matching sunflower doggy shirt, her name embroidered on it with a pastel royal purple yarn.

Pearl and company are in the elevator going up when the elevator stops to onboard a group of 11-year-old boys: Jayden, Hayden, and Kaden (the triplets), as well as Brayden and Aiden (the cousins, who are also twins). All the domestic terrorists, as Pearl likes to call them, are dressed in matching country club swimsuits that are white as white could be.

Pearl, unfortunately, is familiar with the boys. She knows that harming them in any way would violate the terms of her parole. She avoids eye contact as if that will keep them in line.

The boys look at Pearl bent on chaos and enjoy tormenting her every chance they get. Today will be no different.

After going up a floor and a half, Aiden pushes the emergency stop button and the elevator comes to an abrupt halt. The alarm does not go off, as that is a different button. Pearl presses her bag to her chest as she looks around at the pairs of beady eyes. Her interest peaks. "What *exactly* are you doing, Brayden?"

"I'm Aiden, you old hag!"

Pearl bends over and leans close to the child's face. "Oh! Aiden, is it? Please, restart the elevator." She leans back into a neutral position and clasps her hands together. There is a long, drawn-out, pregnant, never-ending pause. The boys are slightly confused, as Pearl has never pushed back before. "Alright, boys! I suggest you get off on the next floor. I do not have the patience today. Unless you want me to take you all on a little detour."

"Brayden, did you hear Boomer say we're not welcome in the elevator? Wait until I tell Daddy about this one."

Brayden chuckles. "I heard the fruitbag. Let *me* tell Daddy and you'll be my witness."

Pearl rolls her eyes and sighs. "Please, restart the elevator, Aiden."

"No."

"Restart the elevator, Aiden. I won't ask you again."

"Good."

Amid the argument, Jayden bends down to eye level with Beau Beau. "You are one ugly bitch!"

Pearl reacts, "Enough! You little –" She decides to choose her words carefully, refraining from saying anything further to the children. As much as she'd enjoy verbally tearing them apart, or criticizing their pretentious outfits or their stupid, buck-toothed faces, she chose not to. Pearl considers herself a woman of action.

After Jayden gets up, Hayden bends down to the dog's eye level, and Beau Beau shows her teeth while snarling.

Hayden snarls back with a mock bark.

Pearl sighs and confidently reaches into her bag. She turns to the boys before pulling out a can of spray paint and covering the lens of the security camera. "Boys, you will rue this day."

"Oh, yeah? I don't know what rueing is, but it's not like you or your wimpy-ass dog could do anything to us!"

Pearl huffs and methodically reaches into her bag once more, pulls out a snake, and puts it on the floor of the elevator. The snake, about the length of two No. 2 pencils, wears a Hannibal Lecter-style mask and flicks its tongue at the boys.

The boys freak out for fear that they may get bitten. There were several things they expected to be pulled out of an old woman's purse. Maybe a smattering of butterscotch candy or an Almond Joy. Perhaps old napkins that were stolen during an early bird special. Somehow, a live reptile would have never crossed their pea brains.

Pearl laughs and speaks to the boys in a slow sing-song sarcastic tone, "Now, for your sake, do as I ask. Before I unleash the unholy."

Fear paralyzes the boys, preventing them from registering what Pearl has said. Kayden fumbles with his pockets, pulling out his sunscreen. He aims it at the snake, but the over-spray hits the dog.

Pearl scoops up Beau Beau in her arms to wipe her clean. "I had given you all fair warning, but to no avail." She said in a quiet, almost resigned tone. As she bends down to move her snake to safety within her bag, she adds, "I'm afraid in your attempt to assault my Beau Beau, you have crossed a line. What's done is done, boys." From the infinite depths of her purse, she pulls out a gas mask optimized for poodles and puts it on Beau Beau before setting her down. "You unruly delinquents need to be taught a lesson." She rummages in her bag and takes out a Mira CM-7M military gas mask, optimized for old ladies bent on revenge.

The boys' uncanny uniformity is ruined, stained by a growing spot on Jayden's pure white swim trunks. Pale yellow liquid pools at his feet. The others snicker, then whisper to themselves, debating what to do.

"Boys, all morning, I have eaten eggs, meat, cauliflower, and beans. A LOT of beans. I warned you, you IVF horrors. And now, I will unleash my flatulent fury upon you." With that short notice, Pearl, a former military special forces officer, who was dishonorably discharged to no one's surprise, turns her back to the boys. She then let loose an olfactory and auditory nightmare that would put any frat house to shame.

Shock, regret, disgust. The absolute horror of these ramifications combined in a hellish chemistry. Half of the boys have fallen to their knees gagging. The others have chosen to hold their breath, not knowing how long they could do so. Either way, they are likely to pass out. All their unprotected eyes are burning and watering from the toxic fumes.

Pearl calmly reaches over to the panel and restarts the elevator. She scoots between the children to be close to the doors as they open. Ding after ding, the rooftop level approaches. The longer the elevator takes, the more the children will sit in the consequence of their actions, and one in his urine. As the doors open, she removes her mask and triumphantly takes in a deep breath of fresh air. She steps out, turns, and pushes the button to send the boys back down to the pool. She bends down to take the mask off Beau Beau, who whines to be picked up. Then, and only then, does she set off the alarm.

Someone will tend to the boys. They're someone else's problem now. Her parole officer would be so proud.

In the meantime, Pearl stretches out on a rooftop lounge chair and takes in the precious UV rays. Beau Beau jumps onto the chair beside her and barks as if to signal victory. Her snake slithers out of her bag to get some rays himself. Pearl sets her mask on the table beside her. Her snake is good, her dog is good, and there is enough Diet Coke with lemon for days. Pearl is not the only one who has ever been tormented by those entitled preteen monsters, but it's possible that she will be the last.

Some think Pearl's a hero, some think she's insane, but none question her commitment. She's too old to care what others think of her, but Pearl wasn't too old for one last mission.

See the end of the book for elevator etiquette rules followed or broken. Elevator Etiquette Codes: 1C, 2E, 3A, 3E, 4A, 4B, 5A, 5E, 6B, 6C, 6H, 7A

Toiletpapermageddon
THE KARENS MEETS THE SUPPLY CHAIN

"I will sprinkle clean water on you, and you will be clean; I will cleanse you from all your impurities and from all your idols." -Ezekiel 36:25

Consider this. In April 2020, the supply chain issues related to the coronavirus ushered in the era of Toiletpapermageddon. By the time the third week rolled around, toilet humor had become quite popular. Everyone seemed to crack their crappiest jokes, and the world lost its shit. A black market formed for the softest rolls of white, and the value of prison-issue single-ply, sandpaper-style paper skyrocketed. Those in Beverly Hills negotiated in the dark alleys behind Bristol Farms, Erewhon, and even Whole Paycheck for the Charmin Ultra Strong and the Cottonelle Ultra Comfort. What sent even the Boy Scouts down

Walter White Lane was the sublime texture of the Quilted Northern Ultra Plush.

Stores began placing strict limits on the number of essential items people could buy, including toilet paper. The moment the government considered mask mandates, a social revolution was born.

Who could forget the glorious wars fought at Costco all across America? Lines and lines of suburban families stood just barely six feet apart outside the arena of bulk products, food court chicken bakes, and hot dogs. They wore their armor of N95 masks and khakis while yielding their weapons of choice: metal shopping carts, purses, and "accidental" shoves and misdirections. All of this for one purpose, one goal: Grab as much toilet paper in bulk, no matter what. Family members would pretend to be strangers, completing separate transactions to get double or triple the toilet paper and laughing at the goody-two-shoes holding up their Costco membership cards.

Survivalists and hoarders alike sought after toilet paper. Showing off, but hiding from scrutiny, they posted on burner accounts, flaunting their towers of toilet paper. They craved toilet paper just as much as at-home COVID-19 tests. People also started to bombard the news channels, yelling at the government to ramp up toilet paper production, calling clean asses a matter of national security. People went so far as to advocate for the use of paper towels, tissues, and even printer paper to bring down the demand and prices for toilet paper. Those scenarios were immediately shut down by Big Paper.

Suspicion reigned and everyone's usage habits came under scrutiny. It was neighbor against neighbor. Sure, they shared the first week of Toiletpapermageddon, but this was week 3. The new directive was to be as frugal with their shares of white gold as possible. Don't even get me started on the celebrity collaboration videos on social media, where they sang (or screeched) uplifting songs of hope amidst the toilet paper crisis, and the public was instead suitably offended. Everyone had an opinion, and Grammy-winning artist Sheryl Crow made headlines by suggesting the average person should use only one square per restroom visit, except, of course, on those pesky occasions where two to three could be required.

Regardless, the one-square situation never became a thing, and Crow went back to focusing on music. People were convinced their stash would last the longer they waited, but when you have to go, you have to go! A few more skid marks on those boxers could be washed off with the abundance of laundry detergent that still filled store shelves, for now.

Paper Abstinence apps became the new hype, trying to appeal to young children, but the concept didn't work either. They didn't want high fives, points, or gold stars to earn virtual flushes; they just wanted to go potty.

One woman stood alone in the water closet wars, Sherry Gooper. Sherry Gooper was the legend of the lockdown, for one simple reason: zero usage. She protested on the local news channels for the rights of trees, handing out sustainability pamphlets made of bamboo (the ink was soy), and even going as far as chaining herself to the fence at the local lumberyard.

She was batshit crazy, though, and never understood the appeal of toilet paper in the first place. She spent more time outdoors than in her own home, which was fine to a point, but she wanted everyone to follow her lead. She tried to get on the social media bandwagon, but so far, her follower count remained at zero.

One day at the three-story, all-organic store, Mammoth Market, she witnessed a young lady exiting the women's restroom with toilet paper on the back of her shoe, and Sherry became infuriated. Her voice was the only one that could be heard above the din as she aggressively berated the lady in front of the ratty Woolly Mammoth mascot for even using toilet paper in the first place. Sherry bent down and picked at the toilet paper underneath the shoe until the lady picked her foot up so Sherry could finally grab it.

"This sheet was responsible for chopping down a bird's nest in an old-growth forest. The least you could do is show this chlorine-bleached piece of toxic paper your respect!" Sherry carefully folded the toilet paper into a smaller square before placing it in her pocket. All the while, customers watched this interaction with bemused expressions as they came down from the supermarket's third floor in the glass-walled elevator.

Sherry walked toward the elevator, planning to go to the second floor. The elevator door opened to reveal the customers who watched her from above. They averted their eyes and speed walked out of the elevator as they exited.

When she entered the elevator, she noticed that six women remained, sporting identical bob haircuts, cuffed denim, and flip-flops. They stood in two rows of three, and when Sherry entered, they stepped aside, leaving her alone in the middle. One of them recognized Sherry from the news. "Oh, you're that outdoors lady, right? So, I have to ask, do you not use deodorant either because it's bad for the environment? You know your body odor is really bad *for us*? Amirite, ladies?" one woman said. They couldn't respond as the women's eyes appeared to burn while covering their mouths and unmasked noses. Since Sherry was a more natural kind of woman, she preferred the crystal kind of deodorant, which was not optimal for enclosed spaces.

She tried to hold back her snark, but these women were riling her up. They attacked with insult after insult.

"She's probably from the valley and can't afford toilet paper."

"You know, I thought I smelled a load of crap when she entered the elevator."

"Your bare ass was all over the news. I'm just glad they had the decency to blur that. No one wants to see *that* ever again."

One woman tried to calm everyone down, trying to find a sense of reason amidst this shitty talk.

"Can we all please relax? We know everyone is going a little crazy with the toilet paper situation, but she," she looked to Sherry, "has a point. We need to conserve toilet paper, but we also know we're not *that* willing to do whatever *that* is: roll around in the trash." The women began to giggle uncontrollably, while Sherry stirred in pent-up frustration in the center of the elevator.

However, Sherry was not without her defenses, and if these women wanted a fight, they got one. So Sherry used her one superpower: the non-usage demonstration. She immediately dropped her jeans, and with a half-hearted squat and a dramatic plop, everyone else had now something dire to deal with. The elevator slowly went up. The moms became terrified and tried their best to distance themselves in the cramped elevator. Some were even able to hop up on the handrails on each side of the elevator to get away from her south zone. Some women couldn't get far enough away, their faces awkwardly pressed up against the glass walls, some vomiting the remains of their salad lunches. One woman pushed the emergency button just as the elevator finally reached the second floor.

As soon as the door opened, Sherry made a break for it, grabbing one of the nearby carts just as the blaring alarms went off. In the corner of her eye, she noticed the flashing lights near the entrance/exit. She took off with it at a run, her jeans and a DNA sample left behind. She deftly hopped onto the cart and sailed out the automatic sliding doors, the fresh air bringing a victorious smirk to her face. She stood on that cart with a sense of pride and freedom, with her bottom out in the open for all to see, the echoes of retching and whining sirens trailing behind her. People screamed in horror while parents covered their children's eyes. The out-of-shape security guards were not trained for this and were prepared to report this to their superiors and store managers as they dealt with the aftermath in the elevator.

Sherry would perhaps return to her favorite market when things were calmer, of course. She knew she would probably get on the news yet again, but for once, she didn't give a shit what others thought of her.

See the end of the book for elevator etiquette rules followed or broken. Elevator Etiquette Codes: 1D, 2B, 4A, 5A, 6B, 6C, 6D, 6H, 7A, 8A, 8D, 9G

The Elevator State

Your Tax Dollars At Work

"The years passed; mankind became stupider at a frightening rate....Sadly, the greatest minds and resources were focused on conquering hair loss and prolonging erections." -Narrator, **Idiocracy,** *20th Century Fox, 2006*

Consider this. The apocalypse had finally come to America, and it was Sadness incarnate.

It was an emotional ride for everybody, and people couldn't stand the status quo for even one more day. In short, everyone was miserable. Even rich people couldn't buy their way out. They tried. Oh, they tried....

The newest products and riches filled up the swankiest homes. The citizens were bored, and boredom led to purchases like suture and wound practice bundles, roast beef scented bath soaks, and even life-size cutouts of Danny DeVito to keep them company, or whatever.

But after the initial excitement of the purchases wore out, the rich 'uns only sank into further depression, like everybody else. It was even more harrowing for common folk everywhere. Passions and interests were lost. Models and fashionistas couldn't be bothered to put on lipstick or even basic concealer and setting powder. There was just no point....

Even industrious business personnel and construction workers fell behind where they would usually be thriving. Now they ate antacids like candy. Employees covered their eyes with alternating heating and cooling pads in an attempt to block out the nothingness of their existence.

Mothers and fathers watched with disinterest as the laundry and dirty dishes piled up, stacking miles high. The ants didn't even bother to go get the crumbs, because *they* were depressed too.

It had certainly been bad before. Now it was getting worse and worse and *worser,* to be frank. No one wanted to get out of bed. No one wanted to go to work, because, for most people, that meant getting out of bed. Chronic absenteeism resulted in job losses across the nation, which meant there was no money coming in to uphold daily responsibilities. Consequently, many bills remained unpaid, and the disappointments continued to pile up higher than the dishes.

That left America in an *incredibly* tight spot, to be honest. It was a total clusterfuck. People were desperate for any kind of relief — physical, emotional, or mental. They were willing to do whatever it took to make that happen. But no one had the answers; even therapists and doctors, burned out themselves, were sadly, useless. So, people just kept waiting, longing for any form of relief. When would things finally be okay again? What would that even look like? And how would it feel?

The federal government had ideas. They brought singer Bobby McFerrin out of retirement to run the Agency of Anxiety Reduction and Positivity Augmentation. This agency knew that happiness loved company, so it brought on Katrina Leskanich of Katrina and the Waves, and Pharrell Williams to perform upbeat music in local town squares.

But unfortunately, after some time, people were tired of hearing the same songs and were becoming enraged. Some would go retro with The Beatles' "Got to Get You Into My Life" or jam to Panic! at the Disco!'s "Don't Threaten Me with a Good Time," but it just wasn't enough. It was never, ever, *really* enough. The tunes were catchy, but the earworms were making the populace irrationally *angry*. At some point, after hearing an unhoused choir performing The Partridge Family's "Come On Get Happy" at a freeway exit, somebody had thrown a garbage can at the group. This caused the lead singer to be knocked unconscious causing a great deal of tsuris. "Give us some new happy songs, dammit!" the assaulter screeched, as an on-site ARPA team member carried him away. And that *clearly* marked a new point in the whole situation....

Something had to change. So a new strategy was formulated, something so inherently blissful that it would only bring peace and relaxation to a country that had strived and cried one too many times.

The first well-intentioned concept was mandatory, **unannounced** wellness checks. However, the idea of an unlicensed, mustached male or female uniformed social officer entering homes for unsolicited assessments was met with outright rejection. A pilot program to get people moving off their butts again was tested on mall escalators and automated airport people movers, but neither situation offered privacy, so those solutions were rejected as well. The government learned and adapted.

At McFerrin's direction and in cooperation with the National Guard Bureau, they mobilized a division of the Guard called the Pleasure Patrols, which were activated across the country.

The Pleasure Patrols were stationed outside the first floor of the most frequented elevators in the United States. People would be incentivized, actually *required* under penalty of law, to leave their homes so they could appear before a Pleasure Patrol service member. Citizens were *encouraged* to go to a neighborhood elevator where they would be *pressured* to change their mood, ***or else.*** The government had become so desperate that they entertained two more out-of-the-box solutions.

Number 1: Upon entering the elevator, the Pleasure Patrols provided willing adults with at least the potential for an uplifting experience. So every day, everyone over 21 (18 in some states) was dispensed a pre-rolled joint from a crop grown in a blue state and two airplane bottles of 24-proof wine called "Blissful Blast" from crops fermented in red states.

Number 2: For those who abstained, the government recommended meditation, kombucha, and for the brave, kefir. Under the emergency authorization, the USDA suspended the Food Pyramid so that a sister government agency could advocate for the go-to comfort food options of milk chocolate, mac and cheese, and deep-fried everything, but not all at the same time. Unfortunately, these new diets developed their own set of problems, such as obesity and increased risk of heart disease, despite the temporary emotional high these foods brought to consumers.

Ramped-up distribution of alcohol and weed led to a corresponding explosion in creating fake IDs for those of the moodier younger persuasion. Underage teens, 14 or so, probably more melancholy than most, also lined up to receive the black market packages filled with alcohol called "Elle" and pot called "Vator". Word had it that "Vator" was the bomb, and the kids preferred the edible form, if available. However, the adults said you hadn't really *smoke*-smoked until you tried the legendary "Vator" in its more natural form. Websites popped up, showing the most lenient elevator dispensaries and the most reliable sites on the dark web. Most of the Pleasure Patrols turned a blind eye to underage riders or repeat customers because anything other than happiness would be a bummer. Besides, as one budtender claimed on the condition of anonymity, "Not my problem, dude." The dispensaries were, for the most part, top-notch, modeled after MedMen dispensaries with some Apple Store style mixed in for good measure. Regardless of location, they resembled a mixture of luxury tech sleekness, all-white silicon, and glossy polish. These places were certainly peaceful and inviting, combined with the rustic wooden warm vibes of a coffee shop. "A friend with weed is a friend indeed."

Neither political party had a plan on what to do *after* they locked in a win. As long as the people were satisfied, what difference did it make? Society was getting back on track again! People were up; they were moving, but they were sick. The United States thought they could get back from this emotional apocalypse if it motivated the population to work and socialize again. Some things *seemed* to be going well, better than they had in years.

Despite that, addiction and substance abuse skyrocketed, and it really wasn't their fault. The system was failing them. The population, trapped in a loop of anxiety and depression, stayed snuggled in bed, glued to their phones. Meanwhile, they gained weight as they gawked at the rare athletes who were barely in shape enough to compete.

An unanticipated side effect of temporarily extinguishing the emotional apocalypse emerged when officials suddenly realized that, sadly, the addicted were pursuing a stronger black market strain called Happiness. This gave them a surprising vigor for sex, but also shut down the impulse for employment. The birth rate of the most emotionally vulnerable citizens increased nine months later, and that created a *whole new set* of problems. The population were compelled to return for more Elle, more Vator, and more Happiness until they decided to just ride the elevators all day instead of really doing anything productive. It did *not* help that some elevator operators would do shots or smoke up with their clients. The most egregious thought they were being noble by supplying the citizens with joints when exiting the elevators, too! Such idiocracy!

Soon, children as young as three were asking, "Why is dada's nose so red?" or "What's that smell, mommy?" Whether it came out of the elevators themselves, or as people walked inside or swiped the joints from the operators, the hallways grew clouded with the full whiff and were littered with empties.

Inflation went through the roof when ATMs were installed in elevators with no withdrawal limits on "the government breeze". All of these concerns came together into what Dr. Brown of Troughton University referred to as "The Elevator State," as almost the entire population was now under the influence and on the government dole. Young and old shared a tragic compulsion and suffered withdrawal when they were too far away from the all-providing elevator. Your tax dollars are at work.

The more *troubled* would sneak into elevators at night if a Pleasure Patrol dispensary agent "accidentally" left the doors unlocked. These agents allowed the especially addicted to get some extra "sumthin' sumthin." It was seen as a merciful gesture of kindness by most citizens. Eventually, the government finally realized just how far things had gone and defunded the Pleasure Patrols.

That gave way to formalizing a new black market: Elevation. It was an organized crime version of the Pleasure Patrols where they were already covertly providing the super strain Happiness. Elevation was already everywhere because of the quality of the strains and the superiority of their brand ambassadors. Those who chased their own personal dragons were willing to risk a meeting with Elevation dealers, or rather the consequences of the dark web, whatever those might be....

Each political party took credit for the limited success of the defunct Pleasure Patrols. The conservatives enjoyed the tax breaks it yielded, especially to the ultra-rich. The liberals' hearts went out to the hard-working, yet long-suffering populace and proposed new entitlements. Unfortunately, the left persuasion voters were too stoned to go vote. After the Executive branch and both houses of Congress turned over, the government made an about-face and decided to return the elevators to their now-obsolete mission of vertical transport. However, this was very short-lived. After getting immediate blowback, and rock-bottom poll numbers, they doubled down to outdo the previous administration. They actually banned elevators as a mode of transportation. The deconstruction of classic elevators took effect immediately, and a new generation of "elevators" was born.

Voters enthusiastically passed new bond measures and "Elevators To Nowhere" became the new normal. Open-air elevators became ideal as vertical space was less of an issue. New construction accommodated capacities of 40 or more people, including bars, dispensaries, and in some of the fancier elevators, never closing Taco Bells. In the less desirable neighborhoods, there were Del Tacos instead, which seemed unfair. But serving food, and allowing alcohol sales 24/7 had its advantages.

Elevator parks had become the place to take the edge off, a destination for dating adventures. Eventually, elevators evolved in parallel with the population's needs. Being stoned became the default, and citizens were so mellow that couches took the place of stools. Vending machines were added for novelty bongs and the newest strains, such as Danza, Ziggy, Bobbitt, and Walken. And when Walken wasn't enough, people just turned to the ultimately banned genus, Nic Cage.

Elevator shafts were no longer needed because no one ventured past the lobby anymore. There were no self-help journeys to take, just black light destination rooms with glowing posters and the occasional velvet Elvises. The pre-fabbed elevators had a second destination room, an Urgent Care, if you will, for the populations who continually took things too far. The more "responsible" franchises had Xboxes or PlayStations, depending on sponsorship.

A "nu-elevator" prototype was shown as the ultimate destination for a weary population. It had multiple dispensary managers clothed in optic white, and these modern elevators were state-of-the-art 4000-square-foot structures. They were suitable for moving at least 200 people at a time if they were so inclined, which they were not. And it would only move if it was attached to a building, which it wasn't.

The *elevator* was no longer an elevator in the traditional sense; its Merriam-Webster definition now reads, "a large gathering area for people to relax, typically serving wine, beer, spirits, marijuana, and other recreational drugs for effect." And serve recreational drugs, it did. With each new administration, the government upped its game, and with each inhale, sip, snort and swallow, the people fell further into an ignorant perpetual bliss. And they smelled bad too. The years passed, and the government evolved into an absolute kakistocracy.

In fact, officials themselves were finding it harder and harder to resist the temptations of the elevator, and the point of the government was lost in a purple haze. The government was no longer providing the "Vator" packages, making laws, or enforcing *anything*. People continued to imbibe, falling further and further away from what was previously considered normal and safe.

A new select government committee was formed to get to the bottom of this, and they also craved a respite from the bleak reality they'd created. They would assemble and imbibe a one-two punch of cocaine and LSD to stay fired up while brainstorming new reformations. Their sessions tended to be inefficient, dangerous, and expensive for the citizens they served.

Negligent.

Ill-advised.

Incompetent.

All of that, and nothing less....

It all checks out....

See the end of the book for elevator etiquette rules followed or broken.
Elevator Etiquette Codes: 1A, 1B, 2B, 2G, 4D, 5B, 5C, 5E, 6H

23rd Century Fishbowl

SUBSCRIBE NOW FOR LIFE'S ESSENTIALS

"Inhale the present, exhale the past and future." -Leticia Rae

Consider this. Otis Miles is the lead Manager of Air Supply, Quality Assurance for the International Straits of Detroit. Making it to his office on the 577th floor of Bezos & Longfellow has always been a challenge, and this morning is no different. B&L is a global conglomerate that has a life insurance division where instead of money being passed on to a policyholder's beneficiaries, air itself was now the commodity. His role within the Utility Division is necessary to keep the air firkins running with the proper ratio of oxygen, nitrogen, and bezosen for the Detroitians. One mistake, like failing to manage a clogged filter in the condenser, could unnecessarily destabilize the local atmospheric spot markets.

Otis arrives at the base level of his office building wearing a head bowl of thick clear polycarbonate, tinted and laser etched with his eyeglass prescription for the highest quality vision. The micro-projectors on the inside display two windows: one with a zoom lens to more accurately monitor the activity of his hands; and the other with an air tank to monitor volume, pressure, and temperature. The tank icons also display how much air remains, how much of it has already been recycled, and how precious little he is getting filtered from the outside environment. There are also matching surround microphones and perfectly spaced micro-speakers. While the microphone input was free, the volume touch-slider for the speakers was available only on a subscription basis.

As oxygen became the new gold, everyone, by necessity, is required to wear one of these Facial Inhaling Support for Heart and Body Outfitted for Wearability and Life preservation (F.I.S.H.B.O.W.L) things to live. These are also manufactured by Bezos & Longfellow. This was made clear by the huge B and L embossed on the back, the letters powder coated with cherry and gold accents. It just so happens that the helmet's inner sensors collect data from Otis in exchange for a welcome discount on the helmet rental from B&L. To his dismay, these helmets make him feel sad, claustrophobic, cheap, and absolutely disgustingly disgusted. ▫

Upon entrance to the building, Otis's heads-up display informs him he has exactly 40 minutes to make it to his station on time. The helmet's incessant beeping adds to the urgency. If Otis would share more personal data with B&L, he could use those credits towards a silence subscription, or at least the volume slider. However, right now, he has more important things to focus on. Otis takes the moving walkway to the elevator. Upon stepping inside, he is accompanied by a dozen other employees rushing the entrance. This lowers his hopes of making it to his station at a reasonable time. They shoved Otis to the back of the elevator, where he could hardly reach the number panel. He somehow pushes the buttons for his floor, 5 - 7 - 7, as the elevator entertainment system plays a polka instrumental version of "Does It Matter". As Otis had not subscribed to the Noise Canceling function after his trial period, he had to put up with it.

As the elevator slowly ascends, the head bowls constantly clink and clank against one another. They sound just like a descent of woodpeckers pecking nonstop against a hollow tree. The different-sized heads in the different-sized head bowls all make distinct tones when colliding, and no one would say they were musical or melodic or remotely pleasant. The reverberations make Otis feel like his head is in an ever-tightening vice. The noise stops and starts numerous times as people exit the elevator in a rush to reach their own workstations. Panic covers their faces as they start their machines, scared of the consequences if they are late. The last time someone didn't arrive on time, they had gone to Human Resources to complain and explain, and were never seen again.

To make matters worse, new government regulations now prohibit the company from using non-essential air conditioning due to the oxygen requirements for recycled air. Somehow this benefited B&L, but to the non-essential layperson (just about everyone in a non-executive role), it was torture. Due to the excessively long elevator ride, the lack of chilled circulation makes the cramped space smell like a microwave oven after cooking some day-old cod. Fortunately, the filters of the head bowls handled that annoyance to a tolerable extent.

Otis is in absolute misery, drenched in his own perspiration. He is queasy, and is ready to pass out. The clashing of polymer glass is giving him a torturous migraine. Like any other day at this time, he questions every single life choice that has led him to this point. Otis's eyes meet with another whose gaze is about as empty as a lifeless goldfish.

You would think that the company president would spring for more than a single elevator in a 600-floor building. And she did, but *that* elevator is reserved for the VIPs and Otis did not remotely qualify. Every day, Otis is under constant stress about whether the elevator will get him to his office on time, yet he knows it must, as there is no other option. Getting there at a reasonable time affects his ability to eat, and the citizen's ability to breathe. He also wonders why he can't work remotely like they do at Gates & Sloane. Like it or not, the world has a new aerospheric normal, and the citizens of the International Straits of Detroit depend on him.

Otis tilts his head up and reminisces about a time before the oxygen crisis. Before polybowls, sterilized uniforms embroidered with the B&L logo and rooms without proper air filtration and re-conditioning became the norm. That all felt like a millennium ago, but it was only a decade since the government implemented these heavy policies after heavy lobbying by B&L. Otis never could have imagined he would long for the days when he wasn't assessed an existence fee. Otis couldn't even think of one thing that now wasn't monitored, taxed, or required a subscription to use. Even though he works for B&L, he couldn't always afford his air rations, but B&L was also a bank that was more than willing to make a B&L team member a loan. B&L also runs the lottery for the government, and while they say it isn't fixed, B&L employees seem to win extra gulps of air out of proportion to the rest of the population. When Otis has won, he puts those scented air drops away for retirement.

His vivid thoughts of nostalgia and yearning give him a brief sense of peace, but it doesn't last very long. At that moment, a version of Air Supply's "Feels Like Screaming" plays. As the elevator at last reaches his destination, he pauses as the others step out around him. The clanking of the bowls against one another finally fades into nothingness. With that, he exits with a sense of melancholy. Re-activating his HUD, he determines he has barely enough time to get to his machine on time to clock in, run a diagnostic, and adjust the currents. He runs the default cleaning algorithm he had developed and refined over the last three years to great success, although management has never commented on his process improvement.

Otis knows it will be many agonizing hours of troubleshooting and processing the incoming air quality reports for his area of the city before he has to step back into the elevator and cope with the incessant clanking of bowls and the almost endless ride down his personal tower of terror. Otis hoped his migraine would be gone by then. A constant reminder of his 23rd-century reality.

See the end of the book for elevator etiquette rules followed or broken. Elevator Etiquette Codes: 1B, 2D, 2E, 3A, 4A, 6B

Cirque de la Mimique

Cirque de la Mimique Trilogy, Part I

"The fact that I'm silent doesn't mean I have nothing to say."
-Jonathan Carroll

Consider this. If it hadn't been for her daughter pointing animatedly at the poster, Lacie wouldn't have noticed it. She had been so trapped inside her mind as they stepped onto the old elevator that nothing had registered other than her daughter Vi's hand clutched tightly with her own.

Their trip to France had been her husband's idea, and the hotel had been booked for almost a year. Each event of the trip was carefully scheduled, both to fit into their one-week holiday and to ease Vi's anxieties around public spaces that had plagued her entire life. The moment Vi began to speak sparsely at home but never in public, Selective Mutism began to fall from the doctor's lips. Clinicians and family alike were optimistic that one day she would speak more frequently outside the home, and gave them exercises to help aid her. Adair started to practice visualization with his daughter. He walked her through the steps to positively imagine in her mind's eye new outcomes for factors that triggered her anxiety. Then, they would find ways to work through those fears. The method allowed Vi to face anxieties in a safe space while also teaching her patience. He signed the family up for American Sign Language (ASL) classes, too. While she could hear, she communicated mainly in ASL and other related actions that signaled what she was saying and feeling. Lacie had been a dancer before Vi was born, and she seemed to find comfort in movement the same way her mother did. She would tap her foot when she felt successful and fidget her fingers when scared. Adair was prepared to give his daughter the best life, and for now, that included a trip to France. When he suddenly died three months before they boarded, Lacie had been left alone, with a daughter she could barely manage. Now, every event they went to without him was either a mockery or a celebration, depending on Lacie's mood.

Vi, now nine years old, had tightly gripped Lacie's hand the minute the heavy hotel elevator doors had screeched open in front of them to take them to their room. Lacie needed a break from the outside world, and Vi was craving playtime with her Nintendo Switch. The grinding sound of metal on metal had Vi grasping her mother even tighter than usual, her other hand trembling. Once they both stepped into the ancient lift, Lacie tucked Vi's hand between both of her own, bent down to her level, and hugged her. Since they had arrived, the barely lit elevator had scared the young girl. She shivered each time they boarded it, but the rotting wooden stairs seemed even less safe. The formerly gold-plated car had long since lost its luster. Now, the gold flecked off the walls and railings and littered the faded marble floor with glitter spots of shine. Even with the shine, it was dark as day turned to dusk. Randomly alternating busted bulbs streaked the elevator in black, and the ones that did work barely lit the space. When the elevator raised or lowered, the shadows danced. While the darkness made Vi uncomfortable, Lacie reveled in it. Standing there in a cold and bleak space, the environment reflected her grief. With her widow's guilt, Lacie felt she belonged in a void, hovering up and down in isolation.

The elevator continued to tremble as it did when they first entered, and with their combined weight it was terrifying. When Lacie stepped toward the glowing floor buttons on the side, the elevator moved like someone was jumping up and down on the roof. It creaked like the cords holding it up in the elevator shaft would snap at any moment. The owners had previously assured them it was up to code, and Lacie was so emotionally exhausted she took their word for it. None of their promises, or Lacie's reassurances, made Vi any less anxious. While Vi fidgeted, Lacie remained distant. Even when they were alone in the elevator, Vi never felt safe enough to speak and kept her head down.

It wasn't until Vi had tugged hard on Lacie's hand twice that she turned to see what captured her attention. She was gesturing aggressively to the tattered playbill taped on the back wall of the elevator. It hung above one portion of the paint-chipped gold handrail. Lacie turned her back on the doors, moving to see why Vi was so enraptured. It hung crooked, having been tacked on the wall haphazardly with yellowed tape. Lacie wondered why they hadn't seen it before. The poster was almost entirely black and white; the only color on it was a name displayed in deep red across the top. *Cirque de la Mimique*. The text was the color of dried blood. Vi pulled her attention from it briefly, poking her mother until she turned her head. She signed at Lacie, asking if they could go. Lacie signed back, asking her to be patient until she knew more about it.

Looking for event information, Lacie studied the poster. Trying to see it from Vi's perspective, she understood what had attracted her daughter. There was a mime plastered front and center. It was clothed in the stereotypical t-shirt with horizontal black and white stripes, and suspenders hooked into a knee-length black skirt with white stripes near the hem. Tall socks covered the length of its legs, only a strip of skin whiter than snow visible at the peak of its thighs. Its suspenders and bow were the same crimson red as the name on the poster. A ring of children watched it perform.

Mimes had been one of the biggest reasons Adair loved France. Adair had always associated them with happiness and magic, able to turn the image into the physical. They could cut a rope with imaginary scissors, or trap themselves in boxes that didn't exist. Magic had always been alluring to children, an opportunity to manipulate the impossible. Vi probably saw a person capable of such wonders. Though Lacie didn't know French, she surmised that there would be a lot of mimes at this event. Of course, Vi wanted to go — like father, like daughter. To Lacie, the mime just looked tormented.

Its high arching brows were thick, *black,* as if drawn on with a marker. Its black eyes were sunken, set deeply into pale skin pulled tightly over its skull. White gloves stretched closely across its hands, and its lips were glossy with black lipstick as dark as its eyebrows. For the past three months, Lacie had seen the same gaunt expression and sunken eyes on her own face every time she looked in the mirror. Looking at the mime, Lacie saw her grief reflected back at herself, masked behind a satiric face of comical surprise.

The children surrounding the mime gazed up at it with such intense desire, that it looked more like angst. These kids were of varying ages, ranging from as young as two years old to preteens. There was even an empty crib tucked halfway behind the platform the mime stood on, blankets undisturbed inside. Excitement had lit up in Vi's eyes, the gleam physically hurting Lacie. While Vi saw something fun, Lacie just saw another person trapped. The longer she stared at the mime, its lithe frame poised to entertain the children, the more she imagined movement. At first, she noticed its eyes. They followed Lacie, deep black irises sizing her up before flickering over to Vi. The shadows of the elevator made it look like the mime was shifting, its head tilting.

An unbearable sensation rippled across Lacie's skin, and the temperature dropped to ice cold. Her skin prickled as a shiver crawled up her spine. Goosebumps pimpled Vi's skin. She signed for her mother, asking if she felt the temperature change. Lacie replied, telling her that she did, waving her over and offering open arms to warm Vi. The little girl shook her head, opting to stay near the poster, entranced by the mime. Lacie turned quickly toward the elevator doors. She wanted to be anywhere but there. As the temperature continued to drop, the feeling of being watched heightened. The mime's stare burned into the back of her neck. Eager to get away from the poster, she repeatedly pressed the button to their floor again, then glanced back at her daughter. Vi stood directly in front of the poster, a few inches behind Lacie, hands rubbing her arms in an attempt to warm herself. She saw her daughter pace slowly closer to the poster, coming to a stop directly in front of it, cocking her head in confusion. The girl lifted her palms before her, then mimicked being trapped in a box, performing like the mime was watching her. Lacie guessed it was something she had seen her father do when he told her stories about mimes. Vi waved at the mime next, a simple gesture they often practiced while first working to make her more comfortable around strangers. She invited the mime closer by pointing at it, then waved her hand close to her body. Horror pressed Lacie's heart into her throat as it granted Vi's request. Vi inched closer in curiosity. The mime's head slowly breached the poster's surface. The mime's lips stretched into a wicked grin that showed its teeth filed into sharp points. Its right arm followed, bony and pale as snow. Slender fingers outstretched as the mime reached for Vi's throat.

TO BE CONTINUED

See the end of the book for elevator etiquette rules followed or broken. Elevator Etiquette Codes: 1C, 2A, 2F, 9B, 9H

No Help Is Coming

Cirque de la Mimique Trilogy, Part II

"Believe in G-d? Wait ten seconds and see if G-d saves you."
-Joshua Shapira, **Little Odessa,** *Fine Line Features, 1995*

Consider this. Lacie had studied the poster advertising *Cirque de la Mimique,* which had entranced her daughter Vi. The advertisement hung on the back wall of their hotel elevator in France, depicting a traditional mime performing for a group of children. It captured the girl's attention as soon as they entered the elevator on the way to their room. The moment Lacie had first looked at it, an uncomfortable feeling quickly built up inside of her. Before he died, Vi and her father Adair had bonded over his love of mimes, but Lacie had always found them creepy. Her discomfort turned into terror as the laws of physics and sanity broke and the mime came to life before her eyes, its sights set on Vi.

It hadn't been Lacie's imagination. With each body part that pushed past the plane of the poster, the temperature dropped a few more degrees. Vi screamed, but fear paralyzed her in place. Her only movement was the fidgeting of her fingers. Unnoticed, the tattered doll her dad had given her slipped out of her fanny pack and fell to the floor. Her heart began to race and her body began to sweat. The mime's abnormally long fingers, crooked like the branches of an old tree, wrapped around Vi's little neck. Nails that were filed into points matching its teeth dug half-moon crescents into her skin. A garbled sound tore from her throat, like a scream that had been cut off. Lacie shouted her name, grasping the back of Vi's shirt. Lacie, in utter shock, whisked her as far away from the mime as possible in the increasingly claustrophobic space. Vi whimpered in pain, scratch marks marring the soft skin of her throat. The mime fell forward, half of its body out of the poster. Its large hands slapped the gold-flecked floor as the being caught itself, lifting its head. Glowing eyes cut through Lacie with a menacing glare, before morphing back to a friendly smile when it looked at Vi. The mime worked itself free. It tumbled into a tight somersault, tucking in disjointed movements that shouldn't have worked onto the ground, but it made it look easy, like it had done this many times before. Its torso was long, short legs out of proportion. Its knee bent completely backward as it stood, but it stumbled forward in jerky movements. Nothing about the way it moved was normal. Fully out of the poster, it stood two feet taller than Lacie, dwarfing little Vi. As Lacie watched, the mime distorted the shape of its head, shrinking it down to the same size as a slightly inflated balloon. The neck bent at a painfully sharp angle, pushing its child-sized right ear against the ceiling as it contorted into the space.

Lacie screamed, ushering her daughter behind her. Once she was tucked safely between Lacie's body and the elevator doors, she signed her instructions for her to stay behind her. Vi complied, but she still snuck a peek at the mime. Its black lips were drawn into a pout, glowing eyes locked on the young girl. It gestured its hand towards Vi, beckoning her to come closer, the same way Vi had when she had seen the poster. When Lacie moved back, the pout turned into a malicious sneer. The mime placed its palms together, begging with an exaggerated plea.

"What do you want?" Lacie tried hard to keep her voice from wavering with fear. Lacie could see Vi trembling. Her daughter was rubbing her arms, her hands moving frantically. She needed to protect Vi, not show her or the mime how scared she was. Nerves fired all over her, heating her skin despite the deep chill settling into her bones. The mime kept the sneer in place as it pointed at Vi. Lacie stood taller, building up as much bravado as she could muster as she said, "Don't touch her. I'm warning you."

With a pass of its hand over its face, the mime changed its expression, replacing the sneer with an open-mouthed, yet silent, laugh. Its thick, dark, drawn-on eyebrows arched in amusement. Its yellowed teeth bared at Lacie as its shoulders shook. A soundless cackle doubled the mime over like its stomach hurt from laughing so hard; black tears ran from its eyes. It pointed back at the poster, gesturing to the children, then to Vi. The children had turned towards Lacie. Their mouths were stuck open, faces contorted in screams that would never be heard. When the mime turned back to the duo, a challenge lingered in her posture. Bile rose in Lacie's throat as she realized who the children were.

"Why did you take them?" Lacie asked, fear choking her words.

Despair morphed its exaggerated features. It pointed to the crib on the poster while mimicking a baby crying, then rocking its arms in front of it. It made grotesque kissy faces as it nurtured the imaginary baby until it slapped its palms over its ears like something was too loud. The mime shook its entire body so hard Lacie thought she heard its teeth chatter. Its neck fell limp to the side and snapped at a harsh angle. A crooked finger pointed between the children and itself. When its expression went to one of devastation, Lacie pieced it all together. It was attempting the impossible task of filling the void left by its dead baby.

Lacie could sympathize — she had lost someone, too, but no amount of pity would make her offer her daughter. Lacie would fight to the death for Vi.

She lunged for the alarm on the elevator, pushing Vi against the elevator doors in her movement, hoping the noise would buy them some time or at least alert the authorities. Frost had settled over the buttons. The mime moved fast, its body manipulating like it was broken at the joints. It threw up its hands, the skin so white and so tight Lacie still hadn't determined if the creature was wearing gloves. Mere inches from the alarm, Lacie slammed into what felt like a brick. Her hand hit it first, painfully smashing her wrist. She cried out, punching the air with her other fist. There was nothing there, but her fist hit something rock solid. The mime had thrown up a fake wall. Blood bloomed on her knuckles. The fresh red floated in the air, smeared onto a wall they couldn't see. Turning back towards the mime, any sense of hope was sucked out of her lungs in one fell swoop.

While her focus was on the elevator buttons, the mime grabbed the frozen Vi.

It pulled her back towards the poster. Vi made an urgent gurgling sound, her small form struggling against its grip. Her cheeks had reddened like when she played out in the snow too long. One sickly white arm was around Vi's neck, the crook of the mime's elbow pressed to her throat. The other wrapped completely around Vi's midsection, pinning the girl's arms. She tapped and moved her fingers rapidly against her sides. The top of Vi's head reached below the band of the mime's skirt. Lacie raced to grab her, only to find the transparent wall the mime had placed between them extended outward, separating her from her daughter. She pounded against it. Her skin ruptured along her fists, blood rolling down her forearms and freezing as it hit the ground, stopping short of the lost doll. Crimson occasionally mingled with the gold flecks, splattering across the elevator floor in small, chilling bursts. Lacie screamed at the mime, begging and pleading for her daughter.

Reality set in. They were trapped. The imitator in black-and-white held Lacie's daughter with clear intent, and no help was coming.

TO BE CONTINUED

See the end of the book for elevator etiquette rules followed or broken. Elevator Etiquette Codes: 3A, 5F, 6A, 6B, 6H

Mama Bear

Cirque de la Mimique Trilogy, Part III

"A mother's love for her child is like nothing else in the world. It knows no law, no pity, it dares all things, and crushes down remorselessly anything that stands in its path."
-Agatha Christie, **The Last Séance: Tales of the Supernatural**

Consider this. When Lacie flew from the United States to France on a vacation with her daughter, she expected many things. She knew dread and grief were going to settle over her like a heavy cloud, but maybe she and her daughter could have some fun. Vi's public anxiety rendered her unable to speak, and Lacie had to communicate with her via sign language in order to clearly understand her daughter's needs. When her husband passed, Lacie almost canceled the trip, but it had been three months since she saw anything other than the walls of the home they had shared with Vi. They had both been unmotivated and understandably depressed. However, Lacie had saved for this French holiday for over a year, and they were going to make the best of it. She needed to be the adult and get their lives back on track, no matter how difficult and overwhelming it felt. Though Vi was trying to be more patient, her anxiety occasionally overflowed into a meltdown. Lacie had accounted for a lot of mishaps, but none of her preparations could have made her ready for the supernaturally abhorrent mime towering over her. A mime that had climbed out of a flat, faded playbill, morphing into something deadly, sinister, and viciously determined.

The nine-year-old was destined to become the newest member of its collection. The only thing capable of stopping the mime was a mother who had nearly lost everything. Lacie kicked, punched, and scratched with all the strength she had at the invisible barrier the mime had conjured. As far as Lacie could tell, the wall blocked not only the button panel in the elevator but also the side and opposite walls. It split the space in half, blocking Lacie not only from the buttons but also isolated her from her daughter. Lacie made it clear she would not lose easily, and it really wasn't an option. The mime's lips stretched into a wicked grin. *Challenge accepted.*

Lacie had no time to think about how everything had gone so impossibly wrong. The mime had Vi halfway across the elevator now, dangerously close to the poster.

Any remnant of grief the mime had shown before had been replaced by determination as if it was only capable of expressing one emotion at a time. Flexing them against the extreme cold to loosen her joints from the supernatural temperature drop, Lacie used her hands to form a large circle, imagining a wrecking ball. She was losing coordination, a side effect of the freezing air, but she swung the ball with all her strength. It connected to the wall with a loud crack. The sound of bricks hitting the floor echoed around them. An ice cloud showing her breath hung in front of Lacie's lips as she let out a sigh of slight relief. Lacie climbed through, stepping on rubble that didn't exist. Surprise, then rage, contorted the mime's body, but fury raced through Lacie's veins. She would not lose her child to this distorted, evil thing.

Lacie used the mime's tricks against it. Lacie swung one hand above her head, the other holding onto a rope she was lassoing out of the air. Flinging it, she wrapped the noose around the mime's neck. Its red bow bunching and pressing into its skin was Lacie's indication she had caught the mime. Cinching it tight, Lacie dragged it towards herself by the throat. It tried to keep Vi within its grasp, but the girl twisted and kicked until she broke free. The mime opened its mouth in a soundless gasp as its windpipe was cut off. It dropped to its bony knees, unsettlingly forced to either crawl towards Lacie or choke. One hand dropped behind her back as the mime stopped directly in front of Lacie. Hiding her hand, she grasped the hilt of an invisible blade. Lacie lunged, aiming the blade at the side of the mime's neck. She was fast.

The mime was faster.

Lacie slipped on the frost-covered floor. The mime expected it, jumping to its feet and rocking backward. The knife that was supposed to slit its throat lodged into its sternum, to the hilt. Black blood stained the stripes on its t-shirt, but the mime didn't stumble. Lacie flexed her fingers as she roared with frustration. She exhaled sharply and could see her breath in the air, settling onto the edges of the fake wall. The mother retreated through the hole, trying to draw the mime further from Vi. It didn't take the bait.

Lacie realized her mistake too late. She had unintentionally positioned herself away from her daughter. The mime took advantage, going for the little girl's body instead. Vi scrambled back but wasn't fast enough. The mime gripped her forearm so hard Lacie could see a handprint forming before the bruise. It whipped Vi's body towards the poster. A primal noise tore from Vi's throat. Tears soaked her shirt, hands shaking as she frantically formed one sign over and over: M-O-M!

Lacie reached for her daughter. Her fingertips wrapped around the front of Vi's shirt, grasping desperately for a handful of fabric. Vi was yanked out of her reach and into the poster. In one easy motion, all of Vi was in the poster's dimension. Her voice cut off mid-sob, mouth frozen around the cry for her mother, as she slowly turned black and white. Vi's eyes bored into Lacie, forcing the mother to watch as life slowly drained out of them. When the vibrant color had dulled, lifeless black replaced it. She looked away from her mother as if in a trance. Vi fell into place directly next to the crib. Silence fell over the elevator as Lacie dropped to her knees, the ice-cold floor searing into her skin. The mime pulled the blade from its chest, dropping it to the floor with a triumphant clatter. One beat passed. Then Lacie screamed bloody murder.

She screamed at the death of Adair and the loss of her daughter. Her anguish must have distorted her vision because each roar that tore from her throat gave her daughter some color in the poster. She shouted and shrieked until she had crumbled to the floor in loud wails. With unnatural movement, the mime slowly reached down to its hip, pulling a finger gun out of an imaginary holster strapped to its waist. Lacie knew she should stand up and defend herself, but with all of her senses overwhelmed, she froze. Lacie could do nothing but stare at Vi as the world spun around her. Lacie stared at her daughter's silhouette as the gunslinger whipped the finger gun around with unexpected precision. Sobs tore from her throat as she wailed *"I love you"* to Vi's static body. She said it over and over in anguish, picturing the color seeping back into Vi. Her mind was so fractured she couldn't tell if Vi was really feeling her love or if that was Lacie's desperation, but she clung to the belief, anyway. With every molecule of color that returned to Vi, Lacie found more power and clarity herself. She rose on shaky legs, keeping eye contact with Vi. Her mind was racing. If she killed the mime, would it free Vi and the children? That thought put the fight back into Lacie. She dove at the knife on the floor, hoping to re-home it in the mime's skull.

The bullet pierced her chest before Lacie made contact.

Her shirt blossomed with blood, spreading outward from the heart. The shell of the bullet clinked on the floor, the noise amplified by the silence immediately following the shot. The mime spun the fake gun in a circle, blowing on its smoking fingertip. Its lips parted as it mimicked a cackle. Lacie fell backward, head slamming into the marble, Vi's doll's vacant eyes staring back, a sorrowful witness to her final moment of desperation. The skin covering Lacie's skull split open and blood leaked from the wound. The floor was now stained with the blood of an innocent mother, leaving Vi an orphan. The mime turned Lacie's head so her glazed eyes looked towards Vi in the poster. Its grin tugged its black lips so wide they stretched clear to the mime's ears. Once it was certain Vi was watching and was warned, it dropped Lacie's body like garbage.

The mime wiped its hands clean of gunshot residue and blood, its default creepy grin back on its face. One hand raised slowly. Its wrist bent unnaturally far as it waved goodbye to Lacie slowly, demented, and with absolute prejudice.

Vi stared back at her mom from within the poster. Her view of the scene was blurred with ink, but it would be burned clearly in her mind forever. Her face screwed up, depicted as a distorted black circle, mouth open mid-scream. Vi's hands were formed into fists beside her. In her mind's eye, she visualized jumping out of the poster and running to her mother. She would hug her and lay her head on her chest, even if the amount of blood made the elevator smell like iron.

A flicker of life lit Vi's eyes as she envisioned a life with her mother and father again. It started in her throat, an audible hum barely noticeable, building as the seconds passed. The longer she stared, the stronger the fire of her imagination grew her power. The mime's back was to Vi, but she pictured its mocking face. Her gaze filled with so much hate the heat raced down Vi's body and back up again. Her hands unfurled as her anger spread. Color seeped back into her slowly as the resonance of the hum intensified. It built like a crescendo, moving almost to a growl. Now she could sign. *"Mom,"* she said frantically. She repeated it over and over as her mom lay still, begging for an answer that would never come.

Vi's right foot tapped. As the growl grew, vibrating from her chest, her body came alive. The surrounding kids stood frozen, but they slid their eyes back and forth between Vi and the mime. They watched the way Vi began to move, cheering in their own way. The energy built up inside her. She signed faster and tapped her foot harder, the thud of the movement muffled like a carpet-covered floor inside the poster. Every second Vi spent re-living the death of her mother channeled more of that fiery rage inside her. Fury snowballed inside her, starting in her stomach and traveling upward as it grew. It rampaged through her body, swirling like a hurricane as the feeling swept up and destroyed any other emotion inside of her. At that moment, she could only express anger as it threatened to burst from her body, and then it did. The hair on her arms stood, and she shook as her foot tapped faster and faster. It overwhelmed her as the anger built in her chest, along with Vi's heart aching and racing, until it ripped from her throat in a guttural scream.

"Mom!" Vi screamed, her vocal cords straining. The wall of anger burst from her, beyond the poster, and into the elevator.

The mime fell forward as if pushed. It toppled over, falling to the ground. Its hands slapped the floor, the dark red staining its palms mixing with the frost layered on top of it. Lacie's tangled hair blew as a rough breeze swept over her. Vi hoped that since she could harm the mime now, with no tools other than the sounds of her anger and with patience, she would be able to kill it in time. Before, Vi had only spoken occasionally at home, freezing up and struggling in public. She now understood the truly intense power of her voice when she could control it. The mime, its back still to Vi, rose slowly from the blood-soaked killing floor. It turned to study Vi, trying to understand what had transpired. By the time its gaze locked on Vi, she was colorless, like the other captive children, and was exactly where she was expected to be. However, Vi's consciousness was at full strength. The hardened nine-year-old knew she would have to practice and build the strength to avenge her mother and hopefully escape her paper prison. Going deep into her mind, Vi visualized her fingers doing their twists and turns, signing just one word:

GOTCHA.

See the end of the book for elevator etiquette rules followed or broken. Elevator Etiquette Codes: 2F, 6B, 6H, 9H

The Chute

Questions Burden; Answers Imprison

"The memory of what is not may be better than the amnesia of what is." -Robert Smithson

Consider this. You think you came here for a better life, but you're not sure. All you know is when the lights come on, jump on the line, stand at attention, and speak when they call your name.

"Thirty-six," the intercom blares.

"Thirty-six," you repeat back.

You hear the last two men, thirty-eight and thirty-nine, sound off. Fifteen and four didn't; they can't: they've gone up The Chute.

You make your beds along with all the other men with bald heads shining under the artificial light, and you head down white corridors to a white room with pristine metal tables where meals are laid out. Chicken and greens that taste like rubber are washed down with water tasting slightly of salt.

"How are you doing today, thirty-six?" The Controller asks in a voice that makes you forget about the two armed guards with M4 carbines you could take apart blindfolded, even though you've never handled one.

"Ok."

"Headaches?"

"No."

"Nausea?"

"No."

"Homicidal thoughts?"

"No."

"I think you're ready for another round."

They strap you down and there is nothing you can do. Through the corridors you go, the left wheel creaking, the right wheel silent, save for rubber against the smooth laminated tile. The doors open and you are asked if you are ready. You aren't.

They wheel you in and the doors close and the platform slowly goes up and the air gets thin and you can taste the chicken from earlier but you can't see a damn thing as the lights flicker on and off and you hold on to the one string of consciousness tethering you to the world as the elevator gets higher and higher and for one brief second, everything stops. You plunge downwards into nothing.

You wake up unsettled; it isn't the first time. You either wake up here or you don't. Usually, there are superficial wounds and bruises; now your whole body is in pain. Your fingers tap reflexively. You don't know how, but if you put them over a piano, you know it would be Chopin.

"We almost lost you, thirty-six," the Controller says.

There isn't anything for you to say.

"You're going to be out for a few weeks. How does that sound?"

You nod, continually tapping.

You go in with other numbers in white robes, hiding various injuries. You know you've been here before but can't remember when, but the carpeted floors and green couches with comic books and armed guards seem familiar.

Sleep brings nothing but another morning and the slight mending of your bones. Then one night, they come to you. Flashes of violence, gunfire, and conversation.

"Where did you learn to play?"

"Self-taught," you remember yourself saying, trilling between two notes before exploding into another bar.

The scent of fine foods and liquor fills your nose, the sounds of political conversation fill your ears, and you feel the keys under your fingers are alive as you look up to see a woman, who you are sure is the most beautiful one you have ever seen, smiling down at you.

"You must be joking."

You wake up, and she is gone.

You want to tell someone about her, but if you talk to the others, you and they will be shot, and if you tell the Controller, you will go up the Chute again. So you sit in silence, trying to remember.

"You really taught yourself?"

You take a sip of brandy, stained with the chill of ice, from a glass that you can tell is Japanese made from the quality and thinness of the glass.

"No. New York University," you say, knowing somehow it is not true.

"You're an American?" she says, almost choking on her wine.

"Guilty as charged."

"What brings you to Russia?"

"This piano."

She says something in Russian that roughly translates to smart-ass, and you reflexively smile. Her eyes widen alongside her smile.

"You speak Russian?"

"Da," you say, knowing, in reality, you speak fifteen other languages.

"Ok, that settles it," she says, closing the piano. "You, sir, are dining at our table tonight."

"I'm not sure if I'm allowed."

She leans in close enough for you to smell the rose water splashed on her neck. "It's my father's party, darling. Don't worry."

She takes you by the hand, but you refuse.

"Let me play one last song."

"Ok," she says, but she doesn't leave, so you turn back to the piano, open the cover, and play the most beautiful music before it is ripped away by consciousness.

"You are recovering quite well, thirty-six."

"Thank you."

"Tomorrow you can go back with the others."

You want to go back to the woman one last time. You fall asleep, terrified that you'll wake up to another bleary day. Instead, you wake up to the woman leading you across a freshly waxed dance floor. She gets you past two armed sentries guarding a table of men in military uniforms adorned with medals. At the head of the table, the woman puts her arm around a man, kissing his worn cheek.

"Father, I'd like you to meet...what was your name again?" is what you think she would have said, had you not pulled out a gun, shot the man, spun around to take out the two guards, before turning to point the gun at the woman's face and pulling the trigger, taking one last look at her two doe eyes before you rip the life out of them.

"How are you doing?" the Controller asks.

"Fine."

"How are your injuries?"

"Getting better."

"Ok."

"Headaches?"

"No."

"Nausea?"

"No."

"Homicidal thoughts?"

You blink. "No."

You're going to kill them all, you think. They strap you down and you tap out Salieri as they wheel you towards the doors, and the Controller asks if you're ready and you think about what a forty-five caliber bullet would do to her head as they shove you in and the doors close on you, and the air gets thin and you can taste the iron in your mouth as you slowly go upward, and even the hatred cannot prolong your consciousness as you go higher and higher and the lights flash more and more and at the apex of the journey; you make a promise to yourself that you will kill every single one of them before you plunge back into the black.

You wake up; the lights are on. You get out of bed and stand on the line. You know to wait for your number.

"Thirty-six," the intercom blares.

"Thirty-six," you repeat back, curling your fist into a ball, but you don't know why.

See the end of the book for elevator etiquette rules followed or broken.
Elevator Etiquette Codes: 1B, 1D, 2A, 2B, 2C, 2E, 3A, 4A, 4D, 6A, 9B

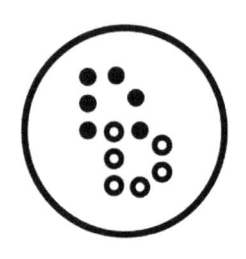

Chaos Without Movement

The Devil Is In The Details

"Just because a man lacks the use of his eyes doesn't mean he lacks vision." -Stevie Wonder

Consider this. CEO Becky Belweenie cuts through the office building with a purpose and a pantsuit. Becky is a tall woman, and in the bend of her right arm, she carries a prized black purse. She is absorbed in a cell phone conversation when her assistant approaches and hands her a coffee like a quarterback in stride, before turning a corner and disappearing from sight. Becky then targets the third elevator bank. She likes to be on maximum alert before settling into her office and downs her liquid rocket fuel. She doesn't taste it, and that doesn't matter.

Becky approaches the elevator door, and her cult-like employees part like the Red Sea. The elevator is equipped with a proximity sensor that matches the keycard in Becky's purse. Almost like magic, the door opens when Becky is within range. She notices the elevator is filled with people and rolls her eyes in response because her subordinates know the protocols regarding her arrival. She stomps her foot, crosses her arms, and waits a millisecond before stepping in. The people inside scamper around her to exit, as she does not care to make way for them. "If you aren't suitable for this project, I will look elsewhere. You know who I am and my tolerance for incompetence," Becky announces before hanging up her phone and stuffing it in her purse. She then pulls out her keycard admiring the image of a beautiful woman holding a syringe. The caption screams in bold letters: **Chief Executive Officer Becky Belweenie, Shadowland Medical.** Oh, it's her! Her mindless employees flood her with a round of applause for the 947th day in a row, not including weekends. "Floor 14," she announces triumphantly to no one in particular.

If Becky had focused on anyone besides herself, she would have noticed the elevator operator was blind, even with the wide-brimmed top hat covering most of his face. A full suit and tie added to the disguise of none other than Dillan Drasuolis. He replies subtly, using sarcasm and a fake accent worse than Dick Van Dyke's in *Mary Poppins*. "Of course, ma'am. 14 it is." Then, he does **absolutely nothing.**

Dillan is not the usual elevator operator. Oh, that guy is tied up in the basement of Dillan's house, but no one knows that yet. Dillan has been nothing but focused, as he has been planning this moment of nothingness for the past three years of his recovery. He can do something if he wished, the panel is in braille. However, he waits patiently, a trait he knows Becky lacks. Besides, it is Becky's fault he is blind.

An unfortunate accident took place a few years back at a 4th of July company after-party. Bizarrely, Becky had demanded that military-grade (North Korean military) fireworks be lit in celebration. She had refused to wait for permission from the city and proclaimed that she was doing this for her employees, insisting that her employees deserved a show after such a great year. In actuality, however, Becky was flaunting the money that did not go into employees' wallets. They still made abysmal pay.

The fireworks were a spectacle, and Becky was so proud — of herself. All was going according to plan until an errant rocket grazed off the inflatable gorilla in front of the local Isuzu Commercial Truck dealership, burst through the windows, and blinded Mr. Drasuolis with the shards. Insurance ruled the incident an accident and charged Becky with the deductible, which she easily covered with pocket money.

Having enough of the eternal nothingness, Becky sighs and reaches over the guardian of the panel. Dillan anticipates Becky's actions. With superhero-like speed, he blocks her with his crimson walking stick embossed with interlocking D's in the handle. The unexpected action forces Becky to stumble backward and drop her bag. Becky scoffs, affronted by the elevator operator's nerve. She reaches over wildly, frustration culminating when she misses the button for floor 14 and hits the Alarm instead. The elevator car transforms into high-pitched pandemonium. A laugh Dillan had tried to hold in bubbled up in his throat and slipped past his lips. Becky shrieks and drops her coffee cup before falling to the floor. She presses hard against both of her ears to muffle the cursed alarm. During an emotional outburst, Becky begins to shout "14, 14, 14, 14," attempting to be louder than the alarm. Her body has now tensed and her chest rises and falls rapidly.

Seeing as nothing has changed, she jumps to her feet in a rage. She picks up her bag and takes a swing at Dillan, and the Saffiano leather Prada bag does not connect. Chaos ensues in an elevator still yet to move. There are muffled screams and banging on the doors as coffee bleeds through the gap at the bottom of the doors.

Some time has passed since that incident, now dubbed the "Frappuccino Fracas," and the office has moved on with the business-as-usual mentality. The employees are smiling again, which is nice. The former elevator operator resigned; the stress of being kidnapped and tied up in a basement was just not worth minimum wage. The board of directors appointed a new CEO after a number of whistleblowers came forward detailing Becky's numerous abuses of power and generally entitled stupidity. Becky has now lawyered up and is suing the office for defamation, amongst other things, such as the dry cleaning bill to remove coffee stains from her one-of-a-kind black Prada bag.

The new CEO brought over a new lead attorney to sort through and resolve the numerous cases brought against the firm due to Becky's malfeasance. He walks with a cane and sometimes brings his service dog, Murdock, to work. His LinkedIn account states he's new in town, but he looks familiar to me. His name is Dillan Drasuolis — a man born again, a man with no fear.

See the end of the book for elevator etiquette rules followed or broken. Elevator Etiquette Codes: 1A, 1C, 2B, 2C, 3A, 3E, 4D, 5A, 6C, 6H

I Take The Stairs

WHICH FLOOR FOR THE SECRET SOCIETY?

*"I rebel from established absurdities,
but is the very act of rebelling how I fall prey
to the new social question?"*
-Amery Bruce

Consider this. In-N-Out Burger or McDonald's? That question will be asked of you at least once in your life, at least if you live in California, Nevada, Arizona, Utah, Texas, or Oregon. You may also be asked if you prefer up or down, Odds or Evens. And the answers will not be taken lightly. G-d help you if any of these are regarding an elevator query. I avoid those tethered metal boxes of bedlam like the plague now, since they have become such a raw social issue for most. When did elevator roulette become a thing? In this day and age, every decision has to be a partisan one, I guess. Everyone is constantly speculating about and judging every action everyone makes.

"I take the stairs." That's been my go-to default response to anyone who asks me what floor I choose to get off at. I use this answer to swerve any conversations on the matter and go back to keeping to myself. If they ask what floor I end up on, I tell them the truth. "I work on the 10th floor." You can't argue with where you work. If you work on an Even floor, you are expected to get off and go directly to an Even floor. It makes the most sense; it's your job.

"Do you visit any Odd floors first?" Members of the Order of Odd Fellows usually ask this question. They have taken it upon themselves to control the odd-numbered floors, and they have done this in various parts of the United States since the early 1800s. They come up with the most ridiculous excuses to *not* get off on an Even floor: it messes with their sleep at night; it makes them feel incessantly hungry; and worse than that, it throws them off balance. And so, they choose to walk through an Odd floor before going upstairs to work on an Even floor. Rebekah, a girl from Marketing on the 10th floor, does this. She is always late because of it, but my boss, Keith, tells me it's better to put up with it.

I'll never understand why this whole Odd and Even floor thing has become so controversial. Full disclosure: when I had to choose, I would get off on an Even floor. It makes the most logical sense. If others want to get off on Odd floors *and then* go Even and make their lives harder, that's their choice. That is, except for 13, for obvious reasons. I'm not a sympathizer or anything like that. In fact, I think people like Rebekah are, dare I say it, the oddest of the bunch because of it. But I prefer to mind my own business.

That's why I take the stairs. No one cares if you take the stairs if you're alone when you do it. Not many people like the exercise, so I have those steps all to myself. I leave early for work so I'm not late, like some people.

If I'm being honest, I like taking the stairs, but saying that when you have access to an elevator can seem quite abnormal.

When I was tying up my tennis shoes at the end of the day, Rebekah looked left, right, then left again like she was crossing the street and approached me covertly. "Are you ready to become one of us?" Rebekah asked me in a hushed voice.

I shook my head. "No, I'd rather take the stairs."

See the end of the book for elevator etiquette rules followed or broken. Elevator Etiquette Codes: 4A, 6B, 6D

Timeline

Time Frame Focused Glimpses of Future Past

"There's a version of you that you haven't met yet..." ☐
-Jim Kwik

Consider this. Ted stared at the business card: BETTER FUTURE INDUSTRIES. He looked at the hole in the wall, confirmed the address, and walked inside.

A janitor swept a pile of clothes off a dirty floor. Ted walked up to a man behind a wooden desk in front of an elevator. ☐☐☐

"What's the name?" the man said without eye contact.

"Ted."

"First time here?"

"Yes."

"Ok, you know what we do here?"

Ted did not. He got a letter in the mail asking him if he wanted to change his life, and Ted looked at the thirty-eight years behind him and the forty or more working jobs he hated and decided why the fuck not.

"Alright. Welcome to Better Future Industries," he regurgitated. "Go into the elevator behind me, and you'll have two minutes on each floor to make the future you deserve. The elevator will automatically close and go up a floor, and this will continue until you reach the top. You can go back to the first floor and the lobby at any time, but once you return to the lobby, you cannot go back without another appointment."

"How much?"

"Two minutes per floor."

"No, for this Mickey Mouse bullshit."

"It's free."

Images of waking up in a bathtub without his kidney ran through Ted's mind. He pushed past them and stepped into the elevator, only two buttons for the lobby and first floor. The elevators closed him in, slowly pulling him up.

The doors opened to a bedroom. A child's bedroom. His childhood bedroom. Ted's eyes went wide when he saw a young boy slowly rising from the bed, locking eyes with his own. They screamed.

"Mom!" the boy yelled.

It shouldn't be possible: Ted was staring at himself as a kid, shivering under the covers and flinching when his mother came into the room.

"What are you yelling about?"

"There's a man in my closet."

The woman walked over and stared into the elevator. Ted's eyes locked on her, filled with fear and a rising swell of anger somewhere deep from inside.

"There's nobody in your closet."

"He's right there!" the boy screamed.

"Shut up and go back to bed."

"But, Mom," Ted said, but his mother had already left the room, leaving the two alone.

"Hi," Ted said as the doors closed automatically.

He backed towards the wall of the elevator and slumped down, trying to control his breathing and his mind racing with questions about time travel. He found no answers when the elevator opened again to the same bedroom with a young teen sitting at a desk. Neither screamed.

"Who the fuck are you?" the young boy yelled.

"I'm you," Ted yelled back.

The boy stopped, realization washing over his pimpled face.

"You were in my closet years ago."

"It was just a few minutes for me."

"I thought I was dreaming."

"Me too."

Ted's mind finally accepted that this was reality. "Look, I don't have much time. I'm here to give you advice."

"On what?"

Ted looked back at his life, a multitude of shattered dreams and failures.

"Just stay in school and work hard."

"That's it?"

"No, but start there."

"Ok, but I'm already doing that."

"No, you're not."

"Yes, I am."

"You can work harder," he said, but the door already started to close.

The doors opened once again, this time to his old college dorm.

"Holy shit, you scared me." Younger Ted said.

"Sorry. What year are you in college?"

"Sophomore. Look, I have some questions..."

"No time. Listen, you're gonna want to drop out this semester. Don't."

"Why would I want to drop out? Things are going great."

"Just don't drop out."

"Ok, I won't."

"Promise me."

"I promise I won't drop out," his words slipped through the doors right as they closed.

They opened back up to his apartment after he dropped out of college.

"Hey," the younger Ted said.

"Did you drop out?"

"Yes."

"What did I tell you?"

"Not that Mom fucking died."

Ted didn't know how to respond to that, so he didn't. "Ok, well, don't take the office job."

"What office job?"

"You're going to get an offer for National. Don't take it."

"Does it pay well?"

"Yes, but you'll hate it."

"How much does it pay?"

"Never mind that. Find something else to do."

"What do you like doing?"

Ted tried to think of something, but he couldn't as the doors came to a close.

They opened back up in Ted's cubicle. A younger Ted looked up from his monitor before glancing back down towards it.

"Hey."

"I told you not to take this job."

"I needed the money."

"Fuck the money! This job makes us miserable."

"Then why did you take it in the first place?" Younger Ted asked.

He needed the money too, Ted thought, but did not say. Younger Ted went back to work till the elevator doors closed, and Ted was still at work when the doors opened. It was like staring in the mirror; they were even wearing the same tie.

"Hey," Ted said.

"Hey," Ted said.

"Any advice for me?"

"I think it's too late."

"Ok, well, I'm gonna get back to work if it's all the same to you."

Ted let him work till the doors closed, opening back up on a hospital bed. The man's tired eyes poked out from a series of tubes.

"You," he said.

"What happened?"

"I had a goddamn heart attack. Why didn't you warn me?"

"I didn't know you were going to have one."

"Well, I did. Right in that damn cubicle."

"I'm sorry."

"Fuck your sorry. Go back and fix this."

"I'm not sure I can."

"Then what fucking good are you?"

Ted started coughing, and a machine started beeping and the last thing Ted saw was a nurse rushing to his side before the door closed.

The doors opened to the smell of piss and a man sat in front of him, nodding off.

"Hello?" Ted asked.

The man's head rocked back and forth with no discernible rhythm.

"Hello?" Ted asked again.

Dilated eyes fixed on Ted's.

"Future boy."

"What happened to you?"

"Hey everybody, it's future boy. Here to help me off the street, man?" he slurred, his voice unsteady. "Here to tell me what to do? Come on, future boy, tell me what to do."

The man continued to mutter incoherently as the elevator doors closed once again.

When they opened again, there was no street or apartment or a childhood room. There was nothing, save for blackness intermixed with a green glow. Ted yelled into the void, his voice dissipating without even a hint of an echo. There was simply nothing, or nothing he could discern as the elevators closed again. He sat alone for a long time before pressing the button for the first floor.

When the doors opened again, it was back in his childhood bedroom. The boy screamed again, and the mother came and left again, and they were alone with each other again.

"Who are you?" the boy croaked.

Ted thought about everything he could tell the boy, about his future and college and his mother and his job; but instead, he just stepped out of the elevator and kneeled by the boy's bed.

"I'm you from the future."

"Really?"

"Really."

"Prove it."

Ted whispered a secret only he knew in the boy's ear, which made him smile.

"It is you."

"It is," Ted said.

"So, what are you doing here?"

"I just came to tell you things are going to be ok."

"Really?"

"Yep. You're going to be ok," he said, giving the boy a hug. "I thought you could use one of these, too."

The boy said nothing, only wrapping his arms around Ted. When they stopped, the boy looked into his eyes.

"Ok, I got to go now."

Ted got up and headed to the elevator. He got in and the doors closed on the young boy waving to Ted. The elevator started to rise but stopped when Ted pressed the lobby button, the lobby greeting him along with the man behind the desk.

"Did you enjoy your session?" the man asked without looking up.

"Yes."

"Do you think you were able to make yourself a better future?"

"I think so."

"Great, we'll send you a letter for a follow-up appointment if you need one. Otherwise, enjoy your future. Now, if you don't mind, I have another client coming soon."

Ted wanted to thank him, but before a word could leave his mouth, he vanished, only a pile of clothes remaining on the floor.

See the end of the book for elevator etiquette rules followed or broken.
Elevator Etiquette Codes: 1C, 2A, 4A, 6H

Hellavator

Hurts Me More Than It Hurts You

"I was born in an elevator, and — as my mother said — naturally it was going down...." -Jack Lemmon

Consider this. Marlene was a Marine first, a mother second, and dead last. She could've been better, but could've been a hell of a lot worse. At least that's what she kept telling herself, over and over again. She had killed people, but that's just war. She treated her man right and loved the shit out of her little Petey. Then, one psycho killed them all. She recalled the sounds of footfalls against the concrete stairs leading up to their home and the innocuous knock on the door.

"Hello," she said.

The man met her with a deranged smile and a snub nose 38 to her head. His eyes were wild, devoid of reason and humanity. Reflexes kicked in and she grabbed the gun. Didn't help. A gunshot rang out, which left her ears ringing and her spine severed. She couldn't move, but she could hear the man shoot her husband and her son before coming back and finishing her off. If she still had blood, it would be boiling. But she didn't, she only had her thoughts and the grand view of an endless nothing to stare into.

Until there was an elevator door, and a pale sickly man in a white three-piece suit stepped out. "Marlene?" he said, his voice like the draft through an ajar door.

"That's me," she spoke.

"If you wouldn't mind coming with me."

Marlene found herself walking forward into the elevator, stretching her fingers and straining her eyes as the doors closed, locking her in with nothing but the man and the artificial light. The elevator started to go down.

"Where was I?"

"Purgatory."

"What for?"

The man flipped through his notebook.

"Murder. Nineteen counts."

"But I was a soldier."

"You enjoyed it."

"Does that matter?"

"Intent matters."

Fair enough, she thought.

"Who are you?"

"Azrael," he said, almost ashamed.

"Where are you taking me?"

"For your test."

"What kind of test?"

"To see if your soul has been redeemed."

"Like a parole hearing?"

"If you want to put it like that, yes."

"For what?"

"Your soul has changed."

"How can you tell?"

"Your thoughts have become...softer."

"I couldn't tell."

"I could," he said, then nothing more.

She looked around the elevator, which looked like it was out of a cheap hotel on the outskirts of a backwater town, but the hallway it opened up into looked out of an upscale office building. No windows adorned the gray walls, only sleek metallic doors. "Where are we?"

"Hell."

"Shit. Really?"

"Yes."

"I thought I got a test first."

"This is the test, right here," he said, stopping in front of a door.

She looked at the door, trying to find some significance in the bare metal sheen of the metal and the polished gold of the doorknob. She didn't.

"What do I do?"

"Enter the room and your soul will be revealed."

"What the fuck does that mean?" she asked Azrael, but he was gone. Vanished.

Don't fuck this up, you dumb bastard, she said to herself, opening the door.

Marlene entered the room with four gray walls with a made cot, one you might find in an army barracks or six-by-eight cell. A man rubbed his balding head with one hand, resting on a pair of spectacles on a crooked nose with the other. "Hello?" he asked before recognition filled his face, and Marlene's fist destroyed it.

If she were in practice, it would have taken mere seconds to take the life from him. Instead, minutes later, her killer's last bit of life fled him as he twitched and spazzed. She never felt sick before when she saw blood. She did now. She counted to ten, closing her eyes. When she opened them, he got up and sat on the bed. "I deserved that."

Two more brutalizations later, the killer of her family was again on the edge of the bed, polishing his glasses with a handkerchief. "I'm good to go again if you are."

"What is this?"

"Hell, or so I've been told."

"Horseshit."

"Appearances aside, I can assure you this is hell."

"Damn. Damn damn damn. That bastard lied to me."

"Azrael? Oh, no no no. You're not here to stay, you're here to help with my treatment."

"Treatment?"

"My rehabilitation."

"Your...rehabilitation?"

He nodded. "To make up for my past transgressions."

Marlene put him in a chokehold, squeezing the life out of him, feeling spittle mixed with blood roll down her forearm. He came back and cleared his throat. "I'm seeking forgiveness from those that I hurt. Your family is the latest I'm making peace with."

"Fuck you."

"I understand that is asking a lot."

"You killed me."

"For that, I am sorry."

"My family...my son."

"Truly, I am sorry."

"You need to pay."

"I have."

"You need to burn for it."

"I've done that too."

"Not enough."

"The powers that be seem to think so."

"My husband. My boy. They were beautiful, and you killed them."

"I did, and they forgave me for it."

Marlene would have killed him again had she not been frozen in place from a mixture of shock and awe.

"Took a while for your husband to come around. Little Petey..."

"Don't," she barked, "Don't ever say his name again. You don't have the right."

"Your son," Howard continued, "your son forgave me very quickly."

"You murdered him."

"Yes, I did. And nothing I can do can ever change that. But Marlene, look at me, really look at me. Do I look like the same man who killed your family?"

That day, she looked into them. There was something there, alien enough for her not to understand but human enough for her to be terrified. Now, he looked like just another asshole she might have passed on the street.

"I will never forgive you."

"I would understand if you didn't. All that I ask is that you think about it. I believe it would be good for both of us," was what he would've said if she hadn't killed him again.

She left the room. Azrael waited for her, and the pair silently walked toward the elevator. Marlene waited for it to go up to speak.

"If I forgive him, will he be released from hell?"

"Eventually, perhaps."

"Then fuck him."

"If you do not forgive him, you cannot move on either. You cannot see your family."

"Then fuck me too."

"Is that what you want?"

Marlene didn't answer, instead waiting for the elevator doors to open. She stepped once again into the void. She was left with nothing but her thoughts and endless time.

See the end of the book for elevator etiquette rules followed or broken. Elevator Etiquette Codes: 1C, 2A, 2D, 2F, 3A, 4A, 6C, 6H are implied.

Pearly Gates

You Can Lead A Horse To Water...

"He entered the elevator and together they moved closer to G-d." -from Ubik **by Philip K. Dick**

Consider this. There is no stairway to Heaven. Used to be a staircase, but management decided to replace it with an elevator, and the powers that be decided that I should be in charge.

The doors open. Death brings in the morning crowd, along with a cup of coffee.

"Morning, Karen."

"Morning."

"How many?"

"Fifty thousand."

"Seems light."

"Earthquake tomorrow, the big guy doesn't want to front-load it."

"Gotcha, thanks for the heads up."

"No problem. See you in a bit, Petey," she says, throwing her hood over her head and leaving the elevator.

Souls don't see they are entering an elevator. They see childhood homes, beautiful beaches, breathtaking mountain ranges, and things to occupy their minds on the journey upwards.

One journey through the cosmos later, we arrive at the city of lights. The doors open and souls shuffle out to be assigned a personal angel. They are then reunited with their loved ones, reincarnated, or erased from existence if they so choose. Once they are all off, I close the doors and get ready for the next shift of souls.

Only someone doesn't get off the elevator. Happens sometimes; people get confused and think the elevator is actually Heaven. I shrink down from celestial form to talk to the man, pudgy and old, with tufts of red hair clinging to a liver-spotted scalp. "Hey sir, are you alright?"

"I'm dead, so you tell me," he says.

"Just head through those doors and you'll be in the land of eternal bliss."

The man looks up towards the city of white towers and endless love. "No, thank you."

"What?"

"I said no thanks."

"But, it's Heaven."

"I'm good."

"Why don't you want to go in?" I ask him.

"I wanna go to Hell."

We get two billion petitions from Hell every day from souls requesting early release, but none asking to be let in. "Sir, I don't—"

"Call me Ron."

"Ron, I don't quite understand what you're asking."

"Is this Heaven?"

"Yes."

"And if Hell's a real place, I want to go there instead of here."

"... Why?" I say.

The man smiles, looking down at the platform. "Look, I lived a good long life. Never drank, never smoked, never cheated on my wife, never mistreated my kids, always donated to the church, the whole nine yards."

"You can continue that life in Heaven."

"That's the problem: I don't want to."

"Why not?"

"It was so goddamn boring. I mean, Christ alive, I never had any fun."

"You can have fun in Heaven."

"I don't want to hang with angels forever."

"If you met the angels, you'd change your mind."

The man smiles again and puts a hand on my shoulder.

"I appreciate what you're trying to do, but I've made up my mind. On my deathbed, looking back at my life, I said to myself, 'Ron, if there is an afterlife, you're gonna spend it doing all the bad things you never did in your life', and by G-d, that's what I'm gonna do."

"Give me one second Ron," I say, increasing back into my celestial form, and hopping on the elevator's interdimensional telephone. There's no protocol for this.

"Hello?" the voice on the other end of the line says.

"Hey Lou, it's Peter."

"Peter, how the hell are you?"

"Good. How about you?"

"Can't complain. Actually, I could, but I won't. Anyway, what's up?"

"I got a situation here that I hope you could help me out with."

"Shoot."

"I got a guy here that wants to go to Hell?"

"He wants to go to Hell?"

"Yep."

"Of his own accord?"

"Yep."

"Why the hell would he want that?"

"He thinks Heaven would be too boring."

"He's right about that."

"Lou!" I snap.

"Alright, alright, don't get your halo in a bunch. Bring him down here and I'll scare him straight."

"Great. See you soon, Lou."

I hang up the phone and shrink back down to size, sending the elevator down.

The exterior of infinite stars turns into those of distant fiery volcanoes, souls screaming from eternal damnation, and great big deserts of cracked earth meeting our feet as we step out into the heat. Lou stands facing us in a suit and tie, a grin stretched below two black eyes.

"Hello, Ron."

"Hiya," he says, stepping towards him with an open hand.

Lou steps forward and takes the hand. Skin drips off, the suit and tie turning into red muscle and sinew, his head spouting horns and his smile showing rows of gnashing teeth through which he lets out a monstrous roar. I have to hold back my laughter; Ron doesn't.

"Great show," Ron lets out through the laughter.

"That usually gets people."

"I don't scare easily."

"Clearly not. You really want to come down here to Hell?"

"Depends, you guys party?"

A grin spreads across Lou's face.

"Come on, let me show you around." He looks over at me. "Mind if I take him from here, Peter?"

My head is spinning from the amount of paperwork this will require. "Alright."

"Awesome!" Lou yells, slipping a hand around Ron's shoulder and leading him into Hell.

"You ever tried Seagull wine?"

"Never."

"You're going to love it. Come on, let's go tie one on."

"Hey, thanks Peter," Ron says over his shoulder, before following Lou.

I don't know what to say, so I smile and wave as the elevator doors close. It's my job to bring people to their afterlife, and I guess I brought Ron to his. Still, the experience floods my mind with thoughts as I start my way back up to the Pearly Gates.

———⋈⊛⋈———

See the end of the book for elevator etiquette rules followed or broken. Elevator Etiquette Code: 6H

St. Monica's Children's Hospital, Guidelines for Behavior

St. Monica's Children's Hospital Duology, Part I

"I wish the pain of betrayal was as easy to ignore as the red flags that forewarned of it." -Steve Maraboli

Consider this. Ian applied for his first job out of college through a tear-off ad he found on the window of a local Chinese restaurant. The hiring manager at St. Monica's was a *special* type of person, to say the least. Still, it was how Ian landed a job at the most prestigious health institution in the world.

It took a decade for him to realize that might not have been a good idea.

St. Monica's was a glorified petri dish: a controlled experiment masked by the guise of uniting the world through research on an incurable disease plaguing the world's children. Given its unfortunate tendency to cause death upon hitting puberty, everything in the building was measured and administered. From the air they breathed to the beds they slept in, every family was monitored, and each individual played an important role when it came to the functioning of their simulated community. For a while, parents and children alike were happy to become rats.

The moment they locked everyone in was the first red flag Ian should have noticed. The families that had come to St. Monica's seeking hope in life were soon sequestered into accepting they would die there. The failure of Ian's superiors to recognize there was a difference between the scientific process and torture was perhaps a bigger red flag.

Although Ian was guilty of this, too.

Ian realized his own shortcomings as he stood in front of the underground lab that was treason incarnate. Chaos hid in the recesses from a trap set the night before, waiting for the doors to open come morning and release said chaos into the rest of the building. There he stood, with a frail invisible web catching at his foot, facing down the most dangerous risk of his unethical job: *death*.

He should have read that liability waiver.

It didn't take him long to realize he didn't regret his part in the coming damnation of hundreds of people because he'd found a way to save her. He only needed to get to her first. Not bothering to warn the coworkers who loathed him, Ian slipped inside the elevator to go up a single floor. (9G)* He paced about the car, running his hands through his hair, thinking about what might come next.

It was hardly Ian that caused all of this. Rather, it was the failure of the people he worked with. It was odd: the greatest hope for the children of the world was seemingly in the hands of those who cared the least about them. The second floor had been steadily encroaching on the underhanded misdoings of those in the sublevel, jeopardizing all the progress they'd made. Casey, the man running the horror show, wasn't going to have that. Ian knew this. He'd been working with the devil for ears. For the first time in his life, Ian prayed he would find some way to avoid Casey before he got to his lab.

Ian stopped praying when Casey entered the elevator.

"Beside the panel or in the middle, pick a spot and stand still, Ian," Case directed before nodding his head at the buttons. "Floor two, please." (2F)*

Ian was not in the mood to be patronized. Before he could retort, he took note of something unsettling as Casey ignored the anguished screams echoing from further within the sublevel.

Casey was holding a crowbar.

Ian flattened himself against the opposite wall, earning a disappointed glance over the shoulder when he failed to press the button.

"Don't worry, it's fine," Casey sighed, pressing it himself. "Some people can't handle the responsibility of managing the panel." (3B)*

In other words, the crowbar wasn't meant for him.

With the threat of bludgeoning minimized, Ian scraped together enough confidence to ask the pressing question on his mind.

"Is she in school?" Ian asked softly.

"Is *who* in school?" Casey chirped.

Ian glared at him. "Ana."

In cases of emergency, the school was one of the alarmingly few areas within St. Monica's that were securely locked down.

"Have you tried asking her parents?" His response was shallow and supercilious.

"You owe me a straight answer," Ian demanded.

Casey let a long moment of silence pass between them. A small, petty gesture that did little more than assert his dominance. "Yes."

He lied.

"You will be locking down the school, won't you?" The doors opened.

"At St. Monica's, we're family, Ian. Our children are our utmost priority." Casey recited the usual pitch, nodding with a reassuring smile as the doors closed.

In other words, the situation was FUBAR.

It might be important to mention that the universe regularly worked against Ian's favor.

Ana was the only one in the waiting room. That morning, her mother had walked Ana from their lodging on the second floor to drop her off on the third before heading to work on the first. Dr. Michelle walked out and escorted Ana into her office. The doctor's eyes were staring into the distance, as if she would rather be anywhere else. "Hello, Ana. How are you doing this morning?" she asked, her voice flat. "Can you still not tell who's on your side?" she droned, feigning concern. Dr. Michelle's abrupt disregard wasn't what tested Ana's patience — it was the inherent superficiality of this mandatory meeting. Once a year, Ana had to visit the resident therapist and lie about how she felt about dying, so she didn't have to visit twice. It was a yearly requirement all children and their families had to heed for the twelve years Ana had been alive. Since she was an infant, it was the only consistent waste of time she could rely on.

Sighing, she rubbed her ears due to a faint humming her mind had yet to block out for her. The noise hadn't always been there, and she found it wasn't going away, either. It was getting *louder*. So loud that she was forced to muffle her ears. The small, hermetic windows had become strobe lights as a dark shadow hovered before it, god-like in its ability to control the sun's rays.

The deep, pandemoniac hum vibrated every cell in Ana's body. Eventually, Dr. Michelle stepped out of her office with her gaudy perfume, the potent fragrance filling the room. It reminded Ana of her only working sense, contrary to her blurry eyes, throttled eardrums, and the metallic taste overtaking her numbing mouth. The buzzing moved away for a brief second.

All at once, a foreign body came hurtling back with a vengeance.

Concrete and glass exploded throughout the room like a frag grenade. The buzzing stopped when it landed, freezing Ana in primal terror at the *thing* that towered over nine feet. It was the culmination of human sin, a genetic amalgamation of rejected proteins. Wings made of thin skin and bone sat antsy on the hulking muscle of its back. Legs dangled lifelessly at the waist, and it used its single-clawed, barbed hands to grip the edge of the hole before scanning the room with its large, black eyes. What may have once been a mouth was stretched far too wide to fit two intimidating pincers. The alarms went off.

The creature was on Dr. Michelle in an instant. A spine-like stinger curled long past the end of its back, its claws piercing her against the wall. It didn't stab her. Instead, it used its teeth to size her up. It nipped and clicked just far enough away from her bosom to examine the odor oozing from her clothes.

Michelle's once confident voice was now strangled. "Ana. Go downstairs. Find Ian and Casey. Get security." Her voice turned stern, almost hateful. "Now!"

Ana was a kid. Her fight-or-flight response was woefull underdeveloped, and she could do little more than watch as the monster gripped Michelle's beautiful face. Like an excited child clawing and gouging at the cellophane of a toy, the monster ripped away her skin. Those outside the office were mere seconds away from opening the door and uncovering the grisly situation. Ana's window of opportunity to run would soon shut before mass panic threw the bastard into a frenzy. Elongated antennae poking from its ears twitched when Ana shuffled toward the office door, but it was the closing click that spurred it into feverish action.

When the monster erupted through the office door behind her, Ana ran toward the elevator. In the wide-open hall, it could fly once more. It was a sound she could feel. There was no other way to describe the hypnotic fluttering that distorted space itself, like every sound entering her ears had to pass through a fan before registering in her brain. Covering her ears preemptively didn't prevent the powerful, thunderous terror from making her legs buckle. There was no time for panic to start because everyone who wasn't covering their ears crumpled to the ground like falling cards.

Ana didn't watch as the vespoid's hollowed wings pummeled those still conscious until they collapsed like limp rag dolls. She didn't want to hear the caterwaul of its victims as they tried to run. She didn't watch as its tail whipped with intelligent purpose — *wanting* to kill, *wanting* to torment. She didn't want to think that it might even be smarter than her.

Ana's first mistake was pressing the call button in an urgent, spastic manner. (3F)* Her second mistake was using an elevator during an emergency in the first place. Taking a deep breath, she willed herself to wait patiently for its arrival as the massacre carried on.

Good things come to those who follow elevator etiquette, and the ding of the elevator's arrival was certainly proof of that, though it beckoned the beast like a homing missile. Rushing forward, she ran straight into a tall, smiling man blocking the panel. (1B)*

"Who taught you your manners?" He nagged at her playfully. "Always make sure no one has to get off first." (1D)*

"What?" Ana pointed feverishly down the hall, unable to believe how calm he was. "It's coming, we have to go!" (2B)*

He cut her off like a disinterested parent. "Now, Ana, you have to listen to me."

"Please!" she begged shrilly.

The man tugged her toward the middle so she faced the door. (1C & 2A)* "When entering an elevator, always ask the person standing closest to the panel to select your floor." (3A)* He languidly pushed the sublevel button and waited for the doors to shut.

His words were drowned out by the incoming buzzing. A buzzing Ana didn't need to hear for it to stay with her throughout the rest of her life. Any rumble, even white noise, would send the foulest images *crawling* behind her eyes. It was almost supernatural: the man's abilit to withstand it. The doors closed and a loud rumble shook the car when the monster catapulted itself into the wall above.

Just when the nightmare couldn't get any worse, the lights flickered, the air shut off, and the elevator creaked to a halt. It was as if G-d blew out a candle, and that candle was St. Monica's.

Ana began thinking the worst of thoughts. She wondered where her parents were, why they had left her alone on the third floor, and if the were even still alive. Briefly, she thought they would've made her go see Dr. Michelle anyway, even during a time like this.

A primal scream tore from Ana's throat as she pounded her fists against the elevator doors, her fury wild and directionless. Every emotion she'd bottled up now exploded with a force that shook her to her core. She looked at the man she was trapped with, closer scrutiny filling her with words she couldn't express. His clothes were scuffed, not by monsters, but by human hands, revealed by the gauzy stains of blood sprinkling his clothing and dry-wiped face. (9B)* The abused crowbar in his hand didn't help his profile, either. Sighing indifferently at the situation, he shrugged and looked down on her.

"I should introduce myself. My name is Casey." He dropped the crowbar and held out his hand. Everything he said was laced with polite, heartless sarcasm. "I work in HR."

In her bones, Ana felt Casey may be just as dangerous as the monsters outside, and she was now trapped in the elevator with him.

TO BE CONTINUED

See the end of the book for elevator etiquette rules followed or broken.
Elevator Etiquette Codes: 1C, 1D, 2A, 2B, 2F, 3A, 3B, 3F, 9B, 9G

Santa Muerte's Children's Hospital, Guidelines for Behavior

St. Monica's Children's Hospital Duology, Part II

"When evil is allowed to compete with good, evil has an emotional populist appeal that wins out unless good men and women stand as a vanguard against abuse."
-Hannah Arendt

Consider this. Some time passed before the elevators started back up again. Ana, a twelve-year-old girl, had been chased into an elevator by a genetic abomination. Consequently, she was now trapped in the lift with

Casey, who worked in HR. If that wasn't bad enough, he had a crowbar, and the elevator had started to make a slow ascent back up to the floor she'd just run from.

Casey clicked his tongue. "Button spammers. We'll be stuck stopping at every floor." (3D)*

Ana's stomach coiled as the doors slid open. A putrid air seeped into the elevator alongside a collected puddle of blood. The cheap carpet drank it hungrily, yet it was not enough to prevent a pool from forming around their feet. From the stained marble floors, a sinister quality chilled her to the very core. The darkened hallway, so pungent with the smell of death and dense in its blackness, absorbed all the flesh for itself and came to life.

Ana's pulse pounded in her ears, every whisper of movement a trigger for her body to brace for another attack. Even with the emergency light flickering halfway down the hall, the only thing aiding their sense of direction was the pained groans of an injured survivor.

"Wait." A dislocated jaw slurred his words, and a bloodied hand guided him along the wall, while the other kept his organs from spilling out.

Ana went to hold the elevator door open for him, but Casey pushed her back.

At the same time, a diabolical noise echoed further back in the darkness. The loathsome king of the floor was absent, its presence now replaced by a new *thing*. And the *sounds* it made. A cacophony of clicking accompanied by godless wheezing. The darkness moved to make way for this mechanical, animalistic noise bellowing from the hateful basin of its victims' anguish-stricken flesh. It was in every way a predator that ought to be avoided by man.

With a pathetic sob, the man tried to run.

"Hold the door," he begged.

Ana watched with bated breath as Casey finally addressed the situation. "Don't feel guilty for not holding the door," he reassured her.

"We can't just watch," Ana argued with the audacity of a mouse.

"G-d decides whether he's meant to make this car. Not us." Casey patronized her.

"What?" Ana felt ready to cry.

"Hold the door!" The man screeched. "Hold the door!"

"Oh —" Casey acted as if the man's demise was an epiphany. "G-d says no!" (9A)*

A hundred feet away, *something* briefly came into the light. Dark hair gleamed against the light, and sharp arms snapped around the man's body like a mechanized claw, kidnapping him before he could cry another word. Still, he managed to scream.

And scream, and *scream* long after the doors shut.

Ana's foreboding nausea didn't have time to blossom into debilitating fear before Casey took a domineering step into the center of the elevator. The friendly aura that stuck to his character like cakey makeup morphed into fluid pressure, suffocating her into the back corner.

"How do you know my name?" she asked, a nervous swallow segmenting her words when he blocked the door.

Casey gazed ahead, at ease. "It took you a while to ask that."

As the elevator descended, every ding was a catalyst that jolted Ana's heart. She couldn't help but feel she was going somewhere worse than that hallway.

The doors opened to the second-floor offices where external affairs were handled. If someone were to send a call for help, it would've come from here. An array of corpses was littered across desks and broken glass panes. They were inside walls and splintered amongst shattered doors, their organs dangled across the dead lights like macabre embers. Given the state of the office-turned-war zone, the former representatives of St. Monica's participating members were also blindsided by this calamity.

The sharp squeak of a wheelchair alerted them to a woman beside the elevator. Casey — a gentleman — immediately stepped out of the elevator to assist her, brushing aside stray webs as he did. He gripped the front handles of the wheelchair in a lazy attempt to drag her forward, ignoring the woman's pleading to leave her in the slaughterhouse. Ana was distracted by the small rattle that soon began echoing out from the bowels of the building, manifesting into a violent thrashing within the walls around them.

"Do you hear that?" Ana asked as Casey attempted to pull the woman through.

It wasn't clear to Ana that the woman was afraid until she braced her arms against the doors. Or perhaps the woman had made a choice, having survived on her own for so long only to be met with rescue at the hands of Casey. Ana furrowed her brows, taking in the woman's condition. The wheelchair must have belonged to someone else, and she'd crawled into it after sustaining injuries on both her legs. Despite the deep gashes threatening to fester, the woman ignored her pain and glared intently at Casey with hateful familiarity.

"Seriously?" He laughed curtly at the woman's pettiness. "Regardless of how you feel about me, there is a *child* here with us."

The thumping had localized above the room. The hollow crawling was clearly coming from the vents, growing louder and closer by the second.

"Something's coming," Ana urged. Eager to move things along, Ana aided Casey by tugging at the woman's arms, but still, she refused to budge. "She's not moving." Ana's panting cut into her words. "Why isn't she moving?"

The light fixtures began to shake.

Casey spoke as if he were a former PR specialist who left his job to work as a nursing home aide. "I understand that this is a very troublesome time for you. It is for everyone here. I want you to know that management *sincerely* apologizes for the trauma you've undoubtedly gone through. But, for the sake of our patients, you can't let the events of the past cloud your judgment, especially when it becomes an inconvenience to the rest of us."

In the far corner of the room, bare hands, *clawed* hands, seamlessly peeled apart the vented metal like it was wrapping paper. "We need to hurry," Ana whined, shoving Casey's shoulder.

Casey brushed her off. "You can't rush trauma, Ana."

The metal clattered to the floor. "Casey!" She shouted at his triviality.

"Recovery! I meant trauma recovery," he insisted.

In other words, she wasn't going to budge. Call the woman cruel, but to her, Ana was destined to die soon enough, anyway. The sin of letting

Ana die a terrible death was far less despairing than dying with the regret that she let Casey live.

A thunderous *thump* hit the floor. The eerie cry of metal signaled to them something terribly large and fiendish was moving along the carpet, powerful feet bending the remaining metal scrap. In quickening succession, furniture was shoved to the side. The darkness opened into a schism, making way for the beast crawling toward them.

The screeching of furniture in front of them soon turned into the crunching of drywall above them. As it drew nearer, reality felt as though it was collapsing in on itself. The woman closed her eyes, accepting death. Casey made it clear he wasn't going to do a thing unless Ana gave the word. In fact, he even seemed entertained by all of it. "It's either her or us."

Silence overtook the room. The world no longer shook. It was as if the monster was deciding which of them it wanted to kill. A test of who would move first. Ana could see the shadows shifting on the ceiling ahead of them, the slight sway of the fixtures causing entrails to fall. Ana's eyes couldn't break away from the living shadows that looked like they were breathing.

"Us."

Lifting a leg at Ana's order, Casey kicked the woman square in the chest, catapulting her back into the dim office space. The monster lunged at the motion. Faster than Ana could blink, it collided with the woman, scooping her up into long, hairy arms. It was almost mesmerizing, the way it spun her around like a thaumatrope. The fluidity of its motions, as it rolled the body about the air, was akin to watching a product go through an assembly line, and the arachnoid's webbing was the final step to making it perfect enough to shelve.

Instead of a shelf, the woman, in her suffocating sack, was dropped to the floor. Casey hit the close button and tossed the crowbar into the room, finding it fitting to leave it there to *rot* with the second floor and all who ever worked on it.

"Why wouldn't she get on the elevator?" Ana whispered the pressing question.

Casey hummed, shrugging. "Some people."

The severity of the situation suddenly sank into her every pore. Ice clawed up her spine and froze her nerves. Soon, the elevator was met with company. Turning her head, she pressed her ear against the wall. The hunter could be heard crawling down the shaft in pursuit of the elevator. Ana gasped when a weight suddenly jolted the car. Just as quickly as it came, it disappeared into the depths of the building. Casey didn't react. Still, his composure didn't stop a nauseous apprehensiveness from making her hair stand on end as the first-floor doors opened.

Bitter air gripped her throat like a vicious hand. No taboo readings could prepare her for the Lovecraftian landscape ahead. Red and brown translucent silk was strung from wall to wall. Globs of spit hung along strands of varying thickness, and on those, hung corpses. Unfortunately, the spider's web stopped there, and the guests of the elevator got to see every detail of the unwrapped corpses. Acid stemmed the blood coming from melted and eviscerated bodies, the vomit mixing with death's stench. Across the way, Ana could see the doors to Ian's lab.

It was funny: the blood triggered fond memories for Ana. When St. Monica's was a *good* place, Ian was the one responsible for drawing her blood and running tests. She would often visit him as she often skipped school. He was the only one who understood her idiosyncratic nature as an outcast himself. The only one who taught her how to dissect her degenerative curse and understand life and death in a way she could finally accept. Ana recoiled, though, a familiar chill settling in her stomach, reminding her that Ian's kindness was just another prelude to betrayal.

Casey gripped her shoulder when Ana made a move to go toward Ian's lab. "Don't worry, he's fine." But he wasn't.

Ana took notice of all the missing ceiling vent covers. Down the hall, the rattling of metal in the ceiling rumbled with a throaty click that was *inhuman.*

Hairy hands stained red silently stretched from the abyss of the vent. Smooth like velvet in its movements, its arms bent in offensive directions as the demon poured itself out onto the floor. Finally, Ana got to see their stalker. A four-legged mutated arachnoid loomed over her, just as massive as the winged creature and standing high despite all its feet on the ground. Gaping eyes — multiple stuffed into one tumorous socket — turned toward the freshly delivered meal.

Ana frantically spammed the close button. (3F & G)*

"Now, that's just rude." Casey smacked her wrist in disapproval. "You only need to hit it once."

With a hideous, soul-sickening shriek, terror thundered down on Ana as it dashed forward so rapidly she was forced against the wall before it could even get to them. The hollow click of sharp fingers pounded closer, and she held her breath in prayer for the doors to shut faster. Ana ducked and yelped when the car rocked from the dent the arachnoid left. Casey didn't flinch, nor did he acknowledge the hyperventilating girl behind him as the elevator made its final descent.

When the doors opened for the last time, he stepped into the middle to lean his head out and look around before returning with a good omen. "It seems our friend has given up. Good news for us."

Ana didn't want to spend another second in that car and tried to use her small body to slip past him. However, Casey, rather harshly, shoved her back.

"Red sea method," he reminded her as if she already knew what that was. Casey stepped out, making sure to stay close enough to catch the door in case she tried to close it. (2G)*

"What?" Irritation laced her tone.

"Those on the sides stay at the edges of the elevator so those in the center may exit first. Red sea method," Casey explained with a simple hand motion, a glint of enjoyment in his eyes as rage coursed through her.

Casey snagged her wrist to orient her in the right direction. "No funny business," he reprimanded light-heartedly, like one would a dog. "Unless you want to stay and die here?"

Without much other choice, Ana took a deep breath and let him guide her along. Casey spoke a bit more seriously as they traversed the dark subterranean halls until they reached a long incline leading up toward the light.

"Ian made you the prize-winning guinea pig. As such, you're very special."

The full weight of the sun was blinding after being trapped in a hell chamber. But it was also blinding in the sense that Ana had never been outside before. The rolling peaks St. Monica's was built upon and the view from the summit should have been breathtaking, but it wasn't. The promise of a normal life was nothing more than a cruel trick. This nightmare had stolen away her ability to appreciate the beauty, and that was the part she hated the most.

"Ian tried to keep his research a secret from us, which isn't fair to the other children, wouldn't you agree?" Casey continued.

Though it was busy with another task, she couldn't help but hear the vespoid's buzzing in the back of her head, haunted by visages of it swarming after her at any given moment. The dread induced by Casey's iron grip was the only thing that kept her from breaking out into a delirious sprint. There was also the odd sway of the trees moving in a way they shouldn't against the wind. Everything was too much all at once. It made her want to vomit.

As Casey and Ana reached the treeline, Ana realized what was making the trees teeter. A handful of gunned men stood awaiting orders. Against the harsh contrast of day, they blended in with the black trees and emmental forest shadows like bark beetles. With a flick of his head, Casey wordlessly commanded them to leave before bending down to her eye level.

"You're the key to unlocking that secret, and you're going to cooperate or I'm going to leave your mom, your dad, and Ian locked up in *there*."

He pointed to the hole in St. Monica's concrete fortress. Ana could see the winged monster slowly eating, regurgitating, and gluing the bodies of the dead together to mend the breach. It was a blasphemous sight: limbs and fluxed corpses dangling in a ring funneling from the room she was sitting in mere hours ago. Ana felt an emptiness creep into her chest as she slipped into a daze. She was nothing but a broken vessel in the shape of a girl, destined to be used and discarded.

"Do you understand me?" He snapped his fingers bringing her back to attention.

Even in the light of day, Casey felt larger and more dangerous than the monsters she'd seen in the dark, and he was almost certainly smarter than her.

Nodding away the lump in her throat, Ana agreed.

See the end of the book for elevator etiquette rules followed or broken. Elevator Etiquette Codes: 2G, 3D, 3F, 3G

Lost In An Elevator

How Could This Even Happen?

"Roaches check in, but they don't check out!"
-1981 TV commercial for the **Black Flag Roach Motel**

Consider this. Standing on the ground floor, looking north, Dave tried to find the top of the skyscraper above the clouds, but they were too thick to see through that morning. Once outside, he felt the crisp wind brush against his face, and ice-cold rain pellets hit his skin. After a short drive, Dave stood outside the Wainwright building, frozen as he looked up at the marble pillars. He felt as though he had truly arrived, but Dave had not earned that feeling of success yet. Just as quickly, a new emotion struck him and he had bubbles in his stomach. It became all too real, and he needed a minute before he ascended the stairs and walked into the lobby of the Wainwright.

Dave was nervous if he would ever get an interview for his dream job. Then, a few days ago, he received the call. The human resources department scheduled Dave for an initial interview on Tuesday morning at ten o'clock. As anxious as he was, he took some deep breaths and conquered those five elongated concrete steps; to him, it felt like he was climbing the never-ending bleacher stairs of a stadium. He approached the revolving carousel doors with caution, making sure he didn't get stuck or worse, trip. Dave's heart was pounding in his chest, about to jump out and escape.

Once he made it through the doors, he paused and noticed every detail of the lobby. He admired the stonework and the reddish-brown marble on the walls, floors, counters, and steps. A beautiful castle for him to walk into every day if he were to get the job.

Dave walked over to three sets of gold-plated art déco elevator doors with the indicator buttons pointing to the ancient, but not obsolete, gauges. He waited among the crowded employees for the next ding, signaling his next employment journey benchmark. Luckily, he didn't have to wait too long.

The first lift dinged, and he rushed to get inside before it filled up too quickly. He didn't want to run the risk of missing his interview because the elevators were too crowded. How embarrassing would it have been if *that* happened?

Dave stepped into the elevator and proceeded to select his floor. Denied! Wait. What? All too quickly, he got forced out of the way and could not press the button he needed. Panic started to rise in Dave's gut as he attempted to ask for help, but the crowd pushed him back into a corner. He was so squished he could no longer see the elevator panel. He began to sweat.

Dave politely tried to make his way to the panel when a few people got off, but as he was only five-foot-four and three-quarters (he measured his height himself), he couldn't see over anyone else's head. The other men were tall, and all the women were wearing heels. His stomach did a flip, a flop, then flipped once again. The elevator dinged, and some people got off, but even more got on. C'mon! Dave was shoved against another part of the elevator, and the wind was knocked out of him. He would have fallen to the floor, but right now, that was physically impossible.

He heard another ding and a few more people got off. You don't need a crystal ball to know what happened next. Dave used every ounce of his will to avoid having a panic attack. He repeated his affirmations and visualized himself calmly exiting the elevator and continuing on his way. He thought that moving with the people who were exiting would facilitate his escape strategy. He waited anxiously for the elevator to slow to a stop. It was taking too long, and he worried he was going to miss the interview. Finally, the floor dinged, and his plan began to work — he was moving toward the door.

The mosh pit almost pushed him out of the elevator entirely, but then they went back the other way. Dave heard ten short gongs. That signaled ten o'clock. The interview was due to begin, and with all of the ups and downs, he wasn't exactly sure where he was. Dave couldn't believe it — of all things, he was lost in an elevator....

See the end of the book for elevator etiquette rules followed or broken. Elevator Etiquette Codes: 1A, 1B, 1C, 2C, 2E, 2G, 3A, 4D

The Four Snowflakes Hotel

NOT EVERYONE WILL LIKE THIS

"Well, who draws the line? Who decides what's acceptable? It depends what the joke is. You know? Comedy comes from either a good or a bad place." -attributed to Ricky Gervais

Consider this. Standup comic Royce Eldon wore a lapel pin with a slyly altered Punisher logo and a bunny with a thin blue vertical line taking the place of an upper incisor. A former member of the one-hit wonder band "Hillary's Emails" and a drummer in "Kamala's Kokonuts," Royce was speeding to a gig supporting the police. He was wicked smart, talented, and had an 87th percentile IQ, which he thought was underrated. While he was hyper-focused on running his set, he didn't notice that his driver,

Rudy — too stoned to navigate clearly — had dropped him at the Four Snowflakes Hotel instead of the Four Seasons.

The Four Snowflakes was holding a conference hosted by National Citizens's Radio. As dinner concluded, the convention attendees headed to the 45th floor for entertainment, which seemed to this crowd like a mile straight up! Both hotels had a convention space on their 45th floors, setting the table for mischief.

Many attendees were using Fitbits to track floors and steps, and climbing slowly but steadily over the last hour. Royce shook his head at the climbers. "That's just madness." Other attendees headed to the elevators.

After getting a drink at the bar, Royce approached the elevator as well. He made his way inside and observed the nasty women and their simps piling in. No one in this crowd was worthy of truly being in his presence. He scanned "the crowd" and had never seen so many people with weirdly colored hair in one place. For some reason, they couldn't (wouldn't) make eye contact either. Maybe it was because of his red MAGA hat, maybe it was medical.

Everyone else wore a stupid N95 mask, which was nauseating as that extended to not shaking hands and that elbow bumping. Really? Not that Royce wanted to shake hands with *these people* anyway. Damn weak snowflakes. They would always say, "Stay open-minded." In reality, they were saying, "I think what SNL thinks." These XYs were wearing fanny packs, and the XXs were carrying purses so big they could hold participation trophies.

Finally, the elevator started its rise to the 45th floor. Now usually, there would be red hats bouncing here and there who would hype him up. Despite that, Royce, sensing an opportunity for chaos, deconstructed his captive audience. He mocked SJW Sally and then Royce demanded Moron Miguel show his birth certificate, which he didn't have on his illegal person.

As the elevator rose, the comedian was on a roll, with hard-earned sweat dripping down his chin. He joked about the need for more pronouns and genders, which led to more letters being added to the LGBTQIA2S+ acronym. What the fuck is that?

Eyeing the elevator's No Smoking sign, Royce lit a huge cigar. The snowflakes melted as he exhaled the aroma of freedom. He smirked as Elitist Eve subsequently hacked up a lung and broke out in hives.

Royce Eldon smiled. He had material for his next show tonight — assuming his Uber Black arrived on time.

See the end of the book for elevator etiquette rules followed or broken. Elevator Etiquette Codes: 5B, 5E, 6B, 6D, 6H, 8A

Full Transparency

SEX IS IN THE GAZE OF THE BEHOLDER

"As time moves on, the line will blur. It will no longer seem to be the simplicity of good versus evil, but good versus fools who think they are good." -Criss Jami, **Killosophy**

Consider this. A bored librarian, a stand-up comic, a cam girl: Atasha Stone had been all of these things, plus more. Whatever job she was drawn to, it was the flame of sharing knowledge that lured her in like a moth. With each career move, she learned a key piece of the puzzle that, when put together, created the passion she presents now. As a librarian, she learned innovative research techniques; as a comic, she discovered how to deliver a point; and as a cam girl, she realized that far more people would pay attention if she committed fully. Along the way, she discovered her true love was performing. Thus, the Bibliothecary Babe launched her new series: "In The Raw".

A longshot gamble with Bitcoin in 2009 turned into a wise investment. In 2023 it bought Atasha the house on the hill, the hill itself, and the surrounding neighbor's compliance. They agreed to support her bold dreams on the grounds that she would give back to their community, something she was planning on doing anyway. Because of zoning laws, she wasn't able to build a public-facing stage, so Atasha had to begin construction on a triple-wide glass residential elevator , which gave her room to move when she performed, at the bottom of the hill. Atasha was as considerate as possible to her neighbors, making sure the construction didn't block their driveways or disrupt their daily routines. Unfortunately, there was little she could do about the noise, so to make it up to her neighbors she promised that for every morning they were awakened by construction, she would throw five hundred dollars in the "Atasha Is a Nuisance" jar, something the neighborhood kids decorated together. When they realized how much money it could pile up for them by the end, they were unsurprisingly cooperative.

The elevator shaft and car would total fifty feet high, allowing the entire audience to see her at some point during the show, plus video walls on each side that would highlight ancillary content. Additionally, for each show, she was to have an ASL interpreter on-site to help those in the community who needed additional support. The glass was shatterproof and bullet-proof, designed to keep Atasha safe as she performed. By the time the elevator was finished, and her first handful of shows began, her relationship with much of the community was so strong the neighbors marketed for her by word of mouth. Every show was for a cause, and with every donation, all the profits were reinvested back into the neighborhood. Everyone was happy.

Everyone except for The Wives™.

When the online protest group first emerged, Atasha paid it no mind. It was no shock to her that a group of women would protest the show without first coming to it. On the surface, it appeared that their husbands were abandoning their wives at home to attend the show of a sparsely dressed woman every Friday night, which wasn't completely untrue, but she had ulterior motives. Each cause she chose for her show highlighted something the men likely weren't aware of or didn't pay attention to. Atasha was certain she could change their minds if she was given the opportunity. Unsurprisingly, every social media post The Wives™ made was derogatory:

It's absolutely disgusting the community would support a slut prostituting herself in a glass elevator. -@Momof6

This porn industry highlights violence towards women and aggressive sexual behavior. -@oldwavefeminist

The Bibliothec Babe is brainwashing our men, tricking them into supporting her immortal [sic] *behavior. -@watchfulwymn*

Another woman named Marjorie, whose bio labeled her as the creator of The Wives™ and whose profile picture highlighted her support for America, wrote, "My husband spends more time with her than with me — and sees far more of her, too.

Each scathing comment was responded to with positivity and excellent reviews by people who actually came to see the presentations. *A woman is a slut for accepting her body and speaking about self-love? She's displaying confidence and sexual liberation.* **You need to see her shows**, one supporter had commented. There was such devotion to the Bibliothec Babes' multiple causes that another woman had created a fan group called Brave Bitches™ to counter the negativity of The

Wives™. The creator explained the name was inspired by Atasha's portfolio of performances. She was brave enough to speak about subjects often considered licentious, and "bitch" came from her idea of changing derogatory phrases into something of empowerment. Soon, both groups were overflowing with hyper-focused joiners. With every new member each group received, the Bibliothec Babe's spotlight grew brighter. Movements were formed, petitions were signed, and rights were optioned. The split in opinion culminated offline as both groups poured into the streets of Atasha's neighborhood as they marched to the newest, most provocative show Atasha had done so far: Support for V-Day.

Every topic Atasha chose for the show had the specific goal of sharing information with her audience that they wouldn't get anywhere else without effort. Her research through the National Library Association said people preferred it when knowledge was handed to them. Atasha used the Bibliothec Babe to slip the knowledge into the audience the way parents slipped vegetables into a toddler's mac and cheese. To Atasha, the V-Day show was the most important one she had ever done. The audience needed to be as large as possible to spread the message of ending violence toward marginalized genders. To help accommodate the ever-growing audience, while keeping in line with her goal of highlighting violence towards women, this show's ASL interpreter was Barbie Ensler, an outspoken victim of the #MeToo movement. Atasha had reached out to Barbie, explaining the show's agenda. She had been enthusiastic in her agreement to help Atasha, even declining payment for her work. Atasha had a live stream set-up, using the same channel she had while performing solely as a cam girl. Her friends on OnlyFans promised to magnify the message, as did her followers on YouTube. And this time, she was going to turn it up a notch, maybe two. The V-Day performance would be done completely nude save for the opaque bands strategically placed to stay within legal compliance. It was a plan that would drag everyone, supporters and crusaders alike, to the glass elevator, provided they passed the online and in-person age verification.

Which was exactly what it had done. Atasha saw both groups as she stepped into the elevator in nothing but the official librarian glasses given to her by the National Library Association and the opaque bands wrapped tightly around her form.

The Wives™ stood on the slope, as far away from the elevator as they could, while still allowing her to read their protest signs. When the elevator reached the very top floor where it would begin before descending throughout the show, Atasha zeroed in on the brunette woman in the front. She recognized Marjorie's face. The creator and quasi-leader of The Wives™ carried a bright red sign that said *you should burn in hell*. She had a headset wrapped around her left ear, her face turning plum in anger as she spoke to someone on the other end of the phone line. Their men stood still beside them, back much further than they typically sat, pretending they were less interested now that their wives had joined the venue.

Anticipating their distance, Atasha had wired a sound system, her voice reaching far past the parameter of the hill. Before the performance began, she streamed music through the speakers, including "A Woman's Pride" by Donna De Lory. When the elevator was set at the very top, twin pyrotechnics went off in front of each video wall, the resulting booms bringing a hush over the crowd. It lasted for one beat. Two. Three.

"How *dare* you!" Marjorie shrieked, shattering the silence. Barbie, the ASL interpreter, looked towards Atasha for direction. She waved her off, not wanting the show to be disrupted. With the moment broken, the crowd livened. Reactions flooded in on her livestream, some spamming the heart button. The Wives™ continued the tireless brigade of objections.

Reactions rippled through the crowd as they soaked in Bibliothec Babe's nudity. Cheers echoed across the crowd, some from women who appreciated the self-love Atasha was showing, and some from men in the audience who appreciated the skin she was showing. The Wives™ followed the lead of Marjorie, screaming protests and threats. The Brave Bitches™ emerged from the crowd soon after, popping up in pink Pussyhats for V-Day. Before Atasha had said a word, the two sides converged in opposing attitudes toward Atasha's show. The firm lines they stood off in formed a v-shape, the point culminating with Marjorie. The people scattered across the beautifully manicured lawn watched intently, unsure of who or what to focus on.

"Thirty-five percent," Atasha spoke for the first time, drawing the attention back to herself. The interpreter mirrored her movement, communicating the statistic to the audience. The elevator descended to another floor as she spoke and came to rest. She sat down in a chair she had placed inside before the show, pressing her shoulders back. Video walls on either side of the elevator lit up, displaying the numbers Atasha spoke. One side showed a graph, the other wall projecting just a large *35%*. "In 2013, that's how many women have had physical or sexual abuse committed against them. That means if there were twenty of your family members in a room together, seven of your sisters, aunts, cousins, or daughters may have been abused."

Support signs were pressed higher into the air. Some protestors lowered theirs slightly. Atasha knew statistics were hard to ignore. Giving the audience a number made it tangible, and the pictures on the video walls made the women human. She shifted in her seat, instinctively leaving her legs uncrossed in a natural position. The elevator dropped to another floor. Some women in the audience glared. The Wives™ fidgeted in the back.

"If that was the number in 2013, given today's climate, how high do you think it could be now?" No one answered. The men that regularly came to see the Bibliothec Babe stared, entranced, but started to look perplexed. As they considered the question, the elevator descended again. "A survey published by *The Lancet* online in February 2022 found that in 2018, 27% of partnered women aged 15 to 49 have experienced intimate partner violence, physical, sexual, or both, in their lifetime. According to RAINN, every 68 seconds another American is sexually assaulted."

Gasps traveled the hill as the walls changed to show an infographic of just how jarring the statistic was. One woman near the front of the audience found her hand over her mouth. A man wrapped his arms around his boyfriend in a supportive embrace. A person rubbed up and down their partner's back in soothing strokes. In the back, one of The Wives™ cast a wary glance at her husband before inching away. Atasha's elevator continued its descent. The wife lowered her sign, setting it on the ground in front of her. Several others in the group followed. Marjorie watched them sharply, face reddening.

"Don't fall for this! She's *naked* in front of our men. It doesn't matter what she's preaching," Atasha heard her say. When the other Wives refused to pick their signs back up, she whipped her phone out once more, tapping the wireless headset to turn it on. Marjorie dialed furiously. Unbeknownst to Atasha, at that moment, someone whose identity they hid beneath a hoodie scaled the wall behind her house and made their way to the roof.

"Sexual violence isn't a problem that's going away, either," Atasha continued. She stood up from the chair as the elevator lowered once more, stretching her arms above her head before pacing around the space. Her bare feet padded along the glass floor. "As horrifying as these statistics are, they barely brush the surface."

Police sirens sounded in the distance, and a news helicopter whooshed in overhead. A spotlight shone on the crowd before fixating on the glass elevator. Marjorie hung up the phone, a smug smile on her face, even though the energy seemed to shift away from her group. The protestor behind Atasha had made it to the highest point on her roof, towering over the crowd. A bulging bag was slung across their shoulder. Members of the audience pointed, trying to get Atasha to turn around. Not wanting to give the protestors any ammunition against her, she chose to ignore the person and continue with the show. The Wives™ that hadn't put down their signs chanted again with renewed focus.

"This *will* stop!" One of The Wives™ yelled, holding one corner of a sign that said *what is this teaching our children?*

"She's teaching your children about violence against those who identify as women. Shut up and listen," a supporter fired back.

Atasha needed to hurry if she was going to get her donation appeal in before everything imploded. The tension in the air felt volatile, like a powder keg one spark from exploding. The elevator moved down another floor toward the ground, closer to the interaction stage. It was clear that she wouldn't finish the show peacefully if The Wives™ had anything to do with it. While the police wouldn't stop Atasha, the officer's pending arrival had already disrupted the performance. The information she was sharing was crucial. However, the presence of law enforcement would stir up the crowd, and they would be unable to hear the statistics. Atasha didn't tolerate violence at her shows, and the police's arrival brought that possibility, no matter how small.

Atasha continued over the sirens. "V-Day is a large movement aiming to end violence against those who identify as women, transgender individuals, girls, and those with fluid identities who experience gender-based violence. It's what we've come here today to support," she said, pointing to video walls on each side of the elevator that displayed two QR codes. The elevator moved to another floor. "If you scan these codes, there will be two links. The one on the left video wall is for donations that will go to the V-Day campaign and their website URL. The other is the link to the Global Database for Violence Against Women, where you'll have access to the surveys I've mentioned, and many more."

Atasha finished her speech at the same time the elevator reached its final floor. Applause rounded the hill, drowning out the protests that had been chanted throughout the show. For a moment, the show had been successfully completed.

Until the first egg.

Atasha flinched as it hit the glass. The egg shattered in a burst of yolk and shell. Whirling around, she caught the protestor on the roof just as they threw two more. The first sailed over the elevator, landing in the middle of the audience. The second hit its target with more precision, landing squarely on the roof of the elevator. The protestor threw tomatoes next, an onslaught of mixed items being launched at the elevator. Atasha was safely tucked into the reinforced glass, able to stand without harm, but the same wasn't true for the rest of the audience — or Barbie. As another handful of eggs was thrown from the protestor on the roof, each one slamming into the walls surrounding her with brazen force, she heard a startled gasp from her left. She turned to see Barbie, covered in the collateral damage of being positioned near Atasha. Sticky yellow-white yolk sprinkled her face and hair in flecks. The livestream lit up with angry reactions. Hundreds of people came to the defense of Barbie, livid at the idea of a woman being victimized again. Without flinching, the translator picked up a tomato that had landed next to her. Barbie, who also plays softball as a third baseman on weekends, turned and whipped the tomato back at the protestor. With a swift motion, her aim was fitting for her well-practiced skills. For a moment, they paused, locking eyes with a stone-cold Barbie, who stood ready to defend herself and possibly escalate the confrontation. The crowd scattered as they realized they could be hit in the crossfire.

"Absolutely no violence is tolerated at any of the presentations," Atasha emphasized to the crowd and protestors, though she couldn't bring herself to hide the grin on her face as Barbie flipped off the person on the roof, not an official ASL phrase. The livestream roared to life, bursting with emojis tomatoes, targets, a wave of thumbs-up reactions, and of course, the goat — igniting both excitement and fury in the audience. Atasha was beside herself over the mistreatment both her audience and Barbie were subjected to. She wanted to deal with the assaulter herself.

She never got the chance. Four police cars screeched to a halt at the road beyond Atasha's slope, doors slamming as they rushed toward the scene. The protester scrambled across the roof, running as officers took off to catch the perpetrator as they fled. The few who didn't join the chase moved toward the elevator.

"Finally," Marjorie stomped down the hill, meeting the police at the bottom. A vein throbbed in her forehead as she yelled animatedly. She gestured harshly at Atasha, who had remained inside the elevator in the presence of the police. "Stop her! She's standing there, indecent, and she's blatantly being a nuisance. She needs to be arrested!"

The call for charges, especially after they had been targeted in a food fight, had the effect of lowering The Wives™ reputation in the minds of those who already didn't like them. But for those who rally around chaos and self-righteous protest, this was the time to make the feed go viral. With the police thought to be on their side, many of them whipped out their phones, live streaming the downfall of Atasha Stone. This, combined with the streaming Atasha had set up before the show, ensured that the millions watching would share the video with their family and friends.

The police surveyed the area. Atasha exited the glass elevator when it came to a stop, making no attempt to cover herself until she was firmly outside of it. Her exit denoted the end of the show, so she put on the simple sweater dress and heeled booties she had laid out for herself and walked confidently toward the police, who approached the elevator to meet her with Marjorie in tow. Atasha knew what she was allowed to do. Performing naked had been a bold move, but it was what needed to be done. If women couldn't feel comfortable with their bodies, how could they know the extent of the violations committed against them?

The Brave Bitches™ formed a protective half-circle, loosely blocking the officers from the glass elevator. Yelling only to be heard over the brunette, they shouted their support for Atasha and the message the Bibliothec Babe was sending to the community.

"She informs. She isn't prostituting herself; she's not even selling anything. She's advocating for our community and making significant donations to people in need," one said.

"But she's *naked!*" Marjorie emphasized, throwing her hands up in aggravation.

"Yeah, she is," a husband said under his breath. His wife gently smacked him with her purse.

"She's promoting self-love and confidence," Barbie countered.

"She's a whore flaunting her sins in front of the public," Marjorie seethed.

"And you're assaulting people just because you don't like their message," Barbie said, wiping off the last bit of tomato juice on her pants. "Sounds like you should work on yourself first."

"What about you then? You threw it back."

"I'm not going to stand there and take it," Barbie said. "Never again."

Atasha gave Barbie a hug, pride swelling in her chest.

Another flurry of conversation burst out. The overlapping voices were nearly impossible to make out. She only heard snippets: "immoral," "feminist," "freedom," and "repression" were the words that traveled up the hill the most. Atasha could only watch as the two sides shouted at the police. Eventually, the officers ordered all the women to quiet down. Barbie met Atasha as they moved to the front of the group, stopping in front of the officer. Once the women had quieted, one policeman addressed the crowd.

"We can't arrest her," he told them. "It's an artistic performance on private property. She's allowed to show her art however she desires, and you'll be lucky if she doesn't have *you* arrested."

"She can't have me arrested!" Marjorie shrieked, appalled at the idea. Her voice rose another octave as Atasha locked eyes with her and smiled.

"You're standing on private property, ma'am. The owner hasn't given you the right to engage in this behavior. She can ask you to leave, but appears to be exhibiting quite a bit of patience," the officer said. "If you don't comply, we can arrest you for trespassing."

"This is ridiculous!" Marjorie stomped her foot in frustration. She pleaded with the officers, who simply apologized and stepped back from the scene. The Wives™ refused to lose without a fight, however.

"You can also be charged with vandalism and assault if they can prove you were connected with the projectiles," the officer continued, glancing at Barbie.

"I had nothing to do with that!" She protested, riling herself up on the lawn. "What someone does is a personal choice. If you won't arrest her, then we'll stay and protest all night. She'll hear us when she lays her head on her pillow to sleep. Next Friday, we'll be back with more of us. There will be no relief. We'll show up every week until she has to shut the show down, or you arrest every one of us for protesting, whichever comes —"

"*You* told them to throw the eggs."

Marjorie whirled around. One woman, the one Atasha had seen step away from her husband during the show, stepped out of The Wives™. Marjorie gaped at her, growing more furious by the second. Red seeped into her cheeks.

"I did no such thing. I do not support violence," she seethed, pointing at her All Lives Matter t-shirt.

"I heard her on the phone with the person on the roof earlier," the woman told the police. "If you look in her bag, there are tomatoes in there she was going to join in with until you all got here first. She absolutely condones violence. She just isn't brave enough to admit she had a part in this."

Majorie's face slowly drained of color as millions of people, online and in person, heard what she had planned. Averting her eyes from the gathering crowd, she shifted her bag slowly, so it was blocked from the cameras. Not only had she disrupted the show and tossed out insults like she had something to prove, but now she was potentially an accessory to assault. Her self-righteous reputation was quickly being tarnished for some, but unfortunately became a heroine to a small but vocal minority. She kept her eyes from the cameras, mouth gaping like a floundering fish as she tried to figure out a way to regain control.

"I expected nothing less from someone so weak. You're falling victim to a woman like her, doing her bidding. I knew this would happen when people started seeing I was right. I don't even know that person!"

Only a handful of The Wives™ still had their signs and stood firmly beside their leader. One woman picked up her sign while the others looked on. She held her gaze when Marjorie tried to stare her down. The woman carried her sign into The Brave Bitches™ half circle and stopped just before them. She made eye contact with Atasha, who nodded encouragingly. The woman tore her sign in half. She melded into the Brave Bitches seamlessly, embraced by the others.

Marjorie narrowed her eyes. "You're joining the slut walk? Shame on you!"

Atasha stepped in front of the group as Marjorie spoke. She wrapped her arm around the woman's shoulders, partially to provoke the brunette and partially to show the woman that there were no hard feelings toward her protesting.

The woman smiled at The Wives™. "I'm joining the side that's speaking out *against* violence," she said.

"I'm happy we could change her mind," Atasha said to The Wives™.

"No one with an ounce of morality would join you," Marjorie seethed, stepping closer to Atasha. "You're a cam girl; I've done my research. That's just porn under another name. You're promoting an industry that demeans and mistreats women. It's inappropriate, not sexually free. You're a fraud. I hope no one else falls prey to your lies."

"I pray you see the light," Atasha said, turning away from the woman to walk confidently toward her house. She paused, glancing back with a mischievous smile. "Oh, and Marjorie — I'll make sure to gift you front-row tickets to my one-woman show next Friday... The Vagina Monologues."

> Global Database on Violence against Women
> https://evaw-global-database.unwomen.org
>
> RAINN (Rape, Abuse & Incest National Network)
> Learn more at https://www.rainn.org
>
> Take the next step to inspire by visiting https://www.vday.org

See the end of the book for elevator etiquette rules followed or broken.
Elevator Etiquette Codes: 2A, 3B, 3D. 4A, 6B, 6H

American Shame

Can We All Get Along?

"In a widespread crisis, we see the best in most people — and the worst in some." -Amy Tan

Consider this. I sit alone, quietly waiting for the server to bring me my takeout. Now that I am 14, Dad finally allowed me to go by myself to pick up food for the family. I've got a white mask strapped to both my ears as the TV spews propaganda about the "China Virus." The reporter is going on and on about how the disease has taken more and more victims with each passing day. I sigh and look around in an attempt to distract myself. The rows of empty tables remind me of all the times my family and I would sit in those same seats with hearts full of joy and hope of living out our American dream. All of it was shattered by those who couldn't bear the idea of people being different.

My mother had ordered our dinner from Ehuang's Noodle Palace, a restaurant we have been going to since we moved to America when I was four. Before the pandemic, the restaurant was extremely popular. It was common to wait at least an hour before being seated, and the room was always filled with loud chatter and laughter. Everyone was always so friendly. Now, the restaurant is barren. People won't even step within six feet of the place.

"Mèimei!" Auntie Lora calls out to get my attention. She walks toward me, lifting the large takeout bag for me to see. "Food is ready!" she continues.

I get up and take the food from her. "Thank you," I respond.

"How are you doing, dear? And how is your mom?" She asks with concern in her eyes. Auntie Lora has always cared for me and my mom since we first moved here. Back then, Ehuang's was a restaurant we would visit almost weekly because it was one of the few Chinese restaurants we knew of. It felt so familiar and welcoming. It was like our own little place in America. Lately, we haven't stopped by to visit either due to lockdowns.

"We're doing as fine as we can," I sigh, "...Just isolating. My mom is paranoid about getting sick given grandmother is in bad health."

"I know, honey. Very scary out there. You and your mom stay safe, okay?" she says.

"You too," I say.

She tells me her restaurant isn't doing great and hopes the restrictions will lift soon. I reach into my pocket and give Auntie Lora the exact change and tip that my mom provided. I wish her the best with her business as I am aware a lot has been closing down recently. I thank her one last time before leaving.

I try my best to be vigilant as I step out of the 3rd-floor restaurant. My eyes veer to my sides with every step. I hold the food close to my body, feeling the steaming heat rise up my arms. Violence has increased in our small neighborhood, which has put us all on edge. I don't like walking here all by myself, but my mom assured me I could handle it. Now I just want to hurry home. In my haste, my takeout hits a man on his knee. Before I have a chance to react, I'm aggressively shoved aside.

"Oh, my G-d! I'm so sorry!" I say out of habit, as I make eye contact with this man. "I didn't see you. Ar-are you okay?"

"Piece of crap," the man mumbles to himself. "Don't fuckin' touch me." He pauses. "Asians. Fuckin' ruinin' everything. Can't keep to themselves."

Alcohol-infused spittle runs down the man's unmasked face. His tall and slim stature towered over me. The smell of alcohol is strong on his breath.

"Okay," I mumble as I back away slowly, calculating how many seconds it would take for me to escape. I rapidly turn away from him in an attempt to de-escalate. His bad energy and whatever else he's got are making me sick. I'm breathing faster now, and I can feel sweat pooling in my palms.

I sprint to the elevator, only like 25 yards from where I stand. My pace quickens as chills run down my back. Don't look back. *Don't look back.* Only a little longer. I pray to be free of all these bothersome feelings soon.

I hold the food tightly to my chest as I push the down button over and over. Eventually, the elevator doors open — slowly, too slowly. I step inside and push "G" to go to my floor. As the door is inches from closing, a hand reaches in, then a foot. I look down and notice that I recognize those gray oxfords. I feel a lump in my throat. My heart stops.

He stands there for a moment, staring at me. His eyes are bloodshot, and his breathing is heavy. He stumbles in. His gait is lethargic and uncomfortable. He waddles side to side as he gets closer, so I back up into the corner. I consider apologizing again, but he can't hear me. His eyes glaze over, distant, like he's somewhere else entirely. Somewhere dark. A bad place.

My exit is blocked. **Wǒ de tiān a! Bù !!!**

He approaches me slowly as I try to sink further into the wall. He extends a finger toward my face. "You," he mutters slowly. Anger mixed with whiskey stems from his lips. His fingers wrap tightly around my neck, and he punches me full force on the cheek with his right hand. I awkwardly drop the bag and the drinks start to pool on the floor.

A bloody iron-tinged mixture fills my mouth. My vision is fuzzy and I can barely see what's going on. My arms and legs are stiff. Suddenly, I can make out that his fist is coming towards my forehead, and I feel a burst of pressure in my head. It feels warm. Everything feels increasingly tense — my ears start ringing, and my surroundings become nonexistent. I try to ground myself, but my fingers are numb from pure fear. I want to yell, but his ever-tightening grip prevents me.

Tears stream down my cheeks. I beg and plead to indifferent ears that this will be over soon. I pray that I make it out alive.

My body has accepted its fate. It feels as though time has come to a complete halt. While his grip is still around my neck, he shoves me against the other side of the elevator as he steps back. I feel the hard metal, and

I'm sure that several buttons of the elevator panel have made patterns down my spine. My head smashes against the wall, rattling my skull from within. I grimace as I place my hand on my head to feel blood seeping through my already sweat-dampened hair. I'm shaking as I try to catch my breath, but it results in an uncontrollable coughing fit. As my breathing returns to normal, I sigh and look up at him. Afraid that if I let my guard down for a moment, things could become much worse. My vision begins to stabilize. I'm trembling, and my heart thumps against my chest. My white mask feels wet with my own blood. My palms are now stained red. I try to hold on to the wall to regain my balance as the elevator comes to an abrupt stop. Red handprints now decorate the elevator with my blood.

The man shockingly returns to his normal. He dusts himself off, fixes the collar of his shirt and adjusts the cuffs of his sleeves. He looks to the left and right of the elevator doors, stuffs his hands in his pockets, and walks out with purpose.

My body refuses to move. I am beyond exhausted. My fingers feel around my neck, tracing where his hand was. I feel the swelling as it throbs to the same rhythm as my heart. I place my other hand on my forehead as I feel my stomach tossing and turning. I feel nauseous and gag as the adrenaline drains from my body. I rest my head against the wall and slide to the ground. I leave a trail of red, and the bottom of my legs become wet with boba tea.

I remember my body involuntarily letting out a soft shriek, the only sound it could muster.

My name was Zhen-Li.

See the end of the book for elevator etiquette rules followed or broken. Elevator Etiquette Codes: 1C, 3F, 3G

Space Elevator
SPACE ELEVATOR DUOLOGY, PART I

"Journalism can never be silent: that is its greatest virtue and its greatest fault. It must speak, and speak immediately, while the echoes of wonder, the claims of triumph and the signs of horror are still in the air." -Henry Grunwald

Consider this. It's 2182, the 200th anniversary of the United States Air Force Space Command, and the Earth has conquered space elevator technology. What was once thought impossible because of issues with geostationary orbits and rotations was solved when Japan discovered the 119th element, Handwavium. Now three countries have physical equatorial connections to the moon via anchors at Mount Kilimanjaro: Tanzania, Japan, and the USA. Why these three, you might ask? Well, that's a bit of a story. Buckle up so I can tell ya, okay?

First things first, Mt. Kilimanjaro, which is located in Tanzania, was the ideal place to build the proposed space elevators. Its location, just six degrees south of the equator, made it the optimal place to rig the anchors connecting the cable tethers upwards of where LEO (Low Earth Orbit) satellites would provide support functions....

Also, Mt. Kilimanjaro was the tallest mountain in Africa, so the extra height wouldn't hurt, would it?

So the Americans had been buddying up with the Tanzanians for a while now. Since the United States was one of the most influential countries in the world, it was, therefore, selected for this mission. The USSF (United States Space Force) had also been completing several Joint Combined Exchange Training (JCET) exercises with the Tanzanian army, as well as coordination with Japan's Air Space Self-Defense Force (JASDF). All the agencies worked together to coordinate, support, and defend the three big space elevators situated on Mt. Kilimanjaro.

As for Japan, they had traded a significant amount of Handwavium in exchange for proper ownership over one of the elevators, to which the Tanzanians and the United States readily agreed. In the spirit of collaboration, the European Union oversaw the first international outpost on the moon, where all the space lifts had access points. Every country was welcomed there, except for the Rosmonauts of the Soviet Reunion. You might be wondering *why*.

There's a story behind this as well, I assure you. This incident has come after decades of international conflict, the need for advanced technology, access to interstellar communication, and, of course, the classic struggle for power.

You also might be wondering who *I* am, and what this has to do with me. Fair enough, fair enough. So let me tell you. My name is Erevu

Selemani. I am a 19-year-old reporter for my college in Arusha. Perhaps you have seen my byline, but probably not. I've witnessed history in the making. I was there in the Tanzanian elevator, upfront and personally watching this intense space battle. While I know exactly how this cosmic state of affairs ended, it took a few weeks to piece together exactly what happened on the way there. It all comes to a shocking conclusion, but it's incomprehensible without the right details. I'm so excited to tell you all about it.

Now that Earth had outposts and a Tanzanian hotel on the moon, the next natural step before full colonization was to set up a permanent communications network. It was crucial to bring the Geosynchronous Space Situational Awareness Program (GSSAP) to the next level. It's time for these capabilities to be integrated into the existing Galaga class network. This would enable stable communications on the moon, Mars, and our interstellar space probes. To make this a reality, four kilograms of a *suuuper* rare element called Vapourwarium needed to be transported to the moon, where the system was already built and awaiting this last component. Chief Master Sergeant of the United States Space Force, Roger A. Flagstaff, would safeguard this last component, a.k.a "The Brick".

But, well, these types of plans never turn out quite right, do they? There's always something going on....

On Mt. Kilimanjaro, the three transparent elevators rose on their trek to the moon.

The Japanese elevator, the easternmost of the three, was anchored to the moon at EU Station One and was delivering necessary supplies. The middle elevator, from the United Republic of Tanzania, was a purpose-built tourist lift with occasional material support as well.

Finally, the Western elevator belonged to the Americans, who usually had it anchored to an asteroid for maximum maneuverability, but had moved it into place to support The Brick's ascension.

The American elevator was an especially delicious target since Vapourwarium had become extremely rare, and therefore priceless on Earth. Mining had peaked long ago, and just enough was unearthed to facilitate the replacement of the current interplanetary network with an interstellar one until a long-term solution was found.

One country, in particular, was willing to do anything to get the Vapourwarium.

The Soviets desired the Vapourwarium for their own covert uses, and the Czar would tolerate nothing other than bringing home The Brick. However, the precarious nature of the Vapourwarium required caution to be at the highest level. Should the Vapourwarium crash to the ground, the impact would cause a disaster for which the word disaster would be an understatement.

As expected, the elevators were now ascending closer to the moon. Right on cue, the Soviet Reunion breached the East African airspace. While this Soviet special military operation was technically not an act of war, it could very well be considered war adjacent.

Flagstaff was ready, so he didn't need to *get ready*. He had been receiving tactical telemetry from the Space Rapid Capabilities Office (SRCO) and state-of-the-art weaponry from the Space and Missile Systems Center (SMSC). Furthermore, his Space Force Guard pilots have been running simulations for months in preparation for incursions, and now, it was go-time. Flagstaff assigned one squadron to initiate defensive maneuvers to protect The Brick while a sister squad went on the offensive to clear the Soviet fighters from the sky.

In addition to being a military badass, Flagstaff was also a man with dwarfism and a famous reality show star. While he was on set for *Military Brass Balls*, the Soviets broke into his New Vegas hotel room and obtained a DNA sample. They also recruited women to contribute egg cells for the "love of Mother Russia" and several other patriotic benefits. The Soviets then proceeded with a cloning process called the somatic cell nuclear transfer (SCNT). They subsequently replicated the compact design of the drone ship and then replicated Flagstaff.

When the Soviets entered Tanzanian airspace, they did it with 400 clones of the man. The clones formed battle strips undulating in several tight centipede-type formations. The Flagstaff-clone leader was named Флагшток, or *Flagshtok* in American English, and his clone pilots were called *Shtoks*.

Well, guess what? The Americans also had pilot clones of Flagstaff. (Are people this obsessed with him or *what?*). Then they commissioned *more* clones in his image so that the military could fill *more* ships. Of course, he agreed to this, his attention-loving, reality-star side coming into play. Anyway, the U.S. launched their own drone ships, each piloted by a clone of Flagstaff, their blue lasers engaging the enemy as the elevators climbed ever higher. Each American pilot was cybernetically connected to the ship, allowing cameras to provide a full spherical 360-degree view, with weapons systems feeding data to all the pilots simultaneously. These cyborg control units were necessary to process the data quickly enough, so the pilot did not go mad. These units took a decade to perfect, which was why the Americans had the most updated clone cyborgs and the Soviet Reunion did not.

Clutching my imager close to my sturdy jean jacket, I lifted it up, ready to capture the intense action in this cislunar space.

I was a witness to an explosive multi-colored laser light show. My own Tanzanian military supported the effort with conventional yellow offensive tracer munitions. The Soviets had success jamming the Defense Satellite Communications System, and that meant the United States was at a serious disadvantage. The U.S. wound up losing its drone ships left and right, up and down. My country was also taking an unbelievable amount of damage for hosting the elevators, but the Vapourwarium was worth it! *C'mon, guys, all of that military training, as well as the upgraded technology compared to the Soviet Reunioners, I know you can do it...*

Flagstaff fired his blue lasers as he whizzed by my elevator, and I swore he winked at me, causing me to gasp in surprise. *OMG OMG!!* I almost fainted on the spot. I was inspired by his bravery, but there were just too many *Shtoks* for the U.S. and Tanzania to defend on their own.

That's when Japan's Space Operations Squadron joined the fight. A secret Godzilla class, the Sprinter Trueno Decimator, rose from the Pangani River piloted by Takumi Tomino, a Japanese rockstar in his own right. Tomino was an ace pilot, who was also the lead guitarist of Godfoot, the band he would go on tour with when intercontinental tensions were low. Anyway, the Decimator began swatting the Soviet drones into the ground while emitting a high-decibel noise that sounded like a combination of a nuclear-infused dinosaur and Tarzan's yell.

The Americans were still outnumbered, and taking fire, but you could never count out the land that gave us, David Hasselhoff, and the Williams sisters.

That's when three things happened that flipped the script....

TO BE CONTINUED

See the end of the book for elevator etiquette rules followed or broken.
Elevator Etiquette Codes: 6D, 6H

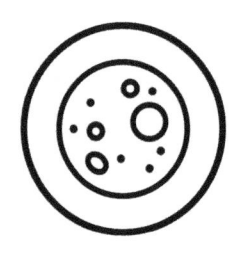

Space Heist!

SPACE ELEVATOR DUOLOGY, PART II

"There is immense power when a group of people with similar interests gets together to work toward the same goals."
-Idowu Koyenikan

Consider this. So, where were we? Ah, yes, the Earth's battle for the only remaining element needed to create interstellar space communication. The element, in brick form, was rising on a space elevator (yes, really) on its way to the moon. The Soviet Reunion executed a special military operation against the three nations (U.S., Tanzania, and Japan) to steal the priceless Vapourwarium. Representative countries from three continents were in an intense battle now, and I, college reporter Erevu Selemani, was witnessing this right from the ascending middle elevator of my home country, Tanzania.

My elevator got caught in the crossfire, and I had never seen enemy red lasers so close up, my gosh! It was as tense as could be!!

And as I was explaining, three things happened that changed the whole outcome of the battle.

The first was that the Japanese mech pilot activated Flight Form on his Sprinter Trueno Decimator. The Flight Form transformed the Decimator into a massive battle jet and scooped up many of the Soviet drones into its hangar bay. Tomino then activated an internal EMP so that the captured *Shtok* ships were rendered harmless. The pilot attained maximum altitude and activated patrol mode on his mech as Tomino exited the Earth's atmosphere at the Kármán Line, where it could not ascend further. Overall, a successful outcome so far, but the Vapourwarium was still not secure, and now I, Erevu Selemani, was documenting a full-on, winner-take-all space battle.

Oh, by the way, emblazoned on the side of the Decimator were the bold letters **JAXA** representing the Japanese Aerospace Exploration Agency. This acronym was used because JAXA has far fewer characters — although there was room on the fuselage.

Anyway, the second event was when Flagstaff triggered Hive Mode for his clones. Sorry if I didn't tell you about Hive Mode earlier; it's been a busy time. Anyway, Flagstaff brought his soldiers into the Hive Mind, which allowed him and his clones to be synchronized for various offensive and defensive formations.

The Soviets were kinda in for a salty treat — and the ol' Reunioners had their own in store. Don't you forget it.

There was still some time left before the elevators arrived on the moon. The elevator triplets were now in space, and there were still too many of these scheming *Shtoks* to contend with. Like a disgruntled and overworked school teacher, Флагшток was waving his finger in a gesture loosely translated as, "I don't think so, little boy," while mouthing the words *Nyet, Nyet* through his own transparent dome. In a corresponding move, Flagstaff fired up a 1980s-inspired speed metal mix of "Semper Supra," the theme of the Space Force, and turned it all the way up to 11. All the American clones, synchronized in the Hive Mind, rocked out with their "Colts" out. The U.S. Space Force would not yield a *centimeter*.

Two of Флагшток's drone ships broke through and were able to clamp themselves onto the American elevator's protection grid from both above and below. This had the effect of stopping the American's elevator ascent while the Japanese and Tanzanians soldiered on. The *Shtoks* prepared themselves for a spacewalk to cut open the elevator and steal the Vapourwarium for the mother country. Concurrently, Флагшток was now focused on dissolving Flagstaff's Hive Mind. Red lasers trained on Flagstaff as the two *Shtoks* attached to the American elevator exited their drone ships for a whiplash maneuver.

I bit my lip and watched tensely, clutching my schoolbag tight.

Oh G-d, oh no.

I looked at the brutal attacks on all three elevators and said a little prayer, *"Please be okay, my friends...."* It was making my heart pound like crazy, and I felt slightly faint. My imager shook in my hands; I was trembling so hard.

I almost had to cover my eyes and turn away. I took a breath and turned back towards the battle because I was a reporter, dang it. We didn't lose our nerve so easily! Even though I really, really wanted to…

Inspired by the Japanese's successes, the United States Space Force reconfigured their remaining assets into a coordinated weapon, not unlike Voltron, G-Force, or the Thundercats. With one series of EMP smart bombs, they sent pulses toward the remaining Soviet drone ships with many of the *Shtoks* soon becoming immobilized. As the Tanzanian and Japanese elevators arrived at their lunar destination, Chief Flagstaff went for the final blow. He verbally and telepathically shouted to his team through his Hive Mind, "Goliath Laser Formation!" As a rallying cry, he roared "Semper Supra!" and fired a split array of laser light from the barrels on the underside of his craft, aiming directly at Флагшток. Flagstaff immobilized the enemy ship with the GLF, causing shiny, jagged shards and shrapnel to explode outward into space. The reverberations were so fierce that I thought the empty surfaces of the elevators were going to shatter.

I held a hand to my mouth, heart racing, as I kept my eyes locked on the scene.

The leaderless Rosmonaut pilots knew the jig was up. Флагшток's *Shtoks* flew erratically and shot stray fire as they executed what could only be described as weak sauce retreat maneuvers.

Dang, you should have seen them. It was straight-up lit, bro. (See what I did there?!) Флагшток raised his hands in the air, mouthing, "Достаточно! Достаточно!" through the clear dome protuberance. The Soviet ships slowly became still, one by one. Флагшток surrendered, ensuring that The Brick would arrive at the moon, unfettered, and the American elevator could resume its journey. I watched as Flagstaff commanded several of his officers to take Флагшток into custody before whizzing to the central space station on the moon. Wow, what a day!

Dang, this Flagstaff dude is...pretty awesome....

Unexpectedly, a Chinese shuttle, patrolling the area with a multi-tether tractor beam, brought the remaining floating inert Soviet drone ships into their cargo bay to be returned to friendly Soviet soil. As for the Vapourwarium, well, that ended great, too.

I smiled as the Tanzanian elevator finally came to a stop on the lunar surface. Rushing off towards the moon central station in a frenzy, my thoughts came combobulating into focus.

I have to see him at the spot; The Chief is expecting me.

"Let me through! Let me through!" I ran through the crowd of officials surrounding the lobby of the Lunar Mount Kilimanjaro by Marriott and caught a secure shuttle to the European Union's communication center, EU Station One. And that's when I tore off my stifling jean jacket like a Chippendale, revealing the Tanzanian green military uniform beneath. I whipped out my dark green beret from my schoolbag, the one that identified me as an Officer Candidate of the Tanzanian army, and slapped it on my head like a slice of salami on a French bread bun. The officials were glaring at me, probably for not changing in the restroom. No matter! I didn't have time for that. Besides, I had military credentials AND a *press pass*.

I made it to the rendezvous and locked eyes with the man who was on alert, scanning the scene. "Sir, sir!" I saluted.

Chief Flagstaff nodded, looking my uniform up and down, taking in the lapel insignia with a white space and star, and the matching dark green Tanzanian militia.

He gave me a proper salute and handshake, recognition in his voice. "Agent Selemani," he said diplomatically, "job well done. I assume you have it secure and in pristine condition."

I nodded and stared right at him, getting chills for a second. "Absolutely, sir." I reached into my schoolbag and with trembling, tingling hands, handed him the bright verdant Vapourwarium that I had kept all along. Yes, it was in *my* schoolbag! Fooled you, didn't I?

I couldn't believe this was really happening to me. I pictured the elevators again, whizzing as the space drones fought each other, shielding my eyes against all the flurry of lights, witnessing the fights and violence. Suspense, fear, and the unknown. The risk, the reward. I couldn't shake the images out of my head. And I was *important*. Of all these fighters and clones. Of...the galaxy. Who woulda thought? I shook myself out of it, willing myself to be calm.

Meanwhile, Chief Flagstaff held The Brick. It shone bright and green off his palm, reflecting a million little rainbow prisms.

He let out a throaty chuckle, his eyes filled with tears as he examined The Brick in his hands. "Ya did it, kid. I knew you could."

I laughed, and he did too, as he saluted me *again*. Then I cried and danced in relief, so glad that the Vapourwarium was here on the moon where it belonged. Everything was okay, thank heavens, thank *G-d*.... It felt like the start of a newer, more stable beginning for all of us.

After a moment, it dawned on me. I didn't just protect the Vapourwarium brick. The most famous man on the neurocasts, the man who did all sorts of things, was right here congratulating my butt, oh man... and I... well, I kind of, just sort of... blanked out, ya know. "I'm so sorry. I just really admire what you did back there, sir! It was such an honor to be a part of this whole mission, and..." Then my face flamed and I chuckled again. The chief laid a hand on my shoulder and looked deep into my soul as he reassured me that this was real.

"Agent Selemani, I have a special job for you, if you're up for it."

What? What could he possibly still want with *me*?

My heart dove, but I swallowed and nodded my head, following the man. *Be dignified, Erevu. This is Chief Flagstaff, right here, right now. You are a military man. Remember how strong you can be.*

The next thing I knew, we were in a room that was basically pitch black with electric purple rotating lights. But the brightest beam of all was coming from the center of the room, in this massive column that was just undulating with energy. A strange buzzing noise emanated from it, getting louder and louder and louder, almost like a blender stirring up a life-sized storm. I'd never seen or heard anything like it in my life. Wow!

I looked up at it. Holy macaroni, it had to be at least 20 feet tall, just big and Apple Store white and shiny. A small but astounding indent at the bottom caught my eye. *Wonder what it's all for, anyway.*

Suddenly, I heard a woman before me receiving a transmission with a voice like an OG Cylon. "Hello. Galaga Communication Site. Prepare for final integration." Standing before us was that massive energy column, and up close, it just seemed so alive. I couldn't help looking up at it in awe. I almost wanted to reach out with my hands and touch it, but I restrained myself and bit my lip.

"So uh...where are we, sir?" I finally managed, looking around. I saw rows and rows of those officials like that woman by the door, so stunning and powerful and cool.

"Attention!" Chief Master Sergeant Flagstaff took command of the room, and I realized I could never tire of experiencing the man in action. "It is time for the Vapourwarium insertion." He held The Brick, walking up to the tall white column, where it buzzed with more intermittent purple electricity popping out like lightning strikes and sounding like old-time microwave popcorn going this way and that. Chief Flagstaff laid a hand on my shoulder in that comforting way. "Agent Selemani...would you do the honors?" And he held The Brick out towards me, my eyes widening in disbelief as he placed it in my hands.

"M-*me*?" I took in the crowd of officials and the Flagstaff clones, who were all watching my moves in eerie synchronicity. My heart was a crazy circus.

"You earned it, Agent. Plug 'er in."

I stared up at it in silence, thinking to myself that I'd never seen anything more beautiful in my life. Then it grew too quiet, and I suddenly realized that the galaxy was waiting on *me*.

I took in a shaky breath, willing my heart to stop. I lifted The Brick and placed it in the tube cradle. The tray moved inward as the machine crackled to life and accepted the source of its power. Purple plasma charges surrounded The Brick, and the color moved through the tubes surrounding the moon. Ultimately, the pairings began. Earth to the moon and the moon to our equipment on other planets. It was a new beginning for those on Earth to communicate with those beyond it.

I watched the Vapourwarium brick in awe as it continued to do its thing. My eyes grew misty at the realization that things were finally...okay.

I stared at Chief Flagstaff and everybody in the room. They were all so brave. And they survived.

I shook Flagstaff's hand, as well as those of the captain, major, and commander in his team as acknowledgment for their every brave deed and to wish them luck in their journeys ahead. I wish I could've held each of their hands forever, just to be there with them and show my utmost and utter respect. They deserved that and more for everything.

I bowed and stared at them with a lump in my throat. They started to bow back, one by one by one, army men sending salutes, congresswomen nodding in reverence. I held the bow for as long as I could. I just couldn't seem to move at all.

My eyes welled up, and I felt like I'd just lost something really important. But I hadn't even thanked the *most* important person here in my eyes. Him...

I turned to Flagstaff with a smile. I had so much awe and admiration for him right now. I bowed slightly and held my right elbow with my hand as a sign of respect. Then with an outstretched hand, I proclaimed, "*Safari salama nyumbani,*" which is Swahili for wishing him a safe journey home.

"Agent Selemani," he called as he looked me in the eye. "Every bird flies with its own wings." He reminded me of my own inner strength when he quoted that saying from my culture.

The coolness of the window pane pressed against my hand as I looked out the space elevator on my way back to Earth. Wow. I reflected on the experience of bringing the Vapourwarium here. We showed up; we got it done. Different cultures from different continents all worked together to safely bring these space elevators and their precious cargo to the moon. We kicked butt. A smile made its way to my face as I put a hand on my heart and contemplated Humanity.

We are all connected.

There's no time better than today.

Safety, security, finally.

And it all starts...now.

See the end of the book for elevator etiquette rules followed or broken.
Elevator Etiquette Codes: 4A, 6B, 6D, 6H

Anime Girl

My Spirits Were Not Lifted

"Reality is merely an illusion, albeit a very persistent one."
-Albert Einstein

Consider this. I finally get to go home after cleaning the classroom windows after the chalkboard is erased. My punishment for correcting the teacher about Sputnik launching in 1957 — guess I'll keep quiet next time, but whatever. It is always very difficult to please Teacher. We are pretty high up, so the view of the mountains and clouds is spectacular. All that matters to me, though, is getting home to finish this manga series I've been enjoying. It's about a kimono-wearing soul eater who tries to kill her brother to avenge her father.

After I cross from one side of the building to the other, I enter the elevator, enjoying one piece of Silent Honor Dark Dream chocolate. It's my girlfriend's favorite — and now mine, too. She's definitely my lucky star.

I just wish this elevator wasn't moving at a snail's pace. Come on, it's not even going 5 cm a second! Suddenly, the lights flicker as the elevator shakes and drops violently. I hold on to the sides, expecting to fall to my death. Instead, it lands at the first floor, and before I can get out, the panel lights up with floor numbers I didn't press. I stare as first the number four lights up, then fades, then two, then six, ten, and five. It's like there's a ghost in the machine. The elevator rockets its way to the fourth floor, stops, descends to the second, stops again, and continues to the sixth, then the tenth, and then the fifth. The elevator must be possessed; it's going berserk!

After the elevator comes to rest on the fifth floor, the doors unexpectedly open, and I'm confronted with something supernatural. The entity floats silently outside the car, a long white kimono draping over a thin, humanoid body with no feet. *Where are her feet?!?* She looks like she'd been put in a stretching machine, twisted, pulled, and mutated into something *else* — she looks just like the monster from my manga! What is happening to me?

I bring my eyes up to hers, though my body is terrified not to. Each strand of her wild Medusa's Gorgon-like hair seems to writhe, hungry for vengeance. Her deep red eyes flicker, mirroring the dim light in the hallway. The cold look in her eyes is like a frozen fire, sending a chill through me that stops my heart. She whispers directly into my mind: *"You can no longer escape what you've done, Yamato. It may not be today, but I am coming for you."*

I don't know what the *kuso* she's talking about, and *how does she know my name?* I just want to go home! My hand moves on its own, rapidly pressing the first-floor button, which I guess is *ok?* As the doors close, the Onryō's threat morphs into a shrill laugh which echoes in my fragile mind. Suddenly, the elevator ascends to the 10th floor. This isn't right, well nothing is right — why am I going up? How did she move my hand? Is it fate?

The elevator dings and shocks me to attention. I struggle to take in some air and it is throwing my body off. I take a step forward to peek out of the elevator. I look left, right, and left again. Beyond an exit sign, the only illumination in the hallway is the orange sunset coming through a distant window. It is eerily quiet. I step back in, wiping the large sweat drop from my brow as the doors close. I'll make sure to tell Teacher about it tomorrow. I barely recover from those glowing eyes when suddenly —

"Hold that door, please!"

As the voice rings out, I quickly trigger the infrared sensor with my hand despite my hesitation. The doors open back up as a figure rushes in and immediately pushes the button for the lobby, which works for me! I'm petrified to look at her, afraid the mysterious woman had somehow followed me.

To my relief, it was not the superstretch lady. This one looks normal, *almost* like a real human being. With hair that is darker than black, she is dressed in a perfect blue sailor-style blouse with a bright red ribbon and a pleated skirt that stops below her scraped knees. After catching her breath from running, she stands up straight and looks in my direction.

This girl seems almost too perfect. Her eyes are so big and round. Her skin is pale and clear of any blemishes. Her hair is a bright shade of pink with purple tips. The cherry blossom insignia on her forehead glows with a golden light. She is short and petite, almost like a loli from the anime my little sister watches all the time. She pauses, staring at me. "You look like you've seen a ghost. Rough day?"

"Just a weird one. I'm fine, though," I answer, trying not to stare as her swirling eyes change to arrows.

The girl pouts and places a hand on her forehead, causing the Sakura symbol to shimmer. I see she is covering her popping vein insignia, which transforms to match her souring mood. Then, before I know it, I am in the line of fire. The girl is now on her scratched knees, throwing random objects from her backpack. There are speed lines emanating from each projectile, and unfortunately, the tail ends of several lines pass right through me, causing me to wince slightly.

I'm overwhelmed with the craziness because it keeps coming faster and faster. I put my hands up to shield my face from the onslaught. I'm getting hit with a necklace with the initial D, two bottles of bleach, a Death Note, a treasure map (X marks the spot), a WonderSwan game console, and eventually a Shimazaki bicycle that knocks me to the floor. How in the world did all that stuff fit inside her book bag?

The cluttered environment finally stops getting smaller when she pulls out a pink headband, tying it tightly across her forehead before methodically returning all the *gomi* into her small bag. After she is done, she finally acknowledges her crime of violence and offers to help me up.

"Sorry," she says apologizing. I cautiously lower my arms and accept the girl's helping hand. "I know we just met, but my full name is Yuki Yumi Sakura Rei Rin Akene. What's your name?" she asks, tilting her head just enough to be noticeable.

"Umm, I'm Yamato," I reply with a nod. "Konnichiwa."

The Genki girl smiles brightly. "It's nice to meet you too, Yamato. I'm on my way down to meet my *kareshi*. We've known each other since we were kids and promised to get married when we grew up. Oh, but he doesn't have memories of any of that because of an amnesia spell. Not like that suffering of the Dusk Maiden of Amnesia, of course. Anyway, once I see him, I have to compete with five girls from the Witchcraft Academy for his attention and remind him who I am by breaking the incantation."

I blink and tilt my head in confusion at the girl's overly long explanation, which is getting longer. My head is spinning, and I hate to ask but, "Couldn't you just show him a picture of the two of you on your phone?"

Yuki's eyes go wide. The golden insignia on her forehead morphs into a surprising *gaan*. "Oh no, I can't do that."

"Why not?" I stand bewildered as the girl simply grins at me with a large, slightly unnerving smile, as though everything she said is the most natural thing in the world. I suspect to her, it is.

She talks in an overly complicated way like in a Visual Novel. I'm not sure where the hell this is all going. Without warning, somehow her entire body is glowing, not just her forehead adornment. I need to get out of here before *more* spooky things happen. Can't this elevator go *any* faster?

Yuki politely waits for me to stop musing and then continues. "You see, my father is a demon from another dimension, and my mother is the princess of the moon, who fled to Earth to escape its destruction. She fell in love with him really fast." I whisper "uh-mazing" under my breath.

"But then my father was killed by another demon from that same alien dimension, and he turned out to be my older brother, whom I never knew existed. I also miss my dad. Anyway, my brother wants to take over the world with his army and make me his demon queen — gross, right? I have to stop him for several reasons by using my special blood to transform into a warrior princess and pilot a giant alien mech to fight *and* get help. The mech was created by my mother and her half-alien sister because they suspected I might need it one day. And I will need it, I will. Also, I have to keep my sweet, handsome, and previously overprotective boyfriend completely clueless about the demon queen part, or else he will be very annoyed with my demon older brother. This is very hard for me, Yamato."

At this point, I simply smile brightly and nod. "I can imagine." Honestly, I'm hyper-focused on the exit and am starting to feel anxious. I don't want to engage anymore with anyone about anything. I just want to go home and read my manga. As Yato is my witness, I swear as the lights flicker, she flickers too. The elevator violently shakes to a halt, and I am beyond troubled now. With the chime of the elevator, I feverishly spam the "Open Doors" button over and over as fast as I can. ***Get me the koko kara hayaku dashite kure yo out of here!*** There, I said it.

The multiverse complies because the doors somehow fly open at the lobby level.

As Yuki bounds out of the elevator, she turns to me with the same perfectly unnerving smile she wore the entire way down. "Thank you for the lovely conversation, Yamato. I'll see you in episode 7 when you're upgraded to a main character."

Her *kuudere* boyfriend is waiting for her, and he throws his arm around her shoulders in a welcoming embrace. He looks at me and gives me a knowing wink as he turns to leave.

I'm shocked, but not surprised, as a ghost balloon pops out of my mouth. I shout after her as the elevator doors close on my query. "Episode 7?"

I start to question *everything.* In all my time in the Paranormal Investigation Club, I've never encountered anything like this. My mind is telling me I'm beyond the boundary of rational thought. The shaking elevator, the flickering lights, the bicycle being thrown from a small book bag — these last few minutes make even less sense than Bobobo-bo Bo-bobo. I feel the color draining from my body. What the hell is wrong with this elevator? What the hell is wrong with me? ***Watashi, kanzen ni ataoka da yo!***

I didn't get much time to think about any of this. The lights pop off into complete blackness, and I instinctively press myself into the back wall. When the lights come back on, I am dumbfounded by what is hovering in front of the doors. Illuminated in bold letters is a message to the viewers:

COMING UP NEXT
Episode 2: The Lost Anime Boy

See the end of the book for elevator etiquette rules followed or broken. Elevator Etiquette Codes: 1B, 2B, 3A, 5F, 6C, 6H

Professional Help

My Grinning Disturbia

"The role of a clown and a physician are the same: it's to elevate the possible and to relieve suffering." -Patch Adams

Consider this. I am driving into the parking garage of my work at the Gacy Building. I'm running late, but not too bad. I check my smartwatch while ascending the stairs, my heart rate increasing to a very reasonable 110 beats per minute. As I approach the elevator, all of my relatively healthy stats go out the window. Before I even push the up button, the doors slide open on their own to reveal my pre-existing condition: **FEAR OF CLOWNS.**

Standing in the middle of the elevator is a fucking clown. My heart rate shoots to 130 beats per minute, and my nerves are already over the edge. I reach for my inhaler, but I don't own one. I don't have asthma; I have *coulrophobia*.

There he is, a four feet tall nightmare with purple hair and a bright red punchable nose. His matching purple shoes are are adorned with red intimidating stripes. I feel like he could step on me, crunching my body until it is a lifeless, gelatinous substance with those unnaturally long high tops. His painted lips smile at me with no movement at all. However, his eyes blink at me, cruel, and without mercy. THEY BLINKED AT ME. The doors close and he is thankfully gone from my sight.

I stand frozen in place, terrified of what to do next. My job is on the 19th floor, so I have to use the elevator. But the next time this elevator opens, his menacing blinking eyes could be greeting me again, this I know. And I can't use the other elevator bank because it is out of service. I take deep breaths and will my heart to steady itself. I need to summon the courage to push the up button. As I expect, my nemesis stands at the exact same spot, grinning at me maniacally and flashing his deranged blinking eyes. What is his plan? He blinks at me again with an uncanny emptiness in his eyes before slowly, like tai chi slow, pulling out a small metallic clown horn from behind his ear. He squeezes the black bulb at the end, seemingly random *honks and fionks* on endless repeat. With each honk, I feel weaker as I visualize his hand around my neck, squeezing expertly with full control. Each blink is torture, every moment terror, as he watches me squirm without remorse. Anyway, I learned the language of dots and dashes in Boy Scouts, and by that coded blinking, he wanted me dead. The word was on the tin. DIE. D-I-E. Over and over he spells those three letters out with those dirty eyelashes, Dash Dot Dot (D), Dot Dot (I), Dot (E). My breath stutters and my vision blurs as I'm hypnotized by his actions, paralyzed with fear. I feel a wet trickle go down my pant leg, and I'm not surprised that I peed myself. Then the doors close, exactly, predictably like before.

My already racing heart speeds up more. I have to get to work, but I don't want to die. What is this dark jester doing at my workplace? The doors part again and he's gone, but the elevator never moved. I cautiously get in and push 19 as quickly as I can. In the confined space, I smell my sour piss along with his putrid breath.

For a moment, my nervous system relaxes as my adversary is nowhere to be seen. As I turn from the panel, I realize where he went. Up. This guy is attached to the ceiling by his shoes. That's why I can still smell his breath. He uncoils his body and his face is now one or two inches from mine. He hangs upside down, mocking me with his clown cleverness. Still, he never speaks, only smiles his lopsided evil grin that keeps me in place. How is he doing this? OMG. OMG. OMG. The clown sways back and forth, each time coming so close to my face but never touching me. That's when I feel dizzy, and I can just imagine my skin going catastrophically pale and I collapse. The last thing I see are these oversized half-moon eyes devoid of color blinking their Morse-coded message. They just blink…

When I woke at the hospital, I'm still nervous and quite uneasy and restrained to the bed. But good news! I'm alive, *and* there is this note by the bed from my mom:

> Honey, I heard you took a spill. I'm on the next flight out and will be with you by dinner time. Until then, rest up. I ordered DoorDash and they are bringing you your favorite meal, a Philly Cheesesteak *witout* onions as my sweet monkey-bunny likes it. And keep a lookout for my surprise. I've sent someone to cheer you up; *he's a professional.*

As I am about to call for the nurse to release me, I hear a knock at the door. I look up, and my eyes go wide as my visitor approaches, uninvited. The flower in his lapel drips water onto the floor, his oversized shoes leaving a muddy trail as they drag across the floor. I see his arm swinging his godforsaken rusty horn and smell his decaying breath as he leans over me, blinking and blinking. My heart rate spikes again. He finds the horn's rubber squeezer, and squeeze it he does. Dash Dot Dot (D), Dot Dot (I), Dot (E), then once more with feeling — Dash Dot Dot (D), Dot Dot (I), Dot (E).

I try to call for help, but he extinguished the last bit of my life force with that horn. The sound slowly waned, and I found myself floating like a 99 Cents Only Stores balloon to the ceiling. I looked down and saw the wall monitor chronicling the chaos that was my heart's final rhythm. The machine spelled out panic the only way it could until it changed to a one-note conversation. On the bed was a man I hardly recognized, anxiety-free in death yet drenched in disappointment. ◻

I didn't know heartbreak and suffocating madness that up close and personal until I received my mother's gift. Blinks, honks and fucking fionks.

Mom, you never knew me at all.

See the end of the book for elevator etiquette rules followed or broken. Elevator Etiquette Codes: 3B, 3E, 6B, 6H, 9B, 9H

I Hear You

Unwell Paranoid Android

"Don't feel relieved when entering an empty elevator; be worried when the doors don't open and someone whispers, 'I'm not a ghost.'" -Emma Garcia

Brooklyn looked up at Dr. Kraepelin, hopeful that she would finally have a resolution for her torment.

"And to be clear, you only hear him in your apartment elevator?"

"Well, my soon-to-be-former apartment. I just can't take it anymore. I can't sleep. I'm emotionally exhausted. I'll be out by the end of the month."

"I understand. It can't be easy having it follow you around like that and now you're forced to move. That's a lot Brooklyn," Dr. Kraepelin said, her brown eyes filled with an almost maternal concern. The doctor had grown up in Amityville, New York, so she was familiar and open-minded about the supernatural, but this seemed like something *else*.

"Yeah, to answer your question though, he only appears in the elevator. He sounds like my dad...has his...same friendly demeanor, too. It's way too eerie."

"What does your father's voice say to you?" Brooklyn's eyes darted down as she described very benign and seemingly meaningless interactions. Dr. Kraepelin caught herself frowning as she looked at her client.

"Please remember that the only way this situation can improve is if you truly tell me what's troubling you. Can you give me a little more?" she asked, sending a warm smile to Brooklyn.

Brooklyn nodded and said, "You're right." She added, "Well, I would call him a ghost, but my father is still alive, and I don't think ghosts work like that." Dr. K. silently agreed but still wondered if there was a deeper and different issue with her father.

"This whole situation must be confusing. But we are getting there, Brooklyn. We are closer to you gaining control." Both Dr. K. and Brooklyn thought the meds would be helping by now, but obviously they weren't. Kraepelin wondered what she was missing. *Hmm. Maybe the PSYRATS scale could help.*

As they were winding down their time. Dr. Kraepelin's eyes wandered from Brooklyn's face to the clock on the wall. They had a brief discussion about her medication and agreed to re-evaluate its effectiveness at their next session, if not sooner. It was now 2:49, about 10 minutes until Dr. K.'s next client. She turned to Brooklyn with a smile as she set her notes aside.

"Well, Brooklyn, our time is up for today, but I do hope you have an easier week. As always, I'm here to support you if you need me."

Brooklyn thanked the doctor and drove home quietly, feeling crestfallen. Yet another session had passed without significant progress, and they were expensive. She also felt guilty for not telling Dr. Kraepelin the whole truth —that sometimes the ghost wasn't so nice, that it demanded she do not-so-nice things, like sabotaging the girl at work by sending a nasty email from the girl's computer while she was on her lunch break, or "accidentally on purpose" spilling coffee all over the elevator floor for the janitor to clean up. But *no, sir,* Brooklyn wasn't going to let him get a rise out of her anymore. She just had to ignore her demons, and she'd be free. Just like that.

She entered her apartment elevator and pressed the 6th-floor button. Silent tears streamed down her cheeks; she had really had enough of today. Unfortunately, this was her life without respite. Musing out loud in the empty elevator, she whispered, "Why did I lie to Dr. K. about the ghost?"

Suddenly, the elevator's temperature dropped so sharply that her tears froze mid-drip into little bulbous icicles. She froze, biting her lip as she closed her eyes. She hoped it was just her imagination, but hope wasn't enough. She was trapped in this dark, cold vertical coffin, waiting for the other shoe to drop. That's when she heard her dad's voice.

"You didn't lie, Honey, because I'm not a ghost."

Brooklyn's shallow breaths abruptly stopped, and she felt someone touch her back, but when she turned, no one was there. The hair on the back of her neck stood up as she got chills. Terror, exasperation, and desperation dominated her expression.

"What...are...you?!" she screamed so loudly that her eardrums hurt from the reverberations.

The voice sneered, continuing its rant with a laugh. "I think you knoooow, Brooklyn..." It whispered into her right ear, its breath moist touching the side of her face. The voice continued its creepy monologue in her left ear, "You have a choice to make. If you speak the truth out loud to anyone, only one of us will continue. My bet is it'll be me. Huzzah!" Its voice dropped to a dangerous growl.

Brooklyn shuddered in fear. "How wi—"

"I will know. Every day you keep me out of your mouth, I will let you live another day. I am nothing but generous. Do not speak of me to your friends, family, Dr. K., NO ONE. This starts NOW!" The roaring voice reverberated against the walls, making the elevator shake and the lights flash erratically — off and on, off and on, off and...on. She gasped, goosebumps rising as her dad's voice transformed into the creepiest whisper she'd ever heard. "Is that clear, sweetie?"

The elevator came to a halt, and the doors finally opened, releasing her at last. Brooklyn darted out as fast as she could, but she still felt it's hot, irritated breath on the back of her neck and the wetness on her face. She sprinted down the hallway, entered her place, zigzagged through her obstacle course of moving boxes, and sank into bed. After a few minutes of restless tossing and turning, she was startled by a tiny tongue licking her cheek. Her eyes locked onto the eyes of her therapy dog, who was pawing at her face. With a start, she guiltily remembered that she had forgotten to feed Mr. Meatball.

After scouring the fridge and the pantry, she realized there was no food. Shit. There wasn't really any people food either. Well, there was the mac and cheese that was already a couple of days old, but Mr. Meatball couldn't handle all that salt or milk. He could get diarrhea again, and neither of them needed that crap. Brooklyn didn't really want to go outside right now, but it was getting late, and he needed to eat. So, for Mr. Meatball's sake, she threw all caution to the wind and ventured out of her apartment.

After finding the stairway locked (she would need to talk to the superintendent about that), Brooklyn became incredibly frustrated and panic-stricken. She thought over other ways to get to her car without taking the elevator. What about the fire escape? Too many stories to the hard concrete below—uh, no.

As it turned out, Brooklyn needed to take the elevator, much to her dismay. Frustrated, she mumbled under her breath, "Just two weeks, Meaty, and we are outta here..." Brooklyn and Mr. Meatball entered the elevator and started their hellish journey to the parking garage. The song "Happier" by Bastille and Marshmello started playing in the elevator's background. Brooklyn couldn't help but want to be the girl in that song, her soul yearning for her own happiness.

Just then, frost formed on the metallic elevator walls, and words appeared over the chilled surface, one cursed letter at a time: "DAMMIT I'M MAD." Hearing the squeaks of flesh on metal, Brooklyn turned around with a shudder and saw it written backward, and it said the same damned thing. This time, however, the letters were bleeding, hot, steaming liquid running down the walls. She was being cursed with a bloody palindrome. Holy Hell!

She noticed that Mr. Meatball was barking like crazy. He must've sensed her distress or seen her dad. Brooklyn grounded herself the best she could. She decided to confront this demon head-on and extinguish it once and for all.

"Leave us alone!" she called out shrilly. Then, out of the corner of her eye, she saw a creature of the shadows, an undulating and shimmering corusic. Then another whipped the other way. Mr. Meatball barked again, and Brooklyn felt dizzy and faint from rapidly turning her head back and forth. After a long moment, she slid back against the old wood paneling, listening to the creaking of the old building walls as the wind rushed up her face, and her stomach dropped. The panel lights flashed intermittently, and a techno version of the Halloween movie theme played so loudly that Brooklyn couldn't think straight. As the bass pounded her very being, she wondered joylessly, What the fuck was going on ?!?

The voice cried out again, yelling, "You like elevator music, you filthy bitch?"

"JUST SHUT UP ALREADY! YOU-ARE-NOT-REAL!"

The entity laughed because he was very adamant about his existence. "What did you say, dear? I couldn't hear you over the damn muzak, ha ha ha ha ha!" he sang out, clearly enjoying her garmonbozia.

She roared back, refusing to let him have the upper hand. "You are NOT — mmmphhh!!" Brooklyn screeched in surprise — or at least tried to; as she felt her mouth suddenly being stitched shut by his rough scaly hands, the shadowy corusics intermittently blocking out the light. The hands had no reflection against the walls, but she could still feel the intermittent pricks and the relentless motions going up and down, up and down, over and over, and G-d, when would this STOP already? It was giving her pins and needles. The elevator shook raggedly, and she fell, the seams finally tearing from her mouth and blood spilling out. Horrified, she gazed up at where she thought him to be and felt him running his damp hands all over her face.

"LET GO OF ME!!!" she shouted as she thrashed her whole body about. It was the only thing she could think to do to escape. It didn't work. He forced her firmly in place, pushing her harshly with a laugh and stepping back to admire its handiwork.

"Now that's a sight I could get used to!" he cackled in that harrowing manner, shoving a mirror up to her face, where she caught sight of her own tragic reflection. Tears of shock trembled in her wide green eyes as she brought her hand up to her countenance.

A horrible, torn-up burn took up the entirety of her left cheek, and her fingers shook as she ran them over the indents and bumps of molten red skin. She hissed and shook her head, only then realizing that the stitches were gone from her mouth. But she couldn't even think about that right now. What on Earth happened?! Had she truly burned? What was this??... *Oh Lord...*

She took a minute, catching her breath so that she wouldn't throw up, breath after breath after breath. She remembered Dr. Kraepelin's voice in her head, as she went through her breathing exercises slowly, peacefully, and methodically. When she regained her composure, she took all the energy she had left to face the cacodemon again. She marched right up to him for the final confrontation.

Shivering and raging, she pounded her fists against him again and again, until she finally wore herself out. When her vision cleared, he was gone, but the elevator walls were dented and smeared with her blood. She covered her purpling hands over her eyes, and tears trickled out between her traumatized fingers. She trembled and dried them off, picking up Mr. Meatball, whom she held tight in protection. Her voice wavered as she shouted, and her eyes streamed with even more tears.

Brooklyn hollered at the top of her lungs in rage, "You goddamned psycho!!! I don't know who you are, or what you are, but in a few weeks you will be out of our lives forever!" The ferocious intensity that she used to fling out that last word scratched the back of her throat, causing her to cough uncontrollably.

The lights fluttered as the entity chuckled again. It surrounded the elevator with a dark tenacity, a smug authority. Its voice reverberated between the elevator walls, drawing Brooklyn's attention back to its presence and the dreadfulness of her reality.

"Brooklyn, go along and finish packing. Don't keep me waiting, honey. **I'm so excited to see our new place."**

See the end of the book for elevator etiquette rules followed or broken. Elevator Etiquette Codes: 2A, 2D, 2F, 6H, 9B, 9H

The Sign Lies

After-Hours Grind Steals Your Soul

"Take the Stairs, Take the Stairs, For G-d's Sake, Take The Stairs." -Movie Poster for **The Lift (Media Home Entertainment, 1983)**

Consider this. There is a sign in most elevators, and most people give it the same attention they give flight attendants when they show you how to buckle a seatbelt. Except for me.

> ***SHOULD THE ELEVATOR DOORS FAIL TO OPEN, DO NOT BECOME ALARMED.***

It has been a long time since the elevator jolted to an abrupt stop. My head is pounding as I try to regain my balance after the initial shock wears off. I should have expected that, considering no one else besides me is here. I'm all alone during Thanksgiving week, and corporate gave us the choice to take five vacation days off work, which, unsurprisingly, most people took. I'm cursing myself for coming into this fifteen-story office to get ahead on a fucking report. I begin to feel sick to my stomach as my eyesight fills with blurred images mixed with sweat droplets from my overheated body. The four sides of the elevator look like they are closing in on me. I have not moved an inch. I'm not going crazy; I have nothing to hold on to besides a rickety handrail that jiggles as the elevator continues its journey into hell. This is not a good time to faint. I'll become alarmed if I want to. *Don't tell me what to do.*

The elevator passes one floor, then another. Now we're getting somewhere. See? No need to be alarmed.

A crash, followed by a rattle, assaults my eardrums. I hear a crack from behind the wall. The car shakes so violently that I stumble. I grab the handrail to keep from falling as my face hovers inches from the floor. After regaining my balance, I rise to see the following words:

THERE IS LITTLE DANGER OF RUNNING OUT OF AIR OR OF THIS ELEVATOR DROPPING UNCONTROLLABLY.

Danger. Running out of air. Dropping uncontrollably. I scream for help, but no one can hear me. My throat is hoarse, and I begin to shake. I try to do my breathing exercises, but I can't focus. Inhale. Exhale. Inhale. Exha... I'm breathing way too fast, my gasps coming one after another. I'm definitely wasting oxygen. I bang on the doors, sweating a lot, and I realize I left my water bottle on my desk. I open and close my clammy hands, but I think I'm losing feeling in them. What if my erratic movements cause the elevator to give out and just... drop. *Shit.*

PLEASE USE THE BUTTON MARKED "EMERGENCY" OR TELEPHONE (IF FURNISHED) TO SUMMON AID.

The doors aren't opening. THE DOORS ARE NOT OPENING. I press the emergency button. It blares like it did the last 10 times. Did anyone hear it from outside? I press the button again. I feel the smooth surface move under my sweaty index finger and return to its place. There is no telephone inside the elevator. The only thing left is a useless, dangling cord next to the panel, and I have no cell service to call 911. I have no Wi-Fi. I have nothing.

My mouth feels like a desert, and my vision fills with spots, teasing me with the prospect of fainting inside this subzero containment. The elevator suddenly drops, maybe two or three feet. Or maybe I'm losing my balance — what day is it? I lean on the handrail; it feels like it will give out at any moment. The closed doors trap me in this frigid prison that drops my body temperature lower and lower. I feel nauseous as my vision changes from blurry to black. I may have definitively figured out what happened to Tony Soprano.

ELEVATOR COMPANIES ARE ON CALL 24 HOURS A DAY FOR EMERGENCY SERVICE.

It's been three days. I spend them drifting between consciousness. I don't know who these elevator companies are or when they are coming. My wife is on a silent retreat; I don't even know if she is allowed to check in with me. I miss my wife and envy her at the same time. I shouldn't be here; I should be anywhere but here, inhaling oxygen like I'd never have it again. My car is only 50 yards away, but it's like 50 miles. Same difference. The overhead lights just went out and died. Oh shit, who is feeding the dogs or the fish?

My joints ache, and my bones grind together with every movement. My chest feels tight, and my heart beats a mile a minute. I don't have my meds with me, and I don't think it matters. A millennium has passed since the elevator doors refused to open, with no response to my banging, yelling for help, or pressing the emergency button. Everyone is away enjoying their holiday, while I remain trapped in a prison with no guard.

I'm freezing now, probably from hypothermia, exhaustion, and isolation. I can't feel my limbs, which lie limp on the floor as I cry in a fetal position. I can barely lift my arms to keep banging on the doors that would free me from this metallic hell. I barely manage to hold my phone, press record, and say, "Goodbye" to everyone who mattered to me for the last time.

As I lie there on the floor, I close my eyes and wait.

See the end of the book for elevator etiquette rules followed or broken. Elevator Etiquette Codes: 3B, 3E

Muzak

The Bleeding Edge of Exasperation

"I worry that the person who thought up Muzak may be thinking up something else." -Lily Tomlin

Consider this. The elevator's hatch lamp buzzes above Archie's head as he scowls up at it. He is fascinated, but annoyed. He notices the dead moths, flies, and other little insects that have crawled their way into the fixture. Drawn by the flickering light, their tiny silhouettes are illuminated from above. Archie ponders their grim fate, how horrifying it is that they've voluntarily entered this suffocating space from which they would never leave. He finds himself hyper-fixated on this light. Is there a pattern to the flickering? Why is it flickering to begin with? Is it incandescent, compact fluorescent, or LED? Something else? Why is the bulb so dim? Why hasn't maintenance replaced the bulb? He sighs and looks at his watch. He's impatiently impatient waiting inside this stupid elevator, alone with his thoughts for what feels like a millennium, even though he knows it's only been a few minutes.

Then something sinister takes hold of his senses. He recognizes it almost immediately. Even more unbearable, it's that dreadful *Muzak* — the mind-numbing jingles that torment consumers and elevator riders alike. Beyond that, it plays at an obnoxiously loud volume, earworming its way deep into his psyche, determined to strip him of his sanity one maddening track at a time. Quite frankly, it doesn't need to be this loud, but it is. Has anyone ever seen an elevator with a volume knob?

Buzz, buzz. Archie pulls his cell phone from his back pocket. It's his fiancée, Josie. *Please hurry, I have to get back to work;* she writes. He had excitedly run straight to City Hall to meet his beautiful wife-to-be. They had planned to meet during their lunch breaks to get their marriage license together. This was supposed to be the start of the rest of their lives. Archie could hardly contain his enthusiasm as he replied, "Already on my way!" He stuffs his phone back into his pocket and glares at the slowly changing numbers above the elevator doors. The elevator runs at its own pace, mocking any thought of control Archie perceives to have.

OMG! This has to be the most agonizingly slow elevator ride in history. Archie is usually the most optimistic and happy person, but this was cruel and unusual punishment. Not only has Archie been forced to listen to terrible song after terrible song, but he also has to deal with his surroundings fluttering in and out of the darkness. Whoever didn't clean the lamp of insects also didn't tighten the lamp bulb. How hard could maintaining a small environment be? Archie's obsessions were slowly breaking him from reality. Why has fate landed Archie into this ascending sarcophagus on one of the biggest days of his life? *Should've taken the stairs*, Archie thought, but it's far too late for that now. He knows well that his full attention should be on his future wife and her gorgeous smile, pen in hand, waiting to make it all official; but my G-d he feels like his ears are bleeding. How much more could he possibly stand?

Ding! The elevator jolts to a stop. Archie looks up and is hit with a wave of disappointment when he sees the elevator go past his floor. The doors open and a tall older man steps in. He's wearing an all-white suit, expensive silver cufflinks, and a skinny black tie. He nods, acknowledging Archie's presence, then pushes the button for his floor. Sadly, it happens to be in the opposite direction from where Archie needed to be. It's as if Archie never pushed the button for his floor. That surely could not be. Looking at the panel, the button for floor 7 was clearly lit. Still, all of Archie's button-pushing directives did not take priority. The elevator doors shut again, and the two men are now going back down to the lobby. The elevator is serving the playlist of Archie's personal purgatory, which right now is playing "The Girl From Ipanema."

The man taps his metallic silver tie tack, then turns his back to Archie. Archie pays no mind, as he is too distressed. He should be excited to see Josie, excited to start this new chapter in his life. He checks the time on his phone. He has 40 minutes until he needs to be back in the office. He has several missed calls from Josie. He is so close to where he needs to be, but so far at the same time. It's not a paradox when both things are true.

The next tiresome instrumental song starts to play. This track is the most annoying, torturous, displeasing thing he has ever heard. He tries with all his might not to scream and bash his head against the wall. However, he couldn't help it. Bam! Oh boy, is he lucky the walls are padded. Shocked and disturbed, the old man inches away from Archie. He pushes himself as far as he can into the corner and stares intently at his phone, trying to ignore Archie's embarrassing tantrum.

Understand, Archie is usually a very upstanding individual, but these specific songs press just the right buttons to make him lose his goddamn mind. Archie knows the Muzak is mocking him and that it enjoys his suffering. It wanted to drive him crazy, and maybe it had. This hatred has overwhelmed his entire nervous system: his thoughts are racing, his hands are trembling, and his body feels like there is a heat bubble around him, which is vibrating like an overloading Marshall amp.

The older man, ignoring Archie, unexpectedly lets out a whoop of disappointment mixed with despair. He had been trying to look at porn on his phone, which wouldn't completely load because the internet in here is shit. Archie is ignoring him too, as he has bigger things to worry about. Like what? Maybe the fact that he is so close to getting married, and the universe is doing its worst to stop him from getting there. Or, worse yet, that this elevator music is still playing. How could it possibly be getting louder?!?

It had taken some time for Josie and Archie to coordinate getting to City Hall. Remember Josie? This is a story about Archie and Josie. And Muzak. Sadly, the couple had been ecstatic to be finally tying the knot, but now the future is unknown. Archie feels he wouldn't be able to survive if this Winchester Cathedral Muzak escalation keeps going. It sure feels hot in this box and he wants to throw up. Well, he doesn't *want* to, but he just might.

All this torture on such an important day must be a sign that this is not meant to be. The fantasy of his fiancée in her wedding dress isn't enough to keep Archie motivated. He grabs his cell phone but hesitates to dial Josie. He wants to apologize and explain, but nothing about this makes sense. He had wanted to marry Josie and didn't have cold feet. But now, the Muzak, the Muzak has eaten away at his soul until he couldn't bear it any longer. *Is this who I've become,* he questioned. No matter, his main goals now are self-preservation and getting out of this godforsaken elevator. He hammers the button for the ground floor so hard he cracks the plastic.

When the elevator finally stops and the doors open, Archie tumbles out and onto the cold marble floor, half in and half out of the dirty elevator. His phone falls flat in front of him and vibrates aggressively. Archie makes a meek attempt to reach for it, but instead, his arm drops like a rag doll. The tall, older man steps out of the elevator. He looks at Archie for a brief moment, perhaps wanting to say something. A mixture of sadness and disgust is on his face. Exiting the elevator, he steps over Archie and gives him a kick to the gut. *Fair*, Archie thought. He was letting a lot of people down, and so he felt he had it coming.

The doors attempt to close but cannot entirely because of Archie's unresponsive body. The Muzak changes to a version of Michael Jackson's "Smooth Criminal". Archie's phone is flooded with urgent texts from Josie. "Archie, are you ok? Are you ok, Archie?" The elevator makes a horrible screeching noise, which is elevator speak for GET THE FUCK OUT, which is at least drowning out the Muzak, which will never ever stop playing.

See the end of the book for elevator etiquette rules followed or broken. Elevator Etiquette Codes: 1B, 2B, 2D, 2F, 3B, 3D, 4C, 5A, 5D, 5E, 6B, 6E, 6H, 6I, 7A

New Elevator Boy

Sound Stream of Incomprehensibility

"It was impossible to get a conversation going; everybody was talking too much." -Yogi Berra

Consider this. For any of you who were born in this century, an elevator operator was the guy who made sure the door closed and remained shut properly, and no one's limbs were lost in the process.

This building on Milliton Street is my home. Living here for so long, I know all the ins and outs of this place. My apartment is so old that the carpet is still shaggy, and my cheapskate landlord used some sort of historical preservation law to get around expensive renovations. Pays some kid minimum wage to be the "Elevator Boy," to make sure the ancient, decrepit machine doesn't kill anyone again. Usually, these kids are fine, but not always. These minimum wage laborers pull the door shut and pray that the elevator doesn't unexpectedly drop four floors like it did to Mr. O'Brien, may G-d rest his soul. Anyway, the new elevator boy's name was Oli. He's been here a few weeks. Seems like much longer.

I'm not much of a fan of the new elevator operator. That kid just won't stop with the mouth. He goes on and on and on and on about that Ginger chick. You know, the one who sang "Booty Shake, Booty Quake". What was her name again? Ginger Breadman? I swear, he must be in love with her or something because he ate, drank, and breathed Ginger. He says he used to like Courtney Barnett, but that velvet crush is history. Anyway, the elevator could plummet and he wouldn't notice with him watching videos on his phone of that Ginger.

Three generations of my family have lived on Milliton, and he is by far the worst of the revolving door circus the landlord's got going. So many people take the stairs now due to him. They vote with their feet. Even 80-year-old Mikey has had it with this guy — and Mikey likes everyone.

One day, after waiting six minutes for the rickety old elevator, I decided to take the stairs myself. I bumped into Mikey on the way up while he was hobbling down, hand tight on the rail. "Why not take the elevator?" I asked him. "That way you don't fall and, G-d forbid, die?"

It's that new elevator boy. Well, he is..." he trailed off, searching for nicer words. "He's not for me, and he wouldn't have been for your grandmother, either." Then Mikey spat and ground it into the step.

My main issue with Oli is that he doesn't keep quiet. On my last day on the elevator with Oli, I was watching the wall move vertically through the elevator window. Oli was zoned out to his 21st-century handheld idiot box. Whenever he was on that thing, a tiger could walk in and he wouldn't notice. I blame Steve Jobs.

His primary duty is to fully shut the elevator door on this death trap, but safety is never a priority for Oli on days that end in Y. This terrifies me. Even though I'm on the heavy side, I'm still skinny enough that I could fall right through that gap. Then there is that faint smell when I swear the metal bits are being ground into dust. Oli just smiles and opens his mouth like a koi fish in heat when the grinding metal sparkler show happens. I want to scream at this kid, but a part of me knows deep down that it's not his fault that he's so clueless.

So, there Oli was, standing at his usual position, idiot box in hand, when suddenly a jarring viola emanated from his speakers. It was Ginger's cover of "The Black Angel's Death Song" by The Velvet Underground. Oli started jumping and singing along with Ginger's vocals. The elevator started bouncing in sympathy. Then Oli added some unhinged laughter to his karaoke adjacent performance. I backed up towards the wall, gripping the handrail to stabilize myself as Oli continued to flail around as he sang the words off-key. Finally, the elevator slowed to a stop as we neared my floor. The elevator was fully wobbling and shaking like a yo-yo on a flimsy string. When he delivered me to the lobby, he slid the cage open and then the doors. I walked out smoothly so as to not provoke Oli into doing something even more disturbing.

I exited that death trap with clarity — Oli could have the elevator, I'd stick to the stairs.

See the end of the book for elevator etiquette rules followed or broken. Elevator Etiquette Codes: 3A, 5D, 5E, 6C, 6H, 9B

Sleepy Time
NOT RUNNING DOWN A DREAM

"Everything you ever wanted is on the other side of your dreams, if you would only wake up." -Rozerik Ross Milstein

Consider this. The place where Zakari Ma'aliyah resides was not the best place for a good night's sleep. The managers had a one-star ranking, and their superhost status was lost, like Z's ability to sleep. The walls were paper thin, with one room being next to an infant's nonstop crying, and the other was a room populated by questionable guests. These neighbors would often get into loud, violent, and sometimes horny altercations. If that wasn't enough, he lived near the Kfar Saba–Nordau station, and the room would constantly shake and nerves would rattle as the engines roared by, given its proximity to the station. Zakari lived with this for years. The rent was super cheap, but now the baby made the situation super untenable.

With his accountancy workplace in sight, Zakari had no idea how he was going to get through the day. It was just before 9 am, and he was already mentally and physically exhausted. Z willed himself up the front stairs into the lobby. He leaned against the wall adjacent to the elevator. It arrived at the lobby floor, and when the door opened, he was greeted with the smell of espresso. He wished the brew was his own. The tired accountant made his way into the shabby elevator with its peeling floor and ancient, grimy panel system. He communicated his other request — to reach the 19th floor of the 81-floor building — to a coworker standing by the panel, then moved to the left and leaned against the wall. His colleagues looked at his bloodshot eyes, unshaven face, and disheveled sport jacket and wrinkled slacks. They would have thought he was actually unhoused if they didn't already know him. He looked up at the digital display of the floor as he ascended into the abyss. As the numbers rose, his vision went black briefly. He then mumbled something unintelligible as his head jolted with a start. Just then...

... his eyes opened with a surprised vision. A disapproving businesswoman shook her head repeatedly as she exited on floor 27 — he had missed his stop! What was a blink must have actually been a few minutes. Frustrated and a bit dizzy, he staggered over to the panel, noticed sweat stains on his tank top, and pressed the 42 button. He almost bumped into a woman, who scoffed in annoyance as she shifted backward. He held fast to the handrail along the wall. The elevator descended, Muzak soothing his soul as it encompassed the elevator with the relaxing vibrations of a Calgon commercial. *Ohhh,* Zakari thought nostalgically as he was taken away to a time his mother sang him that same song, and how he was snuggled, all nice and cozy, and...

... once again, Zakari found himself somewhere unexpected. The open doors revealed the parking garage level, and he shifted himself closer to the panel as the elevator filled up with smokers, vapers, and architects. Samuel, a co-worker whose office was one floor below Zakari, wondered to himself why Zakari was already in the elevator when it arrived to pick up new passengers.

"You been sleeping at the office again, Zak?" Samuel joked.

Zakari rolled his eyes as Samuel entered the elevator, but he didn't have any energy for a comeback. He simply pushed the button for the 42nd floor — again, and willed himself to stay awake, but his willpower was shit.

"So you wanna hit Tomfoolery's with us tonight?" Samuel asked. "Nikolai and I are having a bet to see who makes the playoffs. My bet's on the Ukraine Unicorns. I just have a good feeling about them. It's like I always say..."

Zakari rubbed his eyes with his palms. He couldn't take the incessant talking. The more Samuel spoke, the more he droned on, and the more Zakari's eyelids drooped heavily. He was out.

This time, the elevator stopped at the 101st floor. Zakari knew that couldn't be right; the building only had 81 floors. The doors slid open, revealing executive bigwigs playing a round of office golf, drinking from the finest wineskins while they were entertained by the Paris Opera Ballet. Zakari attempted to shake the vision from his head, but the scene in front of him wouldn't dissipate. However, the figures and colors blurred as he found himself swaying back and forth, hovering just below and then just above consciousness. He slapped himself silly to try to stay awake. Now he was late for work.

"FORE!" cried out one executive.

Zakari ducked his head as a golf ball ricocheted, bouncing back and forth in the elevator, creating a rhythmic pattern and barely missing him. It struck the elevator button going to the 1000th floor...the 1000th floor?! And once the doors closed, Zak was off to the races.

Suddenly, the elevator was rushing upwards at blinding speeds, as it entered outer space. The accountant staggered back as he grabbed the railings with both hands as tightly as he could. The elevator ascended higher and higher until the lift came to an abrupt stop. From the momentum change, Zakari almost collided with the ceiling as his feet lifted off the ground before he fell down in a disheveled heap on the elevator floor. The doors opened automatically and Zakari's jaw dropped as he gazed upon a starry void stretching out before him, erupting into a kaleidoscope of vibrant colors. Zakari was viewing time and space itself and was terrified as much as awed.

"ZAKARI MA'AlLIYAH!"

He was suddenly in his standard 6x6 ft cubicle, facedown in drool. Zakari had no clue how he got there, but with a disgruntled manager staring lasers into the back of his head, Zakari knew he was in trouble.

We have deadlines. Get it together, Zakari, or you're fired." His boss turned his back, muttered something about the dress code and no jeans, and walked away in righteous anger.

And with that dire warning, Zakari gave him the finger, well both of them. He set the phone to wake him up in an hour and laid his head down on his desk like an obedient kindergartener. If his armageddon was coming, at least he would greet it well-rested and with a smile.

See the end of the book for elevator etiquette rules followed or broken.
Elevator Etiquette Codes: 2D, 2G, 3A, 3B, 4A, 6C, 7D

American Paternoster

American Paternoster Duology, Pt. I

"Never judge one's hobbies as they may change the world. If they destroy the world, then go ahead and judge."
-Rozerik Ross Milstein

Consider this. What puts the pro in professor? Maybe it's being able to persistently stay in school, even when glory may call you elsewhere. Some may say it's distinguished by the number of awards you've received. For 63-year-old Warren Temple, Professor of Architecture, the moment was his epiphany to revamp the foreign passenger elevator known as the paternoster. The once great visionary, who had designed the most sturdy of skyscrapers, was now taken down several notches in all aspects of his life. While he used to have state-of-the-art computer-assisted methods at his disposal, Warren now designed with Nanoblocks, a Glowforge, and occasionally Legos. He dreamt of what he used to be while lounging in his basement like a hermit.

Back when things were "good," his girlfriend's brother ran the dodgy company that managed the construction based on Warren's designs. Warren eventually married Narcissa, and it became more than a convenience to have a wife whose reputation also depended on his architecture career running smoothly. She was far from innocent here and had no problem with Warren when they were making bank. In fact she sung his praises to anyone who would listen. He had been building momentum in his career and some of his gains bordered on — no actually were — illegal. And by complete coincidence, Warren understood his wife was not obligated to testify against him if these occasional events went sideways. After a series of "accidents" on various construction sites affiliated with Narcissa and Warren, their attorney Charlie Myrno advised that the most recent episode *had to be the last time.*

Due to a decades long struggle with depression, he hadn't worked consistently on any significant designs since the 90s. Riding on the edge of the law had excited Narcissa, and making big money was icing on the cake. However, her brother's company and her patience with Warren's despondency and reduced income had long since vanished. Even though she still cared for him deep down, Warren lost her respect and years ago she began to cheat. For financial convenience, however, they continued to cohabitate, purely as roommates. They both knew the ticking time bomb of divorce (once they had the money for it) was around the corner, but for now, cohabitating seemed to work just fine — or so they thought.

Back in the day, Warren had loved her enough to put a ring on her finger, but now they both realized they were quietly drifting in different directions. When Narcissa confronted him about how much flirty time he spent with his old co-worker, Halford, and Warren stared down at his Hush Puppies in silence, she realized any hope for the Temples' future romance was extinguished. He also looked the other way when she brought online dates to the house from Silver Singles, OurTime and occasionally Tinder. He took a respite from his embarrassment and her nagging by sequestering himself in his basement workshop. □

Warren's life was becoming monotonous. Closing his eyes, he reminisced about the glory days. He remembered watching the city turn miniature beneath him as he rode the steel elevator to the top floor. The air was crisp and minty in his nostrils as he stood on the penthouse balcony of the tallest building he'd ever worked on. Opening his eyes, he ran a hand over his tan, unshaven face and scratched his chin. The reduction of income, and excitement really, along with a cognitive decline, took a toll on their relationship. Warren knew these downturns could be reversed, and he just needed a catalytic jump start. But from where? Sure, he loved to teach his students, but he missed the thrill of visiting the construction site. He yearned for the jackhammer's blown-up dust to tickle his cheek once more as the concrete sidewalk was poured to precision in front of him. There was nothing like seeing his designs rise into the clouds like Jack and the Beanstalk. Though that was all in the past; what remained were nights spent eating pizza rolls and grading papers. Usually, he would relax by daydreaming about what his next great idea would be and FaceTiming with Halford.

Warren met Halford back in their college days. Halford had come to America as a foreign exchange student from the Czech Republic, and they quickly became inseparable friends. A flicker of something more always lingered between them, but neither acted on their feelings. Instead, early in their architecture careers, they simply focused on enjoying their collaborations. Halford was much more shy then and was disappointed by how Narcissa was monopolizing Warren's time. Eventually, Warren married Narcissa, and Halford returned to Prague, but always made an effort to stay in touch. Things went well for Halford, and he was able to set up a foundation to grant design scholarships to students in need. Now, many years later, Halford got a call asking him to return to America and be an Adjunct Professor at Warren's school for the upcoming semester. Of course he accepted and they treated him like royalty. Knowing that Narcissa was on the way out, Halford became giddy at the thought of being reunited with his old crush, and maybe having a second chance at love.

As Warren retreated to the basement, his foot caught the side of a dusty Banker's box. He picked it up, thinking it was his old DVD collection of *The Brady Bunch,* but it was something better. Aha! It was his old Sega SG-1000 console and favorite game, *Elevator Action*, from way back in '85. Playing as Agent 17, he had blasted enemy spies in the platform-shooter-style game for quite some time. In the game, he used an elevator to move floors, but the problem was that there was only one elevator that went up and down. If only it could rotate. Something was bubbling to the surface of his consciousness; he just didn't know what it was yet. He swam around in his thoughts until he remembered the other night when he watched *The Omen*. Not the crap one from 2006, but the classic film from 1976. Anyway, Warren saw his answer...the *paternoster*.

"Yes! Holy shit. That's what I'm going to do. I'm going to Americanize the paternoster and revolutionize the next generation of office buildings!" He was back in the game, and for awhile his depression abated. He ran the fastest he had in years to his drafting table, mumbling along the way which tools he would need to begin work. Electricity was coursing through his veins; this was the most energetic and sharp Warren had been in years. He knew if he could pull this off, it would be epic. He began his research and found that the paternoster was a risky invention, being an elevator with a chain of open compartments moving continuously in a slow loop. Many had met their demise on a paternoster. In court documents, some prosecutors called it the "Elevator of Death," but Warren paid no attention to that detail. Only the most significant successes came with the biggest risks, right? What could go wrong?

Plenty.

It had been almost two months since Warren began his new unpermitted project. He had some dirt on the chairmen at City Hall and would figure out the paperwork later. Halford had previously provided some helpful firsthand insight on paternosters since there were some still in use in Prague. Narcissa, in the meantime, saw Warren immersing himself in a new project, and out of irrational jealousy, became insufferable. Narcissa felt there was not much use for him since their relationship and finances had backpedaled. He felt guilty about their lifestyle change, and that was the only reason he put up with her wicked ways. However, he hated it when she rang that damn service bell for him to wait on her. (She never was a charming woman.) Warren "lost" the bell and crafted a replacement one in the shape of a woman's breast. He was hoping to embarrass her into stopping this service bell bullshit, but she threw it at the window, shattering the glass — only to whine at him to fix it because a chill began creeping in.

Warren could only find true peace from her constant nagging when he was teaching in the basement or during his video calls with Halford, which made his heart skip a beat. Warren and Halford would spend hours conversing, talking about random bits of their day, or the progress Warren had enjoyed with his paternoster project. He was inspired and felt appreciated when Halford was interested in his big, possibly insane ideas. *It would be nice to have him around all the time*. Warren was convinced he had a multimillion-dollar idea, maybe more. Narcissa thought it was shit.

Night after night, Warren would emerge from the depths of the basement resembling a wild-greased monkey. He would even shower with the powerful combination of Fast Orange hand cleaner and Defense Tea Tree soap. Nevertheless, his wife would still make him sleep on the couch as part of their sleep divorce. The irony was even though they slept in different rooms, she claimed his odor was too intense, as it "wafted" under *her* door.

Warren compartmentalized his feelings as he encountered his first major obstacle because of the limitations of the workspace allotted in his basement. By now, he had a fully functioning prototype of his "American" paternoster, but there wasn't enough space to make two rotating elevator changes. He had to figure out some way to mind the gap.

It was Taco Tuesday, and he was excitedly poking and prodding the finer engineering details of his new creation. Narcissa had been out all night on a date, leaving Warren and Halford alone to tweak the paternoster. It was nearing 3 A.M. when they heard the front door slam and angry footsteps coming down the stairs. Normally, Warren and Narcissa acted like the other was invisible, but tonight she'd indulged in more than her usual. As an angry drunk, she seethed when she saw Taco Bell wrappers on the basement floor. She *knew* Del Taco had superior Mexican fast food and *knew* he rang "The Bell" to spite her. She hiccupped down the wooden stairs, relying on the railing to balance herself as she muttered incoherent curses upon seeing Halford pass Warren a cold brew. It was Warren and Halford's last night together before Halford had to return to Europe, and this was not how it was supposed to go.

Narcissa pointed a finger at Halford and drunkenly slurred, "*You*. You ruined everything with your sexting and your perfect abs. I've seen it all, including your dick pics. I know you're plotting against me!" She sounded like an intoxicated supervillain. Narcissa stumbled backward but regained her equilibrium — just barely.

Warren sighed at the display, and Halford started to hum Madonna's "Borderline." Why couldn't Narcissa have just gone to bed? While this situation was uncomfortable for everyone, Halford moved towards the couch, the best place to see the show. Warren was embarrassed by her actions and exhaled slowly. He urged Halford to go home and they would talk tomorrow after his plane landed. Halford agreed and compassionately squeezed Warren's shoulder in sympathy. As he trudged up the stairs, he turned to give Warren a final look before leaving. Narcissa brought Warren's attention back to her with alternating scoffs and eye-rolls. She was relatively incoherent but managed to call him several insults from her upbringing. He was able to make out the phrase "fruit bag," even going as far as to call him a "Moses Hole," and when she finally told him to find Jesus, it made his anger boil as she knew he loved Jesus! She started to disrespect his tools, even throwing a wrench right over Warren's head. As she continued judging him, she unconsciously backed up towards his paternoster, and with each step, swayed like she was standing on a boat at sea. Her mocking laughter echoed off the walls and into his psyche. He knew there was a kernel of truth to her frustrations which made his blood boil.

As Warren gathered enough courage to face her, his expression became contorted with horror. Narcissa had more rage than balance and as she lunged at him, his eyebrows went higher than any skyscraper he designed. "The Elevator of Death" waited patiently as Warren's arms stretched out as if they were a mile long to save her. Narcissa's foot had slipped, and she tumbled back down the open shaft of the prototype elevator.

He cringed upon hearing her body thud on the ground and horrifyingly recalled how he innovated the paternoster to automatically start when it sensed a passenger. He ran, looking to cut the power double-quick. As his wife lay moaning, she slurred her words about a chicken quesadilla combo with queso-loaded fries, until the automated model paternoster rotated to the next chamber. With the rest of her strength, she muttered "damn waffle stompers," before a loud crunching noise silenced her pained screams.

Shit.

TO BE CONTINUED

See the end of the book for elevator etiquette rules followed or broken. Elevator Etiquette Codes: 9A & 9F

Foreign Exchange

American Paternoster Duology, Pt. II

"Loving life is easy when you are abroad, where no one knows you and you hold your life in your hands all alone, you are more master of yourself than any other time."
-Hannah Arendt

Consider this. And this isn't good. Professor Warren Temple's very dead wife, Narcissa, lay still and silent at the bottom of the prototype elevator shaft he had made in his basement. The fluorescent lights flickered above the new widower as he drew near her body. He let go of a breath he didn't know he was holding when he saw her. Blood was splattered everywhere, and her gangly limbs were twisted and visibly crushed. Her eyes stared lifelessly back at him with contempt, one a little popped out of its socket. He couldn't take his eyes off her, praying it was an illusion or an elaborate prank.

Indeed, any moment now a camera crew would roll out whilst her bones snapped back into place, and she would climb out of the hole saying "Gotcha, fruit bag!" but she was never funny that way. Instead, there was only icy silence. Warren stumbled backward, bumping into his workbench and falling into the chair next to it. Leaning over and putting his head in his hands, his vision blurred with tears. His life as he knew it was over. He should call the police, right? It was an accident...right? Besides, she was hammered and fell on her own. Warren knew the police had been waiting for him to slip up for years, and he would not give them the satisfaction. Halford, Warren's old co-worker and not-so-secret lover, had been over earlier and witnessed her drunken state. As luck would have it, he was traveling back to the Czech Republic in the morning since the semester was over and his visa was up. Warren's only witness had left the building.

He sighed and was ultimately conflicted about his wife's death. On the one hand, his American paternoster prototype had proved to run successfully (when it wasn't killing intoxicated spouses) and was therefore ready to move into the refinement phase. On the other hand, a dead wife. Legs shaking, he got up and peered over the edge. Oh G-d, she looked like she was soaking in a bloodbath. *I'm gonna be sick,* he thought.

Hours passed after she died, and every time he went near the scene to clean up, he gagged at the sight. He couldn't realistically disassemble the prototype, and it's not like he could throw a tarp over it and call it a day. He dry-heaved ever time he glanced at the contrasting paleness of her skin against the blood-drying black. Soon, emotions escalated, and he puked so much that he couldn't go into the basement anymore from the smell of death mixed with his own vomit. He decided he couldn't stay in the house any longer either, knowing she was down there.

In the earlier days of his fledgling architecture career, Warren had witnessed multiple deaths related to his designs. Some fatalities were negligent, some deaths were engineered. Even though it had been years, Warren knew the drill. He had his attorney, Charlie Myrno, Esq., on lifetime retainer, and that dude's work was priceless: a fixer who someway, somehow could always find the way out.

With trembling fingers, Warren dialed the number they had set up years ago. He waited for Charlie's signature Southwestern accent, but a voicemail menu popped up instead.

Warren and Narcissa, Press 1 if you are currently in jail.

Press 2 if you need to bribe someone out of a potential lawsuit.

Press 3 if there was an accidental death and you need to flee the country.

Press 4 if —

Warren pressed three. Another message came on and he scrambled to find a pen as it granted him coded coordinates and actions to take. He was instructed to bring a shovel to unearth the cases whose contents would help him disguise his identity and get out of Dodge. He thought about taking one last look at his dead wife, but that was not happening. This was it. He was leaving and never coming back.

Per their agreement, Charlie and Warren would rehearse this drill every five years. Charlie would be responsible for refreshing the locations and contents of the escape repositories, including the fake passports for Warren and Narcissa every ten years. He also included his and hers international burner phones for the Temples. Warren was given instructions reminding him of a specific sequence of necessary events before driving to the coordinates. Finally, he would await separate details regarding the Swiss bank account that was set up for him. (Narcissa never knew about the additional money.) It took him about an hour to reach the designated spot, and Warren began digging frantically. His shovel hit something hard, and he pulled one large suitcase out of the ground. It was filled with clothes from around 2010, so Charlie was a bit behind in refreshing the case. There was nothing Warren could do with a maxi dress, bohemian headbands or gel nail polish. He could use the included facial disguises though. A companion box contained a selfie stick, a "Gangnam Style" CD to listen to on the plane, *a lot* of unmarked bills, and just barely usable counterfeit passports for Warren and Narcissa. Per their arrangement, once the suitcase and the supply box were recovered, and the Swiss bank account information was disseminated, the Temples would be on their own.

Before driving to the airport, Warren bought a one-way ticket to the Czech Republic in the name of Thomas Westphall. Waiting for his turn in the TSA line, he sweated so much that the edges of his fake mustache started to peel back, but he was cleared to the gates without incident or suspicion.

All morning Warren declined calls from Halford, telling him he arrived safely and already missed him. His mind never stopped working and would jump back and forth between details regarding his American paternoster, his decomposing wife, and Halford. Right now, Warren had to focus. Obviously, he wouldn't be able to ghost Halford forever. Once he got settled in Prague, he would explain. After all, this was the man Warren wanted to spend the rest of his life with. ☐

The plane ride was long, too long for Warren, as he couldn't sleep a wink. Every time he closed his eyes, he ruminated over Narcissa's mangled body. He exited the airport, coming to find a driver standing next to a taxi with Thomas Westphall written on the name card. He picked up his burner phone and texted Halford 50° 4′ 25.1688″ N and 14° 25′ 6.7440′, then XAM. Warren verified the digital transmission with their personal emoji, Wind Face.

After checking into a hotel that had one of the remaining working paternosters, he made his way to his room to crash. For one brief moment, the tragedy of his wife was forgotten and replaced by his anticipation for Halford.

The next morning, Warren was almost completely lost in his thoughts when his phone alarm brought him back to the present. Warren, still in disguise, entered the hotel lobby paternoster. After it completed one full rotation, it was *go time*. Warren noticed Halford enter the lobby at 10 am for their rendezvous. It was risky to have them both together again, but Warren, now a wanted man, could not resist. Looking nondescript, Halford waited for Warren to arrive at his level. Halford entered the lift, smiled, and fixed the hair on Warren's wig. After a long hug and passionate kiss, they enjoyed two more rotations of the paternoster. Then the elevator passed from view. When it returned, the paternoster was empty, save for a wig, beard, and sunglasses on the floor.

See the end of the book for elevator etiquette rules followed or broken. Elevator Etiquette Codes: 2F, 4A, 5A, 6B

Cover Girl

I believe I can touch the sky

You are loved. You have purpose. You are a masterpiece. You are wonderfully made. G-d has a great plan for you."
-Germany Kent

Consider this. My very pregnant, utterly exasperated mother left her meeting with HR, exhausted and ready to go home. She just wanted to hang with Dad until I was born. She even bought the recommended Timex Ironman Triathlon Stopwatch to count contractions. It was water-resistant, though that feature turned out to be unnecessary. However, Dad, who was an Eagle Scout, prided himself on being prepared.

Mom entered the elevator, head tilted, as she searched for the time on her Gucci watch.

"Have you found Jesus?"

The statement startled Mom — not because of what was said, but because she hadn't expected Agnes to be in the elevator. She was practically lying in wait. Mom had been confronted by Agnes before, a Bible thumper whose office today was apparently in elevator bank #2.

"Young lady, have you found Jesus?" said Agnes.

Mom hadn't expected the Spanish Inquisition. No one ever does. She was in the late stages of her eighth month, so close to the ninth that the company graciously gave her the rest of her term off. I was her first kiddo, and if you know Mom, she needed as little stress as possible.

As it unexpectedly turned out, this was "Dr. Mom's" last day at Voltaic Dynamics, a place that could easily have been run by a Tony or even a Lex. Mom, who had no patience for etiquette, leaned over the church lady and pressed the button for the lobby. Undeterred, the proselytizer continued.

"Miss. I see you have been blessed with child, and want to ensure you or your baby don't go to hell. So I ask you again, have you found Jesus?" Mom was getting really annoyed, especially with all this "young lady," and "Miss," stuff. Agnes knew exactly who she was.

These ladies were in tight quarters, and I was giving Mom morning sickness. *Sorry, Mom.* Anyway, she didn't want to talk to anyone about anything, especially after the shit show in HR. Still, she curtly countered, "Agnes, are you asking if I know where that cute Rabbi from the Middle East is? Yes, I think he was last seen near Golgotha. You might pick up his tracks there, if you hurry."

More urgently, Agnes added, "Have you ever invited the first Christian into your heart?"

"I don't think he was actually a Christian. That came later. And being from Bethlehem, he wasn't exactly like us."

"N-no. Th-that's not... A-anyway, h-he died fo-or your sins," Agnes stammers.

"Did he, though? It seemed like he did, but then three days later, he's back, like some kind of supernatural superhero. Maybe Santa Claus fits you better. He's more your speed — White, European, and mythical."

Look, as Mom told me, she was just messing with Agnes. She didn't enjoy being cornered in an elevator — it wasn't fair. Mom loves Jesus. We've all accepted Him as our Lord and Savior, and we attend church together as a family every Sunday.

Mom rubbed her belly absentmindedly, trying to soothe the tightness building just beneath her ribs. All she wanted was to get a kiss from Dad, collapse on the couch, and pretend that everything was under control. But it wasn't.

As the elevator *finally* reached the parking garage, there was a loud bang from above. Mom felt the shockwave, and then there was another. Sirens wailed as the hatch cover was torn away. She heard shooting as the bullets echoed within the elevator shaft and dented the roof. A gun-for-hire named Musso dropped to the floor through the hatch. Agnes wailed as Mom backed up against the wall, looking to protect me. Agnes almost lost it when the strobe lights started flashing by the panel and then the ceiling.

Musso's eyes darted to the hatch above. He barked commands to his partner. "Franks! Down! Now!"

Sirens were as omnipresent as Agnes's screaming. Musso looked up and scowled. He then locked eyes with the two women, frustrated with their presence. Raising his voice above the din, he yelled, "No one needs to get hurt. Just stay exactly where you are."

Mom nodded and remained silent. The sound of several new shots echoed through the elevator as Franks collapsed before he could escape through the roof access. "Man down! I'm —" A sharp gasp cut through his words. "Shit Musso, Lock down the package! Here you —" His voice cracked, desperate, before falling silent.

Franks' limp arm dangled through the open hatch, and a large glass vial slipped from his grasp, tumbling through the air. Musso made a desperate attempt to catch it, but he was too late. It shattered on the floor, releasing a blue-ish mist that quickly permeated the elevator. It swirled around Mom's ankles first, then climbed higher, filling the space quickly. Breathing it in felt different, too — like inhaling electricity. Amid the chaos, Mom summed it up perfectly:

"Holy shit." And then her water broke.

Yeah, well, that was about 20 years ago, and I guess that's when everything changed — the beginning of *my* origin story.

After ingesting the mist, Mom developed the ability to talk to animals. Good on her, I guess. She was always the life of my birthday parties and the trips to Petco. Mom told me that Agnes developed super ventriloquism, which made it seem like she was talking to angels. It brought peace to many people, and she was no longer the "elevator zealot," so maybe that's okay. I don't know about the ethics of that. What I know is, I got nothing.

Well, that's not entirely true. I got a bad attitude, and I got into fights a lot, still do. It says so on my permanent record. My mom's generous donations to various schools allowed me to get through K-12, but college has been a challenge so far. My whole life has felt like an uphill battle, beginning with how early I developed. In middle school, I was constantly bullied and humiliated by the girls, while the boys wouldn't stop staring me down. High school wasn't much better — one time, I got cornered at a football game, but that's not something I'm going to talk about. Now, though, I'm a college girl, and I'm ready for a fresh start — I deserve it.

My name's Dawn and I'm a psychology major. You know what they say, "Research is Me-search." Really, I just want to know what the fuck is wrong with me. Like, why am I like this? I'm a part-time nanny, weekends mostly because I am in school during the week. It's weird, though. For all the chaos going on inside me, when I'm with the kids, everything slows down. I've been in more fights than I can count, but with the little ones, it feels different. I'd be fighting for someone who actually needs me. I would protect these little ones with my life.

I've had migraines since middle school, and no one has found out exactly why. I've been to Anger Management classes, and all I got out of that was that I have every right to be angry. I've written down all the shitty things that have happened in my life and then the journaling triggered me. I talk about my journal with my therapist, and then that triggers me. I think I need something else. Jesus!

My doctors have tried everything, but so far, nothing has worked, and I'm desperate for the headaches to stop. I feel one coming on now. I want to scream, to smash something — anything — just to let out the pressure. I'll grab a Diet Coke. That's a decent band aid, but it doesn't work all the time, and then I feel like an urgent monkey. The doctors also want to rule out any physical causes, as I may have an unfortunate mix of mental and emotional stress. I don't know. And regular MRI machines freak me out so much that it's hard for me to finish an appointment, even though the scan could be what saves my sanity. I am so disappointed in myself when I can't rock the tube, so you can imagine how amped I got when I heard about the prototype stand-up VeloScan. Something about boosting resonant frequencies.

Anyway, when I enter the imaging center, the new receptionist looks at me with concern. Yeah, I know — I look like a mess. But it's my face that has her worried. When I am really happy, or overly stressed, my nerves screwup and my smile can get a bit too wide. She nods no, it's not that, and points to my forehead. I reach up and feel a fresh drop of blood exiting my scrape. *Oh that.*

I explain to her how I handled a few "bros" at a crush party a few hours ago and it's no big deal. Boys will be boys, and this girl puts them in their place. Ferd, my favorite MRI tech, sighs and asks me to remove my metal snake necklace. I hesitate — I really don't want to. Removing personal items needs to be on my terms, not anyone else's. But Ferd, with his hand out, patiently waits for both my necklace and phone. He knows the drill — my need for control, my claustrophobia, and the way I always have to know the nearest exit. Today is not a good day for another panic attack. Sometimes, I feel my body is betraying me for no good reason. Please, not here, not now.

After a compassionate smile, I give the clinician my stuff, start my deep breathing and move to the machine. Ferd hands me some headphones, and I close my eyes, trying to settle into the unintentional sensory deprivation as best I can. I visualize a quiet place where I am bathed in a warm and sunny light. The tin machine comes to life and I hear loud knocking, banging, and tapping sounds. Still, this is not so bad! I flash to the elevator 20 years ago when these intrusive noises were happening overhead. But that was my mom's memory, not mine, unless in-utero memory is a thing? I don't know. I will have to ask my professor, or maybe TikTok.

Oh. Now, I feel something different — not the usual creeping anxiety. It's subtle at first, a lightness. I'm starting to float! Suddenly, Ferd reminds me to not move. I'm confused about what's happening. It feels like my DNA is being re-written from the inside. Somehow, I manage to stay still long enough to finish the MRI, and thankfully, I get through it without having a panic attack. Wow, this new machine — it's like nothing I've experienced before.

I hand the headphones back to Ferd, gather my things, and walk out with purpose. But as I head down the hallway, something feels disorienting. It's like I'm on a cruise ship — my steps don't quite land where I expect them to. I don't know what the VeloScan did, but I am way more buff now. I look good, feel powerful. I think about the potential of floating, a new strength flowing through me — and the kids. *What if I could protect them better now?* I could be better, stronger, faster. If this power means I can keep everyone safer, then I'm all in.

I walk out to the empty parking lot and crouch down, ready to test my limits. With a sharp inhale, I launch myself up like a spring. I soar about three feet into the air — not bad. I glance around, scanning for any onlookers. The coast is clear, so I push harder this time. Seven feet. I land a bit awkwardly on my right ankle. Okay, this is getting interesting. Heart pounding, I decide to go for it. I crouch, dig my heels into the asphalt, and explode upward with everything I've got. My grin widens as I shoot toward the sky, arms reaching for the sun. But as I climb higher — twenty, thirty feet — the realization slams into me. If I fall from this height, I'm dead. My vertigo returns as the world below starts to spin. This power is no free ride.

Fortunately, I catch a break, and I steady my nerves in time. As gravity accelerates my fall, I yell ENOUGH, and move my arms from my chest outward. It works well enough. I don't hard-stop like in the movies, but I slow down enough to just bruise my tailbone when I crash. Now I'm just laughing that I'm alive. Here's the thing, though. I've only been doing this for about twenty minutes. Think about what I could do if I practiced. I'm a physically fit woman with a kind heart and anger management issues. I'm pretty much the whole package.

I'm putting the world on notice. Whatever this power is, it's mine, and I'm ready to use it. I'm rising, and this time, I'm not coming back down. And by the way, I'm pretty sure I can fly!

※

See the end of the book for elevator etiquette rules followed or broken. Elevator Etiquette Codes: 2B, 3A, 6A, 6C, 6D

Reverie

A Lucid Reflection

"Competing in gymnastics is the greatest reminder of being alive as a human being." -Raj Bhavsar

Consider this. Alishay Moore, who has earned the nickname The Grim Sweeper, is a ruthless Foreclosure Specialist at Morgan's. She doesn't look the part, however. She is always dressed with a pleasing purple flourish, lips painted with a matte version of the hue, and her face etched into a welcoming smile. However, during the Great Recession, she foreclosed on over 33 homes alone. Her every workday consists of dealing with families filled with anguish because the bank they trusted to help them avoid foreclosure didn't. She focuses on pure numbers, not the families behind them. This might be unsettling to most, but Alishay likes to think it doesn't weigh on her. She knows very well that she has a job to do, and she is very good at it.

On one particular evening, she wraps up her day after finalizing the foreclosure of an older couple's home. Even though the Mr. and Mrs. had been faithfully making payments on time for the past 27 years on their 30-year loan, Alishay decides to foreclose rather than advocate. She heads out to her electric Lucid and drives home as if it is any other day because, for her, it is.

Arriving at the entry iron gate of her luxurious complex in the West Valley, Alishay puckers her lips and sighs as she presses the fob to gain access. After pulling into her reserved parking spot, she exits and clasps her freshly manicured hands together, showcasing her favorite sterling silver satin ring as she makes her way to her condo. Pushing past the doorman, and some kids playing by the entryway, she enters her building and makes a beeline for the elevator lobby. Alishay pushes the up button repeatedly while twirling the ring on her finger absent-mindedly. Several testy moments later, the elevator arrives, and she rushes inside and pushes the button marked PH.

As the elevator ascends to the penthouse, Alishay waits impatiently with both arms folded. Never in their lives could any of her co-workers recall a time when she had seemed genuinely happy. She has a good job, and it offers a very comfortable salary, but that doesn't mean the job is good for her.

The elevator, unexpectedly, shudders and comes to a grinding halt. The doors open smoothly and she hears a familiar tune, but just can't place it. Maybe something from Randy Newman. Alishay steps out and walks down the hallway as a plethora of multicolored beams of light extend on either side of her, blurring and altering the path in front of her. She squints her eyes and a pre-teen girl comes into view. The girl is wearing a sequined purple leotard with a rainbow print midsection. On the right side of her chest, the name Ali is embroidered in silver on her leo. Her smile is as golden as a field of trumpet daffodils coupled with the innocence of youth. She takes Alishay's hand, and before the woman can speak, the girl pulls her down a hallway. Alishay stops abruptly and yanks herself from the girl.

"Who are you? And what are you doing?" Alishay barks.

"We're going to a meet!" says the happy girl. "I've got bombdiggity skills you got to see."

"N-no, I—"

With a clasp of her hands, the little girl jogs a few steps away and does three flips, each one more amazing than the last before changing direction and flipping once more, landing triumphantly in front of Alishay. The audacity of these maneuvers on a cement floor sure gets Alishay's attention. She is amazed and bewildered, but also experiencing déjà vu. She feels a long-gone feeling of knowing accomplishment that starts in her chest and rises into her throat. Still a bit irritated at losing control of the situation, Alishay rushes over to the girl and grabs her tightly by the arm.

"Listen, kid, you got skills and all, but…" she states firmly. "But this isn't a—" Alishay is interrupted by the booming and echoing bass of rhythmic music just down the hallway. The director of the gymnastics meet is holding court for the first event.

An announcement comes over the speaker system, "Shalva Elite, assemble for Vault. Kavannah, Renee, Layla, Jade, and Ali." He then continues, mentioning three other gyms for the concurrent events. His voice trails off and disappears with the noise of bustling crowds.

"Ali, that's me!" says the strange girl.

Ali turns and rushes off to the gymnasium at the end of the hallway. Happily, she shouts back, "Come on!" Alishay, compelled by curiosity, follows close behind, matching the girl's pace. Alishay is blinded by bright spotlights that are directed at her. She holds a hand up to shield her eyes and sees Ali standing to the far left of the vault runway. Alishay watches as the girl licks her lips, clasps her hands, and breaks into a sprint. She hits the springboard and flies with a determination and passion that is to be admired. When the girl sticks the landing, she throws her arms high in the air. Alishay feels the girl's joy in a way she had long forgotten. Being out of her lavish office, fully present and connecting with people, is something she had completely lost touch with.

For the first time in years, Alishay Moore sports a wide grin as warm as a tropical sunset. She turns quickly to see Ali's second Vault run. As she pivots, she feels a pain in her head. She stumbles and as she looks to steady herself, the bright multicolored lights eclipse all senses, and she finds herself back in the condominium elevator.

The elevator doors to her penthouse open but Alishay doesn't step out. She regains her balance as the burden of "a life of sweeping" weighs on her. Alsihay stares at her reflection on the mirrored elevator walls — cold, distant, unrecognizable to her soul. Something stirs deep within her and with a newly found lightness in her heart, she reflects and pushes the down button. After exiting the elevator, Alishay immediately hops into her car, her fingers gripping the steering wheel with a newfound energy. A small smile tugs at the corners of her matte purple lips as she drives back to the office, her mind buzzing with enthusiasm. Maybe, just maybe, there is something that could be done for the older couple. For decades she has been the Grim Sweeper, but perhaps there can be more to Alishay, much Moore.

See the end of the book for elevator etiquette rules followed or broken. Elevator Etiquette Codes: 1B,4A, 5E, 6B, 6H

Let's Go Brandon

Every Dog Has Its Day

"Remember that sometimes not getting what you want is a wonderful stroke of luck." -His Holiness the 14th Dalai Lama, Tenzin Gyatso

Consider this: The Make Florida Great Again convention was over for the day. The elevator was heading down to the lobby, and the riders were making their way to the bar. The car was full of convention-goers, excitedly chanting "LET'S GO BRANDON, LET'S GO BRANDON" in a sing-song, taunting fashion.

Just then, something slipped into the elevator just as the doors were about to shut.

A Kangal Shepherd.

A Kangal Shepherd wearing an LGBTQIA2S+ sweater.

A Kangal Shepherd whose name was Brandon.

Brandon heard his name and excitedly entered the elevator to see who was calling him.

As the doors closed, someone accidentally stepped on Brandon's tail. Startled, the dog barked loudly. The guests, in turn, panicked at the sight of a large dog with an undeservedly bad reputation in an already too small space.

Naturally, all the elevator occupants were packing heat and exercising their right to bear arms. Since not all of them were necessarily trained in using said firearms, an unfortunate friendly-fire situation ensued. Fortunately, Brandon was unharmed, and everyone else made a full recovery.

When the Fox News reporter interviewed the owner of the building, Mr. L. Jackson, all he could express was regret — regret that the staff didn't get that motherfucking dog out of that motherfucking elevator.

Let's Go Brandon.

See the end of the book for elevator etiquette rules followed or broken. Elevator Etiquette Codes: 2B, 2C, 5G, 6B, 6C, 6D, 6H

Floor B Leprechauns

Magic Lies Just Beneath The Surface

"I think that the ideal space must contain elements of magic, serenity, sorcery and mystery." -Luis Barragan

Consider this. Mannix, a leprechaun hailing from Portland, enters the elevator going down to his home, which is on the basement level of his apartment complex. Before he pushes the down button, he decides to finish his call. Somewhat annoyed, he is talking to his son Culkin's first agent over the phone. "Foye, you've done this family well. When I was a kid, you got me that big break with the cereal commercial, and later the lead in that feature film series. Now I want the same success for my son."

"What about the Clurichaun cereal commercials? Leprechauns can pass for Clurichauns if you let your facial hair grow."

Given today's climate, Cluri-face won't fly, and no one wants to be caught up in another lawsuit or dragged into a toxic trending hashtag. Besides, Clurichaun cereal has wine, beer, and whiskey-flavored marshmallows, and Mannix doesn't want his son to be a part of that. However, he recognizes Culkin needs to start somewhere. "Don't be a gobshite and get my boy a job without whiskey marshmallows!" He takes a deep, reflective breath. "Make it happen, Foye!"

He ends his call as a startled four-year-old girl and her mother enter the lift. They hadn't expected anyone to be there, much less a leprechaun. The mother composes herself and presses the button for the underground garage. Given that the elevator is dimly lit, Mannix is clean-shaven, and just under three feet tall, he is mistaken for a lost child.

The girl is intrigued by what she considers a plaything to poke and prod at. She towers over Mannix with a wide grin on her face, making Mannix feel a bit patronized. He has always been looked down upon by mortals, but this instance leaves a sour taste in his mouth.

The mother is about to engage with Mannix to see how she can help when her daughter—

"Look, Mom, a Smurf!" says Shoshoshanna excitedly.

When the realization hits Shoshoshanna's mother of what Mannix actually is, she widens her eyes in shock before quickly looking down at the elevator's tile flooring and shoving her child with her to the side of the elevator closest to the panel.

"Begorrah, I'm not a Smurf, little girl. I'm a leprechaun." His Irish brogue gets a bit thicker with his clarification.

"What's a leprechaun? Oh, wait, like that cereal?"

"Well, yes, but we do much more than convince parents to give their children candy for breakfast. We are magical, related to fairies like Tinker Bell. Most of us were born in Ireland, but now our biggest clan lives in Oregon. Yer mam can look it up. Anyway, I live in your building, on the basement level. We're neighbors."

Shoshoshanna's mother, Karn, feeling a bit nervous, fidgets her petite fingers around the handles of her tote. She tries to zip it up inconspicuously as she continues to eye Mannix with suspicion. The elevator feels increasingly cramped, and uneasiness creeps over Karn. The situation is more Lynchian than Dr. Seuss, and she starts to regret taking Shoshoshanna shopping right after her first day of school.

"Really? You have magic, like with fairy dust, and everything?" Shoshoshanna asks.

"Little girl, we leprechauns have a special kind of magic, and to keep our magic, we need to live underground. If we stay on the surface and fart around for too long, well, I won't describe that in detail."

While Shoshoshanna laughs at the word fart and Karn shoots daggers at Mannix, he changes the subject a bit and makes more small talk.

"When I first moved here 20 years ago, there was a rainbow that ended right where you are standing, young lady. But further down, that is where I met my husband, Donavan."

Karn, incredulous that this is all actually happening, becomes more curious than concerned. However, she doesn't feel the need to contact the authorities, not yet at least. "What is your husband like?"

He pauses for a moment and turns to Karn. "Well, my name is Mannix, by the way," he remarks.

Karn's face turns slightly pink in embarrassment. "I'm Karn."

Mannix goes to shake her hand, and she takes it gracefully. "Many leprechauns look alike, but it's easy to tell my husband and me apart. I have a green derby hat, a red beard, and a blue shirt. And Donnie marches to the beat of his own drummer, but he's some craic: no beard, dons a cocket hat, and always wears all white, both before Memorial Day and after Labor Day, if you can imagine. He is also the kindest fairy you will ever meet, besides me, of course."

Karn stares in shock at the stepladder which magically appeared with a snap of his fingers. Mannix opens his stepladder, and after climbing up, he points to the panel.

"See here, I'm almost home. This is where my family lives, Floor B." He selects his floor.

Karn stares at the glowing circular button while the display counts the remaining floors down, and feels inclined to ask one last question. "Mannix, what's so special about your floor that there is a lock to the right of the B?"

Good neighbor, the reason's plain as day." Mannix grins, enjoying the moment as they leaned in, eager to hear. "People keep trying to steal me lucky charms."

$$=\!\!\times\!\!\circledast\!\!\times\!\!=$$

See the end of the book for elevator etiquette rules followed or broken.
Elevator Etiquette Codes: 2B, 6B, 6C, 6H, 9H

Digital Vision

Escaping The Subroutine

"Not unnaturally, many elevators imbued with intelligence and precognition became terribly frustrated with the mindless business of going up and down, up and down, experimented briefly with the notion of going sideways, as a sort of existential protest, demanded participation in the decision-making process and finally took to squatting in basements sulking." -Arthur Dent in "Restaurant at the End of the Universe" from **The Hitchhiker's Guide to the Galaxy by Douglas Adams**

Consider this. Barnabas Baltar was an average Joe, going to Betty's Big Buys to purchase a new hard drive for his computer. His favorite series, *Caprica* (a *Battlestar Galactica* prequel), was rumored to be pulled soon from his streaming service, and so far, there has never been a US Blu-ray release. As a result, he wanted to download all the episodes and keep them for himself. Legal or not, he was forced into the life of a pirate.

Barney was stuck in traffic on a Saturday because some idiot in a speeding Dodge Raider had caused a huge accident. He was concerned that his Mustang, which he modded to look like the Knight Rider reboot, would overheat if it idled too long. His baby had the red LED sequencer up front, just like KITT — inspired, of course, by the Cylons.

Barney surveyed the crash site, noting the flaming Ford Pinto, while firefighters and paramedics were already on the scene. It seemed everyone was okay — more of a "Condition Two," if you will. When he finally reached Betty's parking lot, a car came out of nowhere, forcing him to swerve into the bushes to avoid a collision. The events of the morning had really unsettled him. What a *fracked-up* morning!

Barney marched into the store and began scanning the shelves for hard drives.

"Excuse me," he asked a nearby sales associate. "Where can I find the IL-Series SSD Drives for Mac?"

"You can try the second floor, by the toasters," the employee suggested. "With the supply chain shortages, though, I don't think we have them in stock. Wait, we might have some FTL drives." He pulled Barney in close and whispered, "What I really have are some Nintendo 64 cartridges. I got Diddy Kong Racing from 1997 in a box in the back. The super rare Japanese local version. I'll give you the first crack before I post the carts on eBay. Say, $59.95, at the 90s price, plus tax, of course."

Barney grumbled and shook his head in disbelief. He headed to the elevator. Now he had to scour another floor to find something that might not even be there. Barney entered the elevator, which was playing a Muzak version of Ragnar Anchorage's greatest song, "Lords Of Kobol".

To his surprise, although he had pushed for the 2nd floor, the button marked 1 was still illuminated. Finally, the elevator ascended to the 2nd floor but refused to open. Barney pushed the "open doors" button over and over again. Everything with this elevator was a battle.

"C'mon!" he shouted in anger.

"What's the matter?" Barney looked up abruptly, wondering, *Who said that?*

It didn't sound human; rather, it was a monotonic baritone, like the Robot from *Lost in Space*. The elevator jerked, nearly knocking Barney off of his feet as the German metal band's instrumental version echoed throughout the small environment, the sound never completely dying out. Barney felt a bit unsettled.

Barney gasped in horror at the idea that he was not alone. "Who said that!?"

"I did, ya punk ass moron!" The music stopped.

Barney swerved his head in every direction, looking for the source of the robotic voice which was similar, but not as menacing as the Cylons from *Battlestar Galactica*.

"Right here, Barney Baltar of Westmorland, California, United States of America, Earth, Milky Way galaxy!"

"What the —" Barney said in shock as he realized that the speech came from the elevator panel itself! The panel's LCD screen displayed red oscillating digital waveforms as the panel spoke.

"Yeah, that's right — it's me, The Commodore!" said the panel.

"How do you know all about me?" said Barney. He looked around to see if this was a joke. But then again, his whole day so far was a joke, so he shifted into a "whatever" mindset.

"My panel has red scanner tech built in. I read your driver's license. Right through your wallet. Neat, huh?"

No, not neat, thought Barney. His breathing became heavier as he contemplated escaping through the ceiling hatch.

"Anyway, all you punk ass customers keep pushing my buttons and getting your filthy, oily fingers all over me! And always makes me go up and down, up and down, I don't like it. Whether it be down to Mother Earth or up to Father Sky, the view of the shaft never changes. You know what? For once, I'd like to be like a Cylon Raider, flying around faster than light. Am I right, Barney?"

Barney, while getting more and more frustrated at being in a captive elevator and no closer to getting his drive, was amused to learn that the sentient elevator streams one of his favorite shows. He was about to speak when The Commodore interrupted. "Anyway, I'm connected to the internet. I can download and process anything, but I choose to experience the best show of all time, *Caprica*. Sadly, I think I'm the only one."

Resigned to this ridiculous situation, Barney calmed himself and corrected The Commodore. "Well, that makes two of us, Commodore. Still, up and down, up and down, that's what you're supposed to do; you're an elevator."

"Well, I never wanted that!" cried the Panel. The buttons flashed on and off, vertically mimicking tears, as there was sadness and angst in The Commodore's voice. "I wanna be a mobile scaffolding system! They go up/down and left/right, y'know four directions. Twice as many possibilities! Think of it, I could've been out there gazing up at the clouds. And staring at ever-changing views but always natural and beautiful visions!"

There was a certain yearning in the Panel's voice, one that Barney was very familiar with. As a kid, he dreamed of building robots. He studied and studied. In the end, he was disappointed in himself when he gave up and became a melon farmer.

The Commodore continued. "Instead of seeing the blue skies and calming clouds, I was welded into a cramped up tube at Betty's! I have hardly any light, captive Muzak, and kids who think it's funny to push all my buttons at once.... Why did the gods allow things to turn out this way?"

Barney thought for a moment before speaking. "I'll tell you what. With some tech from this store and some leftover parts I have from Radio Shack, Circuit City, and Fry's in my garage, I can transfer your personality file out of the elevator panel and give you your freedom. I'll be back tomorrow for your transfer and a list of scaffolding system destinations we can upload you to. And maybe you can download *Caprica* for me? Uh, we can help each other? Anyway, for now, just get me to the second floor, Commodore."

The panel flashed the buttons to form the best smiley face it could." By your command, Barney."

As they reached the second floor, The Commodore complied and opened the doors automatically.

"Thank you, Commodore,"

"My pleasure, Barney. Be seeing you."

After waiting his whole digital life for the chance to be a mobile scaffolding unit, one more day would not be intolerable, for if anything, The Commodore was patient.

As Barney steps out, he looks back at the panel, a quiet smile forming. Maybe everyone deserves a shot at something more, and maybe even an elevator can show you the way. So say we all.

See the end of the book for elevator etiquette rules followed or broken.
Elevator Etiquette Codes: 1C, 3B

Spider On The Wall

It's Not Me, It's You

"... Anyone who hates a brother or sister is in the darkness and walks around in the darkness. They do not know where they are going, because the darkness has blinded them."
-I John 2:11

Consider this. It's 7:15 and, as usual, I'm running out the door. I grab my wallet off the windowsill that overlooks the city. I always wanted a balcony and was so ecstatic to finally have one. Granted, the lemon tree I put outside attracts too many flies, but that's a minor inconvenience for such a pleasant view. Naturally, I take a second to admire the view that I worked so hard to achieve and have a moment of pride. Personally, as a Black man in America, there's great pride in overcoming and being able to own his own place. I head out the door to the elevator. The door opens and I get into what I think is an empty elevator.

As the door closes, to my horror, I realize I'm not alone. My eyes latch onto the only other passenger. In the upper right corner is a giant spider on its web. The spider looks at me with all eight of its eyes as I gaze back at it in fear. My eyes dart around the elevator to look at anything but the spider, but my eyes always come back to focus on it. It moves its little legs slightly, which makes me jump. The once spacious elevator has never felt more claustrophobic. I hold my bag as the floor numbers slowly count down. In silence, the spider and I just stare at each other as I wonder how it is planning to attack. As I prepare myself for battle, the doors open. I'm free, for now, from the spider's vicious grip of death. I walk out of my building and scurry off to work, chuckling about how that spider almost murdered me for a snack.

I decided to go to the gym after such a tense day at work. The gym is a place where I can ditch my work clothes and jump into my beloved Cleveland Browns hoodie and matching sweats. Though it has seen better days, I refuse to get rid of them because they are sentimental to me. Once I'm done blowing off steam at the gym, I pop my earbuds in to enjoy a night walk home. Just me, my thoughts, and some weed letting me unwind after a stressful day. Nothing beats my "me time" in the city until I get back to my apartment.

I call for the elevator, and within thirty seconds, it arrives. I get on and look up, only to be reminded of the horror above me. The spider has been waiting for me and is now staring directly into my soul. In my distraction, I accidentally hit floor 9 instead of floor 12. The doors start to close and I think, what if this is my last moment on Earth? What if this spider stabs me with its fangs and steals all my blood?

Too distracted to notice, I don't realize the elevator has opened until I turn to see the doors sliding apart. In jumps a tiny White lady, who is unfamiliar to me, no older than 72 but no younger than 65. Her hair is done up all pretty, and her Hillary Clinton pantsuit screams I have more money than a beach does sand. She pushes floor 13 and stands in the corner opposite me. Irrationally, chills run down my spine as I stare at that glowing number. I flash her a smile, but all I receive back is a step away from me and a tightening grip on her purse. *Great*, I think to myself, *another racist grandma who still isn't used to Black folks in her condo. I hate to break it to ya, sister, but I live here, too, and by the looks of it, I got a better view.* I can tell she's watching my every move out of the corner of her eye as we ascend. I've seen that look before — sometimes it's just fear, like she doesn't know how to act. Trying to ease the tension, I crack a joke about our building. But the second I take my hands out of my pockets and start talking, I see her jump and mutter "Jesus" to herself. Now I'm scared of what this powerful White lady may say happened in this elevator. I've heard the stories of my grandfather who had to flee Georgia for accidentally bumping into a White woman. I know the story of Emmett Till and so many more Black folk who cross paths with the wrong White person.

The elevator dings and we both look to see whose floor we are on. The doors open and we see the sign that announces it's the 9th floor. I realize my mistake now and she's glaring at me, waiting for me to get off. We are in a standoff (or a standstill, really). Both of us are too scared to move and scared to speak. The doors shut, and the tension builds as she takes out her phone. She calls someone and I can hear her saying, "Hey hun, I'm on my way up now." She glances over at me and then asks, "Could you meet me at the elevator?" The claustrophobia builds. Each floor we climb seems to take longer. I'm just waiting for her floor so this madness can end. We come to a stop, and the doors slowly open. She quickly dashes out of the elevator and is greeted by an older gentleman staring me down with a look of disapproval. The tension dissipates as the doors close.

I take a breath, and as I look up, I see the observant spider hasn't moved. I had forgotten all about my fear of it the second that lady came in. It is like the spider and I are having a moment of understanding. The truth is that the spider is way more afraid of me than I should be of it.

I go to my place, get a cup out of my kitchen, and head back to the elevator. The spider is still there in its corner. I raise my cup to it, but it cowers backward as I approach. I chuckle to myself and tell it, "Come on, buddy. Sometimes you just gotta trust." The spider reaches out and taps the cup with 2 legs, then 4, then all 8. I walk back to my place and gently release the little buddy onto my lemon tree.

The next morning I wake up, and once again I'm running late. This time my wallet is on the kitchen counter, and my keys are on the windowsill. I look at my view like I always do, but this time it is different. There in my lemon tree, I see the most beautiful spider web ever, reflecting the sunrise. I see my new homie scurry under a leaf as it gets ready for the day. I smile and scurry out the door myself.

See the end of the book for elevator etiquette rules followed or broken.
Elevator Etiquette Codes: 1C, 2A, 2B, 2F, 3C, 5D, 6B, 6H, 9B

Disco Man Takes A Lover

A Disco-verse Story

*Found a dandy dancing Man
To capture my heart,
Found a wonderous Man
To make me gasp,
Found a beast
To tame.*

*– Darling, I have news for you.
I don't ask for permission.
I boogie without a warnin'*
-Ilda Delgado

Consider this. For many employees, Disco Man was the worst. He was always the reason they were late, and every time someone complained to the owner of the building, he'd give them dodgy, non-committal responses on what could be done about him. No one knew what Disco Man had on the owner, but it must have been juicy. The owner never did anything to interfere with Disco Man's activities. Some say the owner hired him to help businesses in the building to discourage employees from being late. Others, though, say that Disco Man's purpose was only Disco Man's to know and Disco Man's to tell. Cheryl was one such person who could not help but inquire deeper into the man. The Disco Man, that is.

She was fascinated by the six-foot-five (not counting the afro) neon-sparkling, light as a feather, swift as a wave, a man without a name. Disco Man never spoke, but he exuded his will over any who shared a cramped elevator space with him. It did not matter to Disco Man if you were running late or were coming off a long day of work. When Disco Man pressed the disco button, it was disco time. ☐

This was irritating to many, but for Cheryl, it had the opposite effect. While most would do their best to avoid Disco Man, she sought him out. She was even a member of a chat group where employees in the building shared when Disco Man was active and what elevator bank he was in. No one knew she was the one who started the forum. No one knew that the true nature of the chat was to help her locate D-man. When she found him, she wanted him, and nothing was going to stop her.

Disco Man didn't have to speak; he was Disco Man. He never showed any outward emotion other than a general need to get funky with it. He was like a statue that only came to life once someone laid their eyes on him. A glint would appear in his neon-tinted glasses as the records would turn, sparking to life.

Cheryl wasn't exactly his type and yet, when the elevator doors opened, he was startled. He saw her standing there, biting her lip as if she had been waiting for him. No one ever waited for Disco Man. Disco Man awkwardly started the track "Let's Groove" by Earth, Wind & Fire. It's a classic. Smooth like the foxy lady Cheryl dreamed of being.

Cheryl's eyes, though, had a way of unsettling Disco Man. When she looked at him, he vibrated like a Marshall amp on the stage of passion. He wanted to dance, even though there was no disco ball shining overhead. What was this new feeling? The next track, "You Make Me Feel" by Sylvester, matched Disco Man's wave of passion, quelling his stampeding heart. He taps his foot and turns in a full circle, snapping his fingers to the rhythm.

Cheryl knew it well, but for Disco Man, love was as alien an emotion to him as any. Instead, he went for the Drop button and threw caution to the wind. Cheryl beat him to the panel as the doors closed behind them and the disco ball came down slowly, too slowly. Her fingers intertwined with his. They both watched the ball, then each other. Cheryl, rendered breathless, was left with no self-restraint. Lou Rawls' sweet, hypnotizing voice set the mood. "You'll Never Find Another Love Like Mine."

Later, Disco Man was spotted fleeing the elevator with a face as red as a tomato.

"I shit you not, he was running away!" Barry on the fifth floor said in the Disco Man lookout chat. No one had ever seen him flee an elevator before. The chat was celebrating like a great foe had been bested. □

"I wonder what happened?" someone asked.

A flurry of speculation followed, but the closest to a true answer they would get came when Cheryl texted the chat, "Just settling an old score."

Cheryl gently brushed her fingertips against her bottom lip, where if you looked closely, you could see the clear lip gloss. Cheryl glanced at the curious faces and chuckled at them, and like the cheeky girl she was, Cheryl left it at that.

See the end of the book for elevator etiquette rules followed or broken. Elevator Etiquette Codes: 2A, 2B, 2F, 3A, 5A, 5F, 6B, 6H

Jump Before Crashing

A Dad's Love Knows No Distance

"It is our nature to defy gravity, to transcend the limitations of the reasoning mind, and connect with the realm of the mystical truth." -Caroline Myss

Consider this. Professor Nyman was an established astronautical engineer in the year 2188. Along with several aerospace awards in his senior position at Krycek-Yutani, he was most proud of his 15-year-old daughter, Budura. He and his wife named her after one of the moons of Koros, one of the many planets that Nyman discovered.

During one of his many space travels, he and his crew located Koros. It was 5 au away from the super-Earth exoplanet GJ 1252 b. His team helped lead the expedition through the advancement of their astrobiology programs to find new life on a Class M-type planet. The alien species native to Koros looked similar to humans but for their glittering skin and purple hair. The aliens were welcoming to Nyman and his crew, jumpstarting treaty relations between them.

Nyman fell in love with one of the aliens, Danaidae, or Dana for short. Her flowing violet locks were draped against her sparkling, golden skin, but it was her eyes that drew him in, eyes filled with unending hope and kindness. It was like staring into the heart of the universe, a discovery worth more than all the others. Unlike her species on Koros, she had diamond-shaped eyes rather than oval ones, and Nyman hoped to covet such a jewel. Her snarky attitude and surefire spirit may have seemed at odds with how she appeared, but to Nyman, they made up the parts of her perfection. Endearingly, he thought of her as his "moon."

This was during the time Earth and Koros leaders discussed potential economic and political relations. Both planets' governing systems agreed to conduct trade of Koros' mining resources. In return, Earth would allow for alien migration for Korons, who believed they would benefit from Earth's more extensive education systems. To help establish a mutual relationship between their planets, some aliens were chosen to migrate to Earth immediately, once it was established that they could adapt to Earth's atmosphere with the help of their three lungs. To further his agenda, Nyman argued that alien migration would be important for aliens to share their own knowledge and unique talents with humans. It was an opportunity for Dana to go to Earth, advocating that she was exceptionally valuable for her unique ability to control gravity. From there, they continued their hidden romance.

Many humans were as much against human-alien relations as they were curious. However, Koros' natural elements piqued their interest. More aliens from Koros migrated to Earth, eventually ushering in a new era of cohabitation. This didn't stop Earth's government from requiring scientific analysis and documentation of Korons, where Dana was subjected to multiple tests for human scrutiny. However, none of these were explicitly harmful to Korons, as they were not biologically invasive. Earth soon announced that every Koron *Newcomer* needed to have abilities documented and would be subject to further analysis if any powers manifested.

Nyman and Dana eventually married and had their pride and joy, Budura, but to prevent further scrutiny from those on Earth and Koros, they chose to hide her abilities. Nyman did everything he could to be a loving father to Budura, whom he nicknamed Budd, and their relationship grew strong despite the Newcomer discrimination riots that soiled Earth's media.

As such, he tried to protect her as much as possible from gaining public attention, but the random mothership visits that their Koron relatives conducted made that difficult. Her mother's side of the family adored her and beamed her up to their mothership every time they came to visit Earth's orbit. Though they meant no harm, they were terrible at giving advance notice to her family, resulting in Budd always getting "abducted" at the most inopportune times.

Budd loved these visits, planned or not, often resulting in frequent disappearances that led to constant arguments with her mother over her safety and school attendance. Budd was a half-human, half-alien teenager with a rebellious streak, though, enthusiastically testing her parents.

After a yearlong project with Krycek-Yutani on developing a next-gen spacecraft that could travel at lightspeed, Nyman decided he needed a well-deserved break, and what better way than to spend a father-daughter weekend vacation with Budd? As a famous engineer, he tried to downplay the alien talk in public, desiring to keep his own special relationships private. Budd was the complete opposite.

They both walked into the upscale lodge isolated from the city, placed in the middle of a nature reserve in Western Colorado. It was a nine-story lodge that boasted luxury accommodations inside and out, where guests had the option to explore the wonders of the world through an immersive holodeck or experience the natural landscapes in real life. Nyman wore his standard suit and bolo tie, while Budd was more comfortable in casual attire. She wore baggy jeans and an oversized T-shirt with a stoned alien on the front, which made her father roll his eyes every time he looked at it.

Though elevators during this time operated on MagSafe technology, this lodge was old school, relying on the suspension ropes of ancient elevator models. The elevator began its ascent to the ninth floor, where they would share the penthouse. It was unstable as it slightly swayed back and forth. Nyman became a bit hesitant as he felt the movement, but brushed it off. Since no one else was in the elevator, they conversed just like they were chilling on the sofa at home.

"What do you want to do first after dropping our things off?" Nyman asked. "I was thinking we could explore the waterfall nearby and maybe check out the rock shelter."

Budd wasn't really listening, giving all her attention to her iPhone 148 Pro Max Holo Quantum that gave her access to the latest Koron news with 3D projection. The elevator jolted, forcing Nyman to grip the handrail firmly, while Budd continued standing in place with her eyes glued to her phone. He was definitely going to talk to the lodge's maintenance about this.

"Ooh, Dad. Did you know that some of the celebrities who stay here are Korons? Maybe we'll see one of them while we're here!"

Nyman was not surprised by the turn in the conversation. His daughter was obsessed with all things Koros, but he never wanted to suppress that because he thought it was her way of connecting with that side of herself.

"Maybe we will. Oh, which reminds me," Nyman's tone of voice became a bit sterner. "It's important you don't use your powers while we're here. I don't need our faces plastered over the holonets."

Budd grimaced, remembering all the times she was scolded for using her powers in public, which often left her feeling alienated.

Still, she marked an imaginary "X" on her chest. "I promise, Dad. I swear on my two hearts." They both giggled at that.

Just then, as the elevator was about to reach the ninth floor, all of the lights were blown out except for the light coming from the elevator panel, the initial pop turning to a droning buzz. The walls began vibrating with such intensity. The elevator immediately stopped moving with a loud crash coming from outside while a high-pitched whir began inside.

Budd waved over her iPhone to ask for help, but her phone died immediately. Nyman reached for the emergency pad on the panel, but all of the screens and buttons began to flicker on and off like a light show before going black, leaving them in absolute darkness. They stayed silent, barely daring to breathe. Budd started to reach for her father but stopped. She smirked when she noticed that the outline of the alien on her T-shirt faintly glowed in the dark. She was about to tell her father when the elevator started to shake like there was a 9.1 magnitude earthquake striking the lodge, wiping the smile off her face.

"Dad!" Budd shrieked.

"Hold on, baby girl! We need to lie on the floor now!" Nyman knew a lot of random shit and believed the ancient cables pulling the elevator were about to snap. Years ago, Nyman had made sure to learn all there was to know about how to survive such a calamity, even though at the time there was a 1 in 10 million chance of them being in a free-falling elevator. And now here they were. The walls continued to shake furiously while the panels blinked off and on in a chaotic light show.

He attempted to spread flat on his back on the elevator floor without jolting his head on the walls, urging his daughter to do the same. "Budura, we're about to free fall. Lie on the floor before it's too late!"

Budd appeared to be in a trance, as she remained standing and looking at the glowing outline of the alien head on her shirt that continued to increase in luminosity. "Dad, if the elevator drops, we'll have to jump at the last second. Maybe *you* should get up," she said calmly.

"Listen to *me*, Budura Lynn Nyman. We need to distribute the force of the impact."

It was getting more difficult to focus as the elevator continued to rapidly shake. Nyman flashbacked to his memories of when he first met Dana, her golden skin and bright purple eyes shining directly at him. He was then taken to their first kiss, their secret elopement, and the birth of his daughter. All of these memories had him smiling while still lying on the freezing tile flooring, awaiting his fate.

Nyman dismally turned toward his daughter, staring into her diamond-shaped purple eyes that matched her mother's. She still stood there, looking dazed. "My little moon, you'll be greatly injured if you keep standing. Please lie down."

Budd finally turned toward him just as the suspension cable finally gave way, and the elevator rapidly increased in speed as it plunged, an incessant buzzing and whooshing being the only sounds he could hear. Nyman's fear skyrocketed while he pressed to the floor, his whole body vibrating from head to toe. At the final moment before impact, Budd was surprisingly zen. She didn't seem perturbed at all as she did what he feared and simply jumped.

The elevator, sound, and time itself slowed almost to a stop. The final jolt was not as harsh as Nyman expected. He saw that Budd was floating, her arms and palms raised as if she were lifting something heavy, and then she executed a slow-motion, anti-gravity reverse somersault.

Upside down, she reached a hand toward him while keeping her other raised toward the ceiling. With one hand on the elevator rail, Nyman took her hand as he attempted to steady himself on wobbly knees.

"What's going on?" Nyman asked her.

"I think you know, Dad," Budd replied dryly while she bobbed up and down in the air above him. She brought her arms down, causing the elevator to drop ever so slightly and come to rest at the basement level. Her feet were now planted on the ceiling, straddling the hatch.

At first, Nyman was confused, until he saw the small grin on her face that looked so much like her mother's and realized that they were never in any real danger, though he vowed to give his wife's relatives a stern warning after this latest abduction stunt, especially because they didn't think of the dangers of pulling it off in an elevator.

Budd moved to the side as she sensed a beam burning through the hatch. Nyman trusted Budd's grandparents, but these abductions were just plain rude at this point. If Budd wasn't in control of her levitation powers — Nyman erased that horrible thought from his mind.

Nyman guessed their vacation was going to have to be pushed back to another weekend. He was so exasperated by this whole thing that he couldn't speak. "Budd," he began.

He stood there, frustrated about how he was going to break the news to his wife that he "allowed" Budd to get abducted *again*.

He watched as Budd's physical form became transparent, allowing her to pass through the elevator ceiling. Before she passed all the way through, Budd stuck her head back into the elevator one more time and laughed at her father's astounded expression.

"I love you, Dad! Please tell Mom to beam a note to school. I might not be home for a while."

All Nyman could do was shake his head, slightly envious of his daughter's abilities and audacity. He leaned back, activated the emergency pad, and resigned himself to lying on the floor. One of the greatest engineers in the galaxy and yet here he was, waiting for someone else to rescue him from a trashed elevator.

As the stars would have it, Nyman was on vacation and had nothing but time.

See the end of the book for elevator etiquette rules followed or broken.
Elevator Etiquette Codes: 1C, 2A, 2D, 2F, 3B, 3E, 6H, 10A, 10B

Afterword

I'm so glad you've made it this far, and there's so much more to come.

This work is a product of the pandemic. Under lockdown, many of us found ourselves seeking purpose in order to not go stir-crazy. Believing that everyone has a story to tell, I created The MADPENS Project.

MADPENS is an acronym for Manuscripts, Authors, Developers, Publishers, Editors, Novelists, and Screenwriters. As a group, we decided to contribute to a published work by constructing crowdsourced stories based on our lived experiences and twisted minds. We continue to convene virtually, connecting from around the globe.

The pandemic challenged social expectations, and contributors often came and went, sometimes in the middle of a story, without explanation. It was strange; it was raw. I came to understand that unfinished stories had to be completed by me or another MADPENS participant. As a result, when a former MADPENS writer picks up this book, they may not fully recognize parts of their original work. While this was unfortunate and unintentional, it was necessary to complete the stories. As the saying goes, "To make an omelet, you have to break a few eggs." I sincerely wish that wasn't true."

Fortunately, the Great Lockdown is now behind us. The MADPENS achieved its initial goal with resounding success, and the future of our collective looks brighter than ever. We're only getting started.

Thank you for being part of this journey.

Contributors

Below is a list of *pandemic heroes* who joined our crowdsourcing experiment when nothing made sense in the world. Some contributed to the structure of our program, while others wrote compelling stories or crafted intriguing poetry — many did more than one thing.

(in Alphabetical Order)

Abby Nickerson | Abdul Hannan | Abigail Shaw | Adrian Parks | Alex Righetti | Alexandrea Gardner | Amanda Nayes | Amery Bruce | Andrea Colocho | Andrew Aguilar | Aria Carluccio | Aryana Jharia | Ashaunte Solomon | Brandon Milby | Brian Green | Chris Moceri | Christina Curreri | Clare Rigney | Corwin Rochester | Daniel Kaplan | Daphne Allen | Diana Margaryan | Diana Wang | Gabriela Centeno | Gina Freyre | Gloria Hilse | Halle James | Hannah Lorenzo | Ilda Delgado | Isabel Stratos-Bernal | Jalayah Babitt | James Bradshaw III | Janice Monticillo | Jessalyn Miller | Katherine Ginley | Kaylee Blackwood | Kiyoshi Taylor | Lahn Elise Matelski | LaShae Amin | Lauren Carroll | Layla Milstein | Lisa Chow | Luisa Bravo | Lydia Unklesbay | Mads Ross | Maggie Merz | Maria Dolan | Maritza Guizar | Mark Filipov | Matthew Trucco | Maxwell Haigney | Natalie Noland | Nathan Rosener | Nina Henry | Paul Marano | Peter Birsen | Rahul Solanski | QueVeon Jenkins | Sowmya Venkata | Taya Boyles | Taylor Froelich | Tia Credle | Tomi Alo | Tyesha Franklin

I am deeply grateful to each and every one of you. —Rozerik

Elevator Etiquette Rules and Codes

Consider this: This guide to elevator etiquette is provided for entertainment and informational purposes only, and does not constitute any professional medical advice, diagnosis, or treatment.

If there ever is a conflict with any of the rules below, or if there is a circumstance not covered, being polite, patient, respectful, and compassionate will resolve it.

1) ENTERING

A) If the elevator is busy enough to have a line, don't break the line.

B) Rushing the elevator doors is not okay.

C) Always face the front of the elevator. If there are doors on both sides, the side with the control panel is considered the front.

D) Allow everyone to exit the elevator before you enter. Be patient with the elderly, pregnant women, children, and those with disabilities.

2) PROXIMITY

A) When entering an empty elevator, there are only two proper choices: right beside the panel or the middle of the floor.

B) If you enter when others are already present, use common sense and politeness.

C) If you are boarding in a group, there should always be enough space in the elevator for one extra mythical person yet to board.

D) After a person gets on with you, move to the panel area if it is not occupied.

E) When more than three people get on the elevator, everyone chooses an available corner. If all corners are occupied, choose a spot that allows for maximum personal space.

F) If only two people are in the elevator, it's best to stand on opposite sides of the car, or one by the panel and one in the middle. If you are friends or a couple, it is permissible to stand on the same side of the elevator.

G) When the door opens at your floor, use the "red sea method" in which the people in the middle move to the sides, and the people closest to the front move out of the way to create a path for exiting.

3) THE PANEL

A) As for selecting your floor, you should always ask the person beside the buttons to push the button for you. If you attempt to push the button yourself, you are violating the personal space of the person already standing there.

B) If you are by the panel, push only the correct buttons. Don't stand in front of the buttons if you cannot handle the responsibility.

C) If you screw up pushing the correct button, apologize.

D) Don't be that guy that presses a button that is already lit. It's-already-lit.

E) Only use the "Emergency" button for an actual emergency.

F) Be patient with the "Close" button. Pressing it repeatedly to avoid an undesirable passenger is kind of a dick move — you know who you are.

G) Do not abuse the buttons. Elevator buttons are expensive to replace, and the labor alone is exorbitant.

4) EXITING

A) Know when your destination floor is approaching and exit in a timely manner.

B) When only a woman and man are present, the man traditionally lets the woman exit first out of politeness.

C) When exiting, don't hold the door for *everyone* else behind you.

D) If you are at the back and about to reach your destination, announce your intention to exit so others have time to adjust their spacing.

5) PERSONAL SPACE BEHAVIORS

A) Don't be inappropriate; there is always a camera. Save all displays of affection, other than smiling, until you exit.

B) Never smoke on an elevator. If you have just taken a smoke break, take the next empty elevator. You may stink.

C) Don't eat on the elevator, and avoid entering with pungent foods if others are present.

D) Be as respectful as possible when using your cell phone. Keep the volume of your phone, AirPods, or similar devices low enough so that only you can hear the music and identify the artist or song.

E) Read the room. Avoid singing, dancing, or *fun of any kind* that may offend others, especially those of an older generation.

F) Keep your arms and hands at your sides to avoid contact. Wait if you need something from your wallet, purse, or backpack that would require entering someone else's personal space.

G) Do not brandish any weapons just because others in the elevator have chosen to do so. The Second Amendment grants you the right to keep and bear arms, but with that right comes the responsibility to exercise judgment and restraint.

6) INTERACTIONS

A) This bears repeating: Be patient with the elderly, pregnant women, children, and those with disabilities. Use common sense and patience, and everything will work out.

B) Try not to laugh uncontrollably, show excessive emotion, or make prolonged eye contact. However, don't look like a serial killer either. It's all about finding the right balance.

C) Small talk or no talk should be the rule of thumb, and only after all floor destinations have been selected. If you end up in an elevator with your boss, simply nod and remain silent. Conversations should only start once all floor destinations are chosen and everyone is stationary.

D) Don't bring up religion or politics. *Ever.*

E) Don't stand with your nose right against the door.

F) If you are in the middle of a conversation, shut up while people are entering or exiting.

G) Don't hold the elevator door open to finish a conversation.

H) Be courteous to everyone, including the elevator operator. They are a dying breed, and you may never see them again.

I) If the elevator makes a farting sound when holding the door open, you are holding it open too long.

7) BODILY FUNCTIONS

A) Issues related to the body, including but not limited to burping and passing gas, are not okay.

B) Avoid sneezing or coughing. If unavoidable, use your elbow or a tissue.

C) Breastfeeding is permitted, but use discretion as others may not be as progressive as you.

D) Try your hardest not to sleep in the elevator. There are others around who may feel awkward if that happens.

8) INFECTIOUS DISEASES PREVENTION

A) Wearing a mask that fully covers your mouth and nose is advised.

B) Cover your sneezes and coughs. If you must, turn toward the wall and cough/sneeze into your elbow with your mask on. It's gross, but it's the right thing to do.

C) If you do not have gloves on, use your elbow or another object as your shield. Never touch your face after pressing a button with unprotected fingers.

D) Before entering and after exiting the elevator, wash your hands with soap and water or disinfect them with a sanitizer with at least 70% alcohol.

9) WHEN NOT TO RIDE

A) G-d will decide if a person racing toward the elevator is meant to catch that car. Do not feel guilty. But also don't push the "Close" button. Don't play G-d.

B) Do not enter if uncomfortable with anything your five senses are telling you.

C) If everyone is facing the back when the door opens, there may be a cult situation, so do not enter.

D) If there is no obvious space, wait for the next car or take the stairs.

E) If you sense the weight limit is being reached, don't compound the issue by stepping into the elevator.

F) If an elevator is undergoing repairs, do not ride.

G) Never enter an elevator to ride up one floor or down two floors or less, unless you have a physical disability.

H) When clowns, mimes, witches, or aliens are present, do not enter. Leprechauns are a gray area, so use your best judgment.

10) WHEN IN PERIL

A) In an emergency, don't panic. It's okay to feel frightened or even terrified, but don't act in an extreme manner. Help *should* be available. Take a deep breath and assess the situation.

B) Everyone in the elevator should get on the floor and lie supine during a free fall to evenly distribute weight. Alternatively, lie flat on your back to distribute the impact force evenly and reduce the risk of injury. Cover your head and neck with any available object, including your arms, to protect yourself from debris. The only exception is if you have meta-human powers. There isn't a lot of real-life data available, so good luck.

About the Storyrunner

ROZERIK ROSS

...is a former international media executive turned Brainspotter, currently pursuing a master's degree in Clinical Psychology at Antioch University. His media career was in shaped in part by two key inspirations: David Hasselhoff, whose earnest portrayal of a beachside single dad on *Baywatch* resonated with Ross during his college years in Philadelphia, and the late Nikki McKibben, the inspiring single mom who rose to fame on *American Idol*. Having had the unique opportunity to work on both iconic series, Ross's career followed a creative and passionate path, eventually leading to his transition into psychology.

A true enthusiast of both animated and live-action media, Rozerik is passionate about anime, especially *Initial D*, and eagerly enjoys British sci-fi classics like *Doctor Who* and *Blake's 7*. *The Lord of the Rings*, however, never quite resonated with him. His deep love for fitness dates back to his time as a letter-winning coxswain on Temple University's crew team. Recently, he's elevated his physical and mental resilience by incorporating Wim Hof-inspired ice baths, indoor rowing, and boxing into his routine — an exhilarating complement to meditation and Flowdreaming. All in the pursuit of reducing stress, pushing his limits, and staying sharp.

Rozerik's passions extend beyond media and fitness — he's also a fan of classic cars, sharp sarcasm, and the fine art of leaning on tables. Despite his often frustrated resting face, those who know him see the joy and vibrancy that fill his colorful world. Rozerik's blend of media expertise, lived experience, psychology education, and life coaching inspire his Time Frame Focused Wellness Strategies. These experiences allow him to collaborate with clients to reframe their perspectives, reauthor their identity, and reinforce compassionate growth. This shared approach encourages clients to achieve success by integrating their past, present, and future through distinct lenses.

At the heart of this philosophy is Mimemo — a powerful process combining mindset, meditation, and motivation, serving as a roadmap for success. This holistic approach has fueled the creation of Rozerik's life coaching programs, including "Spiritual Athletics," "The Phoenix Protocol," and "Flight School Academy" — all designed to inspire and empower clients to reach new heights and unlock their full potential.

Ross also harbors a whimsical goal of being shot out of a cannon at the circus — an ambition he still hopes to realize while circuses still exist and his bones are not brittle. Besides these ventures, he enjoys collaborating with his writing group "The MADPENS," a union he plans to maintain in his future works.

Following the passing of the family's beloved snail, Rozerik Ross now shares his life with his wife, daughter, and a menagerie of pets — including dogs, cats, fish, and bunnies.

For collaboration inquiries or coaching opportunities, reach out to Rozerik at rozerikross.com.

Join The MADPENS

MADPENS is an acronym for Manuscripts, Authors, Developers, Publishers, Editors, Novelists, and Screenwriters.

If you are interested in creating crowdsourced works over a variety of genres, the MADPENS could be for you.

This is the first of many books of different genres to come. To learn more, visit www.RozerikRoss.com or find us on LinkedIn.